Forming Ethical Identities in Early Childhood Play

Forming Ethical Identities in Early Childhood Play breaks new ground in three inter-connected aspects of the broad field of early childhood studies: child–adult play, superhero play, and moral development. The author convincingly demonstrates through compelling examples why and how adults should play with young children to create with them a 'workshop for life'.

In showing how child–adult pretend play can form what he calls 'ethical identities', Edmiston contests many of the common assumptions about play and moral development. Aligning himself with those postmodern, post-structuralist, feminist, and Vygotskian scholars who have challenged dominant assumptions about early childhood, he draws in particular on Bakhtinian theory to argue that pretend play can create a social aesthetic space in which children and adults can co-author understanding and, over time, shape and form ethical identities. In a chapter on 'mythic play' Edmiston confronts adult discomfort over children's play with pretend weapons, as he encourages adults both to support children's desires to experience in imagination the limits of life and death, and to travel with children on their transformational journeys into unknown territory. The book's final chapter considers what early childhood institutions might look like if they applied the framework developed within the book to recognise play's potential as ethical pedagogy.

This book provides researchers and students with a sound theoretical framework for re-conceptualising significant aspects of pretend play in early childhood. Its many practical illustrations make this a compelling and provocative read for any student taking courses in Early Childhood Studies.

Brian Edmiston is Associate Professor at the School of Teaching and Learning, Ohio State University.

Forming Ethical Identities in Early Childhood Play

Brian Edmiston

Routledge
Taylor & Francis Group

LONDON AND NEW YORK

For Michael, Zoë, and Pat, with whom I continue
to learn the value of playing at life

First published 2008
by Routledge
2 Park Square, Milton Park, Abingdon, Oxon OX14 4RN

Simultaneously published in the USA and Canada
by Routledge
270 Madison Avenue, New York NY 10016

Routledge is an imprint of the Taylor & Francis Group, an informa business

© 2008 Brian Edmiston

Typeset in Baskerville by
Keystroke, 28 High Street, Tettenhall, Wolverhampton
Printed and bound in Great Britain
by TJ International Ltd, Padstow, Cornwall

British Library Cataloguing in Publication Data
A catalogue record for this book is available from the British Library

Library of Congress Cataloging in Publication Data
A catalog record for this book has been requested

ISBN 13: 978–0–415–43547–5 (hbk)
ISBN 13: 978–0–415–43548–2 (pbk)
ISBN 13: 978–0–203–93473–9 (ebk)

ISBN 10: 0–415–43547–1 (hbk)
ISBN 10: 0–415–43548–X (pbk)
ISBN 10: 0–203–93473–3 (ebk)

Contents

Illustrations

Figures

Tables

Introduction by the Series Editors

Gunilla Dahlberg and Peter Moss

Brian Edmiston's book – *Forming Ethical Identities in Early Childhood Play* – is the fifth book to be published in the series 'Contesting Early Childhood'. The purpose of the series is to question the current dominant discourses in early childhood and to offer alternative narratives for the area, which are growing out of a multiplicity of perspectives and debates. We want the series to contribute to a politicisation and democratisation of early childhood, through helping to make more widely visible the plurality, diversity and complexity that is flourishing in the field. Rather than searching for answers to the technical 'what works?' question, our hope for the series has been to increase awareness of the wealth of possibilities available to us. If the series contains one key message, therefore, it is that early childhood education faces political choices about policy, provision and practice – and that this is a thoroughly good thing.

Forming Ethical Identities in Early Childhood Play has a different focus from the previous books in the series. Rather than early childhood institutions or populations of young children, Brian Edmiston's book is primarily about a child, Michael, and his father, Brian. It offers an account and an interpretation of Michael's play, especially with his father, between eighteen months and seven years. It is a case study that is vivid, moving and deeply insightful, both because of Brian's ability to reflect deeply on the play and because of his use of a wide range of theoretical perspectives. Like others in the series, Brian works with poststructural theorists such as Foucault. But he makes particular use of a theorist not represented before in the series, the Russian philosopher and literary critic Mikhail Bakhtin (1885–1975), and his theories of ethics, discourse, narrative, authoring and dialogism.

In the attention paid to ethics, this book complements an earlier book in the series *Ethics and Politics in Early Childhood Education*. Both books reclaim ethics as central to early childhood. This is a matter of the utmost importance at a time when the field has come to be dominated by a discourse of technical practice, with its instrumental preoccupation with the production of predetermined outcomes, that attempts to ensure individual children follow a known and linear pathway to achieve a sequence of normative stages.

Both books, too, reject an idea of ethics as being a matter of conforming to universal principles, legal rules or moral norms. But whereas in *Ethics and Politics* we paid particular attention to the ideas of Emmanuel Levinas, in particular his concept of the 'ethics of an encounter' with the importance it attaches to respecting the absolute alterity of the Other, Brian Edmiston is inspired by Bakhtin's thinking on ethics. For Bakhtin, 'a person's actions are ethical when they are "answerable" to anyone who "addresses" them about the consequences of those particular actions' (p. 27). Being answerable is more than being responsible: 'when people are answerable their ethical understandings are affected and transformed because they allow themselves to be addressed by another person's ideas that dialogically affects and shapes the framework they use to make meaning'.

The book also highlights another aspect of ethics, ethical identities and how play can promote the formation of such identities:

> I argue that people's ethical identities are how they frame their relationships to the world in terms of malleable frameworks which can guide both the daily actions of an ethical self and their evaluations of their own and others' deeds in terms of their 'rightness' and 'goodness'. . . . When people play together they make meaning together to co-author possible selves and over time possible ethical identities.
>
> (p. 32, p. 35)

A particularly fascinating aspect of the book is how the author, basing his work on many years of play with his son and other children, comes to look critically at 'the contentious issue of superhero or war play'. As a result, he re-conceptualises such apparently violent play as 'mythic play', and shows its value: 'mythic play, based as it is on narratives of power, is significant in forming ethical identities' (p. 8). Overcoming his initial ambivalence or outright resistance, Brian comes to see the potential of this play for the child, understood as strong and competent in the sense of being an active meaning maker; Brian shows how Michael's fascination with monsters and heroes enables him to construct complex and positive ethical identities (and Brian's account of Michael at thirteen speaking out against the Iraq War as part of a delegation to a Congresswoman's office speaks volumes for how 'war play' at three does not presage 'war behavior' in later life).

In developing his ideas about ethical identities and the capability of children to author such identities from an early age, the book picks up on two other themes in the *Contesting Early Childhood* series. First, it adds to the growing body of literature that questions the truth claims of child development, by offering a critique of the 'dominant modernist theory of moral development':

Children are viewed as locked into their interrelated stages of cognitive, affective, and moral development. . . . Young children are regarded as not-adult individuals at the start of a long march toward a mature application of universal ethical principles. The discourse of developmental theories assumes that because children construct understandings, moral and otherwise, it takes individual children time to learn to be 'good' and that what is considered 'appropriate' behavior varies by stage of development. . . . [T]hough valued as a useful activity for generic development, the imagined spaces of play are not embraced as sites for the exploration of ethical issues or for moral development via child–adult play. . . . The moral ability to take another's point of view is not expected until the preschool years are long passed.

(pp. 276–7)

But when Brian Edmiston looks at what is happening in Michael's play, including that between the two of them, and when he uses other perspectival lenses to interpret what he sees, he finds a far more complex situation, with a young child deeply engaged in exploring complex ethical situations – perspective-taking and authoring understandings and identities. Drawing on Bakhtin's theory that a person's actions are ethical when they are 'answerable' to anyone who addresses them about the consequences of their action, Brian concludes that:

Over time, pretending to be other people [mythic heroes, as well as destructive monsters] can assist children to take up other perspectives that refract with previous discourses, not to advance them through a particular moral stage of development, but rather to become answerable for their actions as part of developing a disposition to answer people who address them.

(p. 281)

Second, the book adds to the discussion about how we might choose to understand early childhood institutions. While the book is primarily focused on parent and child interactions in the home, it also pays attention to the institutional settings that form part of the lives of most young children today, at least in the rich countries of the North. In a final chapter on 'ethical pedagogy', Brian suggests that 'play as an ethical pedagogy creates spaces in early childhood settings for child–adult co-authoring of ethical selves and identities'. This will not happen by chance, but requires particular ways of working: a 'pedagogy of listening and radical dialogue', such as is found in the early childhood services of Reggio Emilia, discussed in detail in earlier books in the series (Dahlberg and Moss, 2005; Rinaldi, 2006).

Brian Edmiston is here, we think, describing one of the many largely untapped possibilities of early childhood institutions, that they can be loci of ethical practice. In so doing, he contributes to a narrative that contests an over-simplified and impoverished image of the early childhood institution as a technology for producing a narrow range of prespecified outcomes. Instead we can think of these institutions as public spaces, laboratories or workshops where children and adults engage together on many projects – including the co-construction of knowledge, values and identities. Through his discussion of the intersection of ethical with socio-cultural identities, Brian enriches and makes more concrete this idea of the early childhood institution as a place of identity construction. He also recognises that alongside these valuable possibilities, there are risks in such settings due to the unavoidable issue of power relations between adults and children and the potential they offer for adults to govern children in ever more effective ways: 'ethical pedagogy requires adults in preschool classrooms to share power with children as much as possible in order to create trusting collaborative relationships and spaces that will support children's ethical explorations with each other and with adults' (p. 264).

Forming Ethical Identities in Early Childhood Play pays a great deal of attention to one young child, who is clearly recognisable with no attempt made to hide his family identity or his relationship to the author. In reading the manuscript and in exchanges with the author, it has been abundantly clear to us that Michael – who is now in his late teens – has been an understanding and willing subject in this case study, and has participated fully (along with other family members) in the preparation of this book. Any initial concerns about potential exploitation or breach of privacy are fully answered; instead we welcome this opportunity to hear so clearly the voice of the young child – as well as his voice as he passes through childhood into youth. We would therefore like to end this introduction with our thanks to Michael for his essential and generous contribution to the book.

References

Dahlberg, G. and Moss, P. (2005) *Ethics and Politics in Early Childhood Education.* London: Routledge.

Rinaldi, C. (2006) *In Dialogue with Reggio Emilia: Listening, Researching and Learning.* London: Routledge.

Chapter 1

Ethics in play

I believe that maturity is not an outgrowing but a growing up: that an adult is not a dead child but a child who survived. I believe that all the best faculties of a mature human being exist in the child, and that if these faculties are encouraged in youth they will act well and wisely in the adult, but that if they are repressed and denied in the child they will stunt and cripple the adult personality. And finally, I believe that one of the most deeply human, and humane, of these faculties is the power of imagination.

Ursula Le Guin, 1979, p. 44

Introduction

When my son, Michael, was three he turned into a Tyrannosaurus Rex. Right in front of my eyes, as he looked at a book on dinosaurs, his face, body, and voice changed. He loved everything about T-Rex from the powerful legs that it used to pound after any other dinosaur that crossed its path to the nine-inch-long razor-sharp teeth that could rip apart its dinner before gulping it down. Michael seemed to become this 'king of tyrant lizards' when he strode on his tip-toes, held up his first two fingers, and roared. Even at the dinner table he pretended to be this creature as he ate his food with his first two fingers and his teeth.

I was faced with a question that the parents, teachers, and care-givers of so many young children must answer. How should I respond to this apparently violent play? Should I just let him get on with his pretending or should I try to manage his play? At different times, adults will do both. In doing so they follow the advice of most play theorists. Despite the noise and movement that can be annoying, children are, after all, 'only playing'. Because their play is understood as vitally important for their development, it should be encouraged and not banned. On the other hand, children have to learn appropriate social behaviors for particular situations. So play will, at times, need to be controlled. Eating like a dinosaur was not going to go down well with Michael's grandparents whom we were due to visit; and it certainly would not be well received in our favourite Saturday morning restaurant. This book, however, does not address these two alternatives. Instead this book describes and analyses a third alternative – how I played with Michael.

In this book I use examples from a long-term case study of playing with my son (Edmiston, 2005), as well as with other young children, to analyze how extended child–adult play can promote the formation of ethical identities (Edmiston, 1998a; 1998b; 2000) and to develop theories about play, ethics, and pedagogy. Between the age of eighteen months and seven years I encouraged Michael's play and regularly played with him. I made meaning with him not only about the stories that we read and the movies that we watched, but also about life and ethics. As I wrote drafts of this book I often talked with Michael about past events, read him draft descriptions, and asked for his reactions.

One of this book's strengths is that it provides readers with multi-layered analysis of the significance of a child–adult relationship that is interwoven with playful interactions. At the same time, as with any theorizing based on case study research, its implications are necessarily limited. As a child in a middle-class home with academic parents, Michael's experience was atypical. Though this book is unique in describing a father's play with his son, it only briefly touches on issues of gender or class in play. The examples in the text are not intended as recipes, nor is the book presented as a prescription for how adults ought to play with boys or with children in general. Rather, as long-term research I have used a case study to generate new theory by contesting many of the implicit assumptions of the existing theory and research of play, ethics, and pedagogy.

As a teacher–researcher I had engaged in reflective practitioner research into using play and drama with children for curricular purposes in my own classroom with children aged seven, eight, and nine as well as in other teachers' classrooms (Edmiston, 1993; Edmiston and Wilhelm, 1996; 1998; Edmiston and Enciso, 2002). I was comfortable playing with school-aged children, taking field notes, tape-recording, and using reflective analysis to guide my practice. Inquiry as a father-researcher was more seamlessly woven into the fabric of everyday life than it had been in the classroom. Though I had originally intended to document my interactions with our daughter Zoë, who is four-and-a-half years younger, after over five years of tracking my interactions with Michael I had largely stopped keeping records by the time Zoë was three.

The writing of this book has been a topic of family conversation since its inception. Aged seventeen, at the time of writing, Michael has read and approved the manuscript. His sister, Zoë, now aged thirteen, and their mother, Pat Enciso, have also read the sections where they are referenced.

From when Michael was very young he wanted me to play with him rather than watch from a distance as he played. I mostly recorded our interactions in notebooks because using a tape recorder or video camera was largely impossible. Michael rarely stayed still as we played and if he noticed a recording device he would become more interested in it than in imagining he was elsewhere. It was not until he was older that I could have discussions with Michael about the project. Aged seven I asked his permission to share some of his drawings as I interviewed him before making a scholarly presentation. He knew that the words I wrote down carefully were going to be quoted and he changed his register accordingly. Michael, Zoë, Pat, and our children's cousins who are referred to in a later chapter, have all formally signed consent forms. However, they did more than consent to participation in this project and approve the references made to them. All have been highly supportive throughout and have been eager to see the manuscript in print.

Ethics in early childhood

In recent years, scholarly attention has refocused on the ethical dimensions of schooling while stressing that learning and teaching are social practices within cultural institutions (Dewey, 1909/1975; Ayers, 1994; 2004; Jackson et al., 1993; Noddings, 1984; 2002; Wolf and Walsh, 1998; Sockett, 1993; Brooks and Kann, 1993; Buzzelli and Johnston, 2002; Dahlberg and Moss, 2005; Wortham, 2006). Most adults in early childhood institutions assume that children will develop into rational morally objective thinking individuals, either because the adult facilitates whatever individual moral reasoning a child is assumed capable of, or because the adult just tells children what is right and wrong. Such assumptions, which are based in a largely acultural and only minimally social view of learning, are pervasive despite feminist critiques of the atomized view of the individual self that stress the importance of social relationships (Midgley, 1981/2003; Gilligan, 1982; Noddings, 1984; Walkerdine, 1988; Tronto, 1993; Hauser and Jipson, 1998; Sevenhuijsen, 1998; Butler, 2005) as well as postmodern critiques of the modernist theory of ethics underlying such views (Best and Kellner, 1991; Bauman, 1993; 1995; Levinas, 1989) and more general postmodern, post-structural, and critical reconceptualist critiques of the universalizing, objectivist, normative, and rationalist theoretical assumptions of child development (Lather, 1991; Kessler and Swadener, 1992; Day and Tappen, 1996; Packer and Tappen, 2001; Cannella and Bailey, 1999; Soto and Swadener, 2002).

The dominant early childhood discourses of hierarchical stages of cognitive and moral development (Piaget, 1975; 1962; Kohlberg, 1984) assume that young children are too egocentric to be capable of cognitive and moral reasoning and thus unable to develop ethically until they are older (DeVries and Zan, 1994; Gibbs, 2003). Similarly, despite the narrative turn in moral development theory (Tappen and Packer, 1991; Day and Tappen, 1996) and a postmodern critique of the didactic nature of character education (Nash, 1997) as well as a focus on the need to situate moral education within a relational caring community (Noddings, 2002), many parents, teachers, and caregivers think that children will become moral simply by being told to be virtuous (Lickona, 1991; Kilpatrick, 1992; Brooks and Kann, 1993).

Drawing, in particular, on Bakhtin's (1981, 1984a, 1984b, 1986, 1990, 1993) poststructural theories of ethics, discourse, narrative, authoring, art, imagination, dialogism, and the self, I propose an alternative to the dominant moral developmental and character education theories and pedagogies: the formation of ethical identities through play, especially child–adult pretend play. I align myself with those scholars who have applied a Vygotskian and Bakhtinian analysis to moral development (Tappen and Packer, 1991; Day and Tappen, 1996; Tappen, 1997; Buzzelli, 1997). In complementing Bakhtin's theories I draw, in particular, on inter-related social constructivist theories of development, imagination, and play (Vygotsky, 1967; 1978; 1986), post-structural analysis of power relationships (Foucault, 1977; 1978; 1980) in early childhood settings (Dyson, 1997; Dahlberg et al., 1999; Grieshaber and Canella, 2001; Tobin, 1997; 2000; Mac Naughton, 2000; 2005), as well as a social positioning and cultural anthropological analysis of improvisation, agency, and identity formation (Davies and Harré, 1990; Harré and Langenhove, 1999; Holland et al., 1998; Holland and Lave, 2001).

In early childhood institutional settings adults are largely seen as facilitators of children's play with limited adult participation being encouraged by most scholars (Paley, 1986; Jones and Reynolds, 1992; Bennett et al., 1997). The adult's primary role is a 'play watcher' so that children will become 'master players' (Reynolds and Jones, 1997). The adult role of 'guide, friend, counselor and facilitator' of children's play means that 'intervention should be of the gentlest kind . . . lying in the provision of appropriate materials for learning, and the structuring of the classroom context, both social and intellectual, so as to make learning more likely and attractive' (Meadows and Cashdan, 1988, p. 3). Smilansky (1990) suggests that adult participation should be as 'play tutors' in order to enhance cognitive development. Similarly, Shefatya believes that adult 'intervention should be skill oriented and not content orientated . . . with sensitivity to the child's level of play development and in congruence with the content that the child is trying to express' (1990, p. 153).

Research has shown the benefits of adults playing with children in terms of improving communication and developing intimacy (Kelly-Byrne, 1989), engagement with and interpretation of literature (Wolf and Heath, 1995), literacy learning (Kendrick, 2003), and extending learning in general

(Tizard and Hughes, 1984; Sutton-Smith, 1993; Kitson, 1994; Wood and Attfield, 2005). Despite a turn toward social constructivist theory in early childhood (Bennett et al., 1997, p. 14), concerns that adults may over-power children have meant that adult–child play in general tends to be minimized, dismissed, or discouraged (Brown, 2003; Bennett et al., 1997; Scarlet et al., 2005). As Bruner put it, the romanticism of Rousseau, combined with a view of play that wanted to relieve children of adult pressure, created an ideology that, 'real play had to be free of all constraints from adults and be completely autonomous of their influence. True play, in a word, came entirely from the inside out' (1986, p. 79).

In this book I develop a theory and pedagogy for the formation of ethical identities in early childhood play through three intersecting strands: play, ethics, and pedagogy. I use the terms ethics and ethical interchangeably with morality and moral though I tend toward the former usage because, for me, those terms carry fewer negative connotations. Adults' tendencies to moralize in their interactions with children assume an adult moral superiority that I dispute. Likewise, adult reliance on a moral code often infers an even more universalizing authority than assumptions about the need to adhere to predetermined ethical rules, both of which I resist.

This introductory chapter provides both an overview of the book and an introduction to the major theoretical ideas about play and ethics that ground the premises of this scholarship. In chapter two I examine the contentious issue of superhero or war play that I re-conceptualize as 'mythic play' and contrast with everyday play. I show why mythic play, based as it is in narratives of power, is significant in forming ethical identities. In chapter three I discuss the formation of selves and identities and how they may be authored in pretend play. In chapter four I examine how children's ethical identities may be co-authored through child–adult play. I consider the implications for adults' ethical identities when they are committed to playing with children. In particular, I analyze how my own ethical identities have been challenged and changed through play. In chapter five I synthesize the theoretical frameworks developed in the book and consider implications for pedagogy in early childhood institutional settings. I explore what play as ethical pedagogy might look like if teachers, parents, and care-givers were committed to sharing power with children and changed their practice in response to the theoretical ideas and practical approaches outlined in this book.

Play

Binary thinking about play

My attempt to make sense of Michael's play and respond, when he pretended to be a T-Rex, was more problematic than it may seem. Anyone who talks or writes about play, whether in an academic, daycare, or family setting, is unavoidably using a term that is populated with other people's assumptions and beliefs about the value of play in different situations and relationships (Bakhtin, 1981). Understandings of play are linked to various images and experiences about what is wise parenting, nurturing care-giving, or good teaching.

In both professional literature and everyday usage, when people talk or write about play the dominant way of thinking is in terms of binaries. Play is framed as an activity set apart from real life (Huizinga, 1955; Winnicott, 1971; Bateson, 1972). Huizinga argued that human culture emerged out of the human instinct to play but he did not see play as part of cultural reality. Play is a special, irrational, fun activity that is different from 'ordinary' life (p. 4). Winnicott regarded play as essential for creativity, communication, and psychological health but bracketed off from real-world appraisal. For Winnicott, playing, creative, and cultural experiences like art occur in an intermediate area between inner and outer reality (p. 15). Bateson regarded play as essentially an ironic communication about reality (p. 180). Such binary thinking leads to divisions of activities, whether those of adults or children, into being either play or not-play. As Pateman puts it, 'play is not *for* anything; it just *is*' (1991, p. 143).

Helen Schwartzman (1978), a cultural anthropologist, in summarizing the dominant play theories stressed that our understanding of play has been 'most significantly influenced by shared attitudes of what play is not. Play is not work, play is not real, play is not serious, play is not productive – therefore play is not important.'

So where do those views of play leave a child who wants to pretend to be a roaring T-Rex? Unfortunately, the child is often ignored, controlled, chastised, or excluded by adults. It is hard to see violent play as serious, productive, real work. And where does such a discourse position any adult who wants to pretend with the child? Unavoidably on the margins of dominant assumptions about the value of play and what constitutes appropriate behavior.

There is no agreed-upon definition of play. As Bennett, Wood, and Rogers note, play research 'has been bedeviled by the search for a definition of what play is and what it does for the child' (1994, p. 4). There is a pervasive assumption from an adult point of view that play is important only when it is functional in the sense that it is facilitating development (Piaget, 1962). Play is seen as preparatory for the future (Spencer, 1873; Erikson, 1963; Sutton-Smith, 1994) or as a 'rehearsal for life' (Erikson, 1972; Glasgow Koste, 1995). Developmentalists regard playing with objects and people as important because such interactions are regarded as promoting cognitive, emotional, social, and moral development. Through play with objects like blocks and water, children learn about the physical world. Through pretend play, alone and with others, children are socialized; they learn about and can practice appropriate adult social roles as well as appropriate social behavior (Smilansky, 1990). Over time, as children become more cognitively adept, and more empathetic, they are viewed as progressing through predetermined 'stages' of cognitive and moral development. This functional view of play values children pretending to be kind doctors, brave firefighters, good cooks, or helpful car drivers. Pretending to be an attacking, fighting, killing, T-Rex is more troublesome in terms of social norms.

A functional view of play leads to assumptions that play is childish and not really for adults. Thus, it is hardly surprising that adults (whether academics, parents, or care-givers) tend to regard pretending to be dinosaurs (or even pretending to cook) as unimportant in comparison to 'real' activities like actually cooking family meals, productive tasks like putting away toy dinosaurs in one's room, or the serious learning of academic facts from a book about dinosaurs. Because children want to play, playing is legitimated by becoming the 'child's work' (Paley, 2004). As Schwartzman (1991) put it, 'play becomes domesticated, idealized, romanticized and defined as the work of children.' Play is regarded as happening in the special province of childhood; not a space for adults to enter into with children.

Generations of teachers and parents have regarded pretend play as a 'not adult' activity that occurs in a domain of 'childhood'. Play becomes valued when it becomes more serious and productive in games, and thus more adult-like. Adults are encouraged to play games with children and help to organize children at play but they are not encouraged to pretend with them. When I was a young child I was told to 'go off and play' with the assumption that I had to leave the social world of adults in order to pretend. When I was older, adults would play card or word games with me and my siblings. At school we played sports organized and refereed by adult teachers. When our children were in preschool they had 'free play' time when, provided they were safe, they could be silly and do whatever they wanted. They also had 'organized play' time where they were provided with objects to play with and make discoveries about. All these views of play are firmly located in a Piagetian theory of education.

Piaget (1975/1932) incorporated play into his theory of development. He regarded games with rules as a higher form of play than pretending. He assumed that development precedes learning and that thought precedes movement so that children's actions, including when they play, are expressive of thoughts that match their stage of development. For example, he conceptualized that young children have to play with water or sand or shadows in order to express their ideas. Like 'lone scientists', they discover for themselves an object's physical properties. Similarly, he argued, when children pretend to answer the phone or cook for a family they are learning about social roles. He assumed that adults in the same activities have much less to learn than children because adults have already developed under-standings of physical concepts like gravity or adhesion and social interactions like having dinner together. When Piaget watched children play he saw largely imitative repetitive activities that fulfilled a child's need to 'assimilate' ideas. Occasionally a child experiences 'cognitive dissonance' and has to 'accommodate' a conflicting discovery but Piaget theorized that, on the whole, children do not seek out such variations when they play. Further, Piaget argues that young children play with objects because their thinking is 'concrete'; only older children have developed the ability to think abstractly about gravity or social relationships.

Piagetian constructivist theories of development can all too easily leave adults feeling superior to children and disconnected from their play worlds. The ossification of Piaget's assumptions into a rigid stage theory can leave adults assuming that children are on a different 'level' to them; thus a young child's thinking is 'undeveloped' and less abstract because it is anchored to specific situations and objects. Further, a codified approach to what is or is not 'developmentally appropriate practice' (Bredekamp, 1986) can lead adults to exclude themselves from interactions. Though it may be amusing, it is difficult to categorize as 'appropriate' an adult pretending with a child to be fighting dinosaurs.

Playing as an attitude to activities

Some scholars, including Garvey (1977), Schwartzman (1978), Moyles (1989), and Thorne (1993) have critiqued the play/not-play binary. Pelligrini has criticized the tendency to dichotomize activities into play/not-play and instead has proposed conceptualizing play as on a continuum of 'more or less play' (1991, p. 215). At the heart of this critique, as Bruner et al. stressed, is a recognition that 'the main characteristic of play – whether of child or adult – is not its content but its mode. Play is an approach to action, not a form of activity' (1976, p. v). Lurker (1991) similarly argued that play is a function of our attitude; we are playing when we have a 'play attitude' as opposed to a 'survival attitude'. As Garvey puts it, 'All play requires the players to understand that what is done is not what it appears to be. It is this nonliteral attitude that allows play to be buffered from its consequences' (1977, p. 7).

Fromberg (1987; 1992) incorporates the stance of play as an attitude to activity into her definition of play when she includes the following characteristics:

- *Symbolic*, represents reality with the possibilities inherent in an 'as if' or 'what if' attitude;
- *Meaningful*, children use play to connect or relate experiences;

- *Active*, children are engaged in doing things;
- *Pleasurable*, even when children are engaged seriously in an activity;
- *Voluntary and intrinsically motivated*, whether the motivations are curiosity, mastery, affiliation, or others;
- *Rule-governed*, whether implicitly or explicitly expressed;
- *Episodic*, characterized by emerging and shifting goals that children develop spontaneously.

Once I could conceptualize playing as an attitude toward any activity, I was able to accept and value the reality that Michael, aged three, wanted to pretend or imagine for 90 percent of his waking hours. As he talked, moved, read, drew, ate meals, interacted with other children, rode in the car, went for a walk, or watched movies, he played. Further, I could shift into play mode with Michael by adopting this playful attitude toward his activities.

Play worlds and everyday life

People play in the 'subjunctive mood' (Turner, 1992). When people play they act 'as if . . .', for example 'as if I were seeing dinosaurs' or imagining 'what if . . .', for example, 'what if I were a dinosaur' (Bruner et al., 1976). In pretend play people pretend together to move and talk and interact as if they are whatever people or creatures they want to be, in any time or space, engaged in any imagined activity.

Any activity is playful when it has an 'if' dimension. However, the actual physical and social worlds of everyday life do not disappear when we play. Though still present, they do begin to recede. Being playful hints at, and makes reference to, the possibilities of other ways of being, other parallel worlds where we could have different lives. A playful attitude can create imaginary spaces that exist in imagined play worlds. As Vygotsky put it, 'in play a child creates an imaginary situation in an imaginary illusory world [where] unrealizable desires can be realized' (1978, p. 93).

When people play together, pretending that they are elsewhere, every-day life dims in the light of an imagined world that seems to materialize and take on a parallel brighter reality. When we play with children we enter the 'if' dimension to find ourselves on pathways to imagined worlds which for a time can be experienced as more real than everyday life. Jokes can invoke a world where existing social relationships have been inverted. Stories can paint pictures of times and places where we would have to be very different people if we lived there.

Play worlds are created and entered in imagination. A play world begins to take form when people pretend that they are actually there. The external actions in pretend play are the external objectifications of a world conceived in minds, language, and interacting bodies.

Children do this with little effort and move effortlessly between play worlds and the everyday. Adults tend to resist the imaginative leap especially when they feel that other judgmental adults are watching them. Like Alice going down a rabbit hole or stepping into a liquid mirror, entering a wonderland play world can feel unnerving or even dangerous for adults. It can also feel childish and silly. It's only children who would expect to enter a wardrobe to find the world of Narnia. Yet pretending with children opens up possibilities that are unavailable without play.

Adult play

Adults play more than they realize. People begin to play every time they joke, tell stories, play games, mimic others, put on a costume for a fancy-dress party, or imagine possibilities. Vygotsky recognized that imagination is 'play without action' and that 'play is imagination in action' (1967, p. 539). Unlike children who are often very physically and socially active as they play, unless they are sharing a skit or staging a formal performance as actors or dancers, adults rarely use imagination socially to embody other worlds.

Adults are good at imagining using only the mind, for example, as they watch television and movies or read. Nearly all young children learn to imagine with mimimal movement or noise, as Michael did. However, this does not mean that being silent or still while imagining necessarily indicates any particular mental, physical, or moral development. Learning to control bodily movements so that others find it 'appropriate' is an indication of having learned particular social and cultural rules of behavior in particular situations. It does not indicate that these behaviors are 'good', 'better', or more 'advanced'.

Playing as a workshop for life

Over time, I came to regard our playing not as an escape from reality but rather as an ongoing 'workshop for life'. Adults as well as children can explore various personas and over time form and shape ethical identities. The metaphor of play as a rehearsal for life captures the functional aspects of children's play when children try out adult social roles. However, Vygotsky was adamant that 'to consider play as the prototype of a child's everyday activity and its predominant form is completely incorrect' (1978, p. 101). Certainly, regarding play only as a preparation for adult social life did not capture the complexity of Michael's play. The play I describe in this book illustrates the exploratory meaning-making possibilities when children (with or without adults) play together to imagine that they are the people and creatures inside fantastic narrative worlds.

When children, and adults, imagine that they are other people or creatures they try out 'possible selves' (Marcus and Nurius, 1986) in 'possible worlds' (Bruner, 1986). They do so intentionally because a person cannot be made to play. Vygotsky realized that in play, will, movement, and thought are inseparable. As he put it, 'internal and external action are inseparable: imagination, interpretation, and will are internal processes in external action' so that the child 'in wishing carries out his wishes; and in thinking, he acts' (1967, p. 550). Of course, imagined actions and worlds will include all sorts of 'impossibilities' when set beside the physical, social, and cultural realities of people's lives.

Pretend play allows people to explore possible identities as they imagine 'what they might become, would like to become, or are afraid to become' (Marcus and Nurius, 1986, p. 73). Playing opens up imagined spaces beyond the constraints of the actual physical and social worlds where children and adults live. For over five years, Michael's explorations led us into territories inhabited by a myriad possible selves embodied in the deeds of monsters, heroes, and people from mythic tales in imagined worlds as diverse as the *Ramayanna* to the *Odyssey* and from *Frankenstein* to *Star Wars*.

The everyday physical and social worlds do not disappear when people play. Rather, as Vygotsky (1978) recognized, when children play, their attention is more on the meaning of things and actions in imagined worlds rather than on actual objects and movements in the everyday. Children create an imagined world when they play. Adults playing with children have to be ready to do the same.

Rather than focus on actual events, children focus on the meaning of their actions and the objects they use. As Vygotsky puts it, 'In play, action is subordinated to meaning, but in real life of course, action dominates meaning' (ibid., p. 101). There is a divergence between what a child sees and the meaning of objects and actions. 'In play thought is separated from objects and action arises from ideas rather than from things' (ibid., p. 97).

In this sense, children are thinking abstractly when they play because they are always creating symbolic meaning rather than literal meaning. A stick becomes a sword and a doll becomes a child. Further, when they play children can explore their relationships with one another and with other people. In Vygotsky's famous example, when sisters play at being 'sisters' they can be 'a head taller' and thus older and taller and smarter or more socially adept sisters than in their everyday lives as well as being in places where they have never actually been (ibid., p. 95).

Playing creates the opportunity to play with possible selves and identities. When girls play at being sisters, not only can they try out the social role of sister, acting as a sister self, but also the social identity of sister. Even children who actually are sisters can pretend to be sisters. In imagined play spaces, anyone can explore a sister identity, and thus what it means to be a 'sister' in multiple possible situations. As Vygotsky argues, sisters who play at being sisters 'are both concerned with displaying their sisterhood . . . they enact whatever emphasizes their relationship as sisters vis-à-vis adults and strangers' (ibid., p. 95). They can see the world through the eyes of sisters who relate to one another and other people differently as they create and experience scores of activities and events that are unlikely or impossible in everyday life, ranging from going on vacation to adopting a child. When children explore what it means to be a 'kind' sister or a 'mean' sister then they are playing with different possible selves and exploring possible ethical identities.

As Dyson puts it, pretend play 'provides a forum for children [and adults] to create imaginary situations where they 'are "free" from the constraints of concrete objects, real actions, and indeed their own voices [and bodies]. They infuse their own intentions – their own meanings – into those objects and actions' . . . in a space where 'pretend' identities are appropriated (1997, pp. 13–14).

When children play, in imagination they fully enter worlds that may be as engaging and complex as the cultural narratives that they draw upon which include their re-told experiences, the stories they have read, and the movies they have watched. When adults play with children they can likewise enter those worlds not to observe but to participate with children, not only to listen but to interact and shape meaning, and not only to enter imagined space-times but to explore possible ways of acting and identifying with other people in the world.

Ethics

The dominant modernist discourse of ethics shared by people as diverse as academics, educators, parents, legislators, lawyers, priests, and business people, unquestioningly assumes that moral individuals follow core universal, objective, abstract, and rational principles and rules that tell people how they ought to behave. Immanuel Kant's Enlightenment moral philosophy is at the core of a theory of ethics driven by universal rules. Of particular importance is his idea that humans ought to direct their actions according to a rationally derived categorical imperative. An individual knows how to act by applying their reason to discover universal moral laws that they then use to direct their will in following those laws 'which I regard as applicable universally, to everyone and not just me' (Grayling, 2003, p. 152).

Any group's particular core ethical principles and rules are ideally stable and pre-existing. They are codified over time by rational people in authority who have created laws, regulations, moral codes of conduct etc. to apply to everyone in the group. The interpretation of regulations and gradual changes to rules occurs over time through rational exchanges that seek to make guiding principles applied more universally and more impartially. However, when adults regard children as not being rational then it is easy to justify excluding them from any discussion about what actions are reasonable or right within a pre-existing rule. An example would be, 'we don't use pretend guns'.

Groups are seen as formed by autonomous individuals who ought to show one another mutual respect. Children have to learn to respect others because they are not regarded as being born with an inner 'moral compass' that guides their actions. As a member of any group (ranging from public society to a school classroom) it is an individual's duty, so goes the argument, to implicitly or explicitly agree to adhere to the group's principles and rules which create order by providing adults with clear predictable behavioral expectations. Rights are granted to individuals because of their reciprocal acceptance of their responsibilities under the pre-existing rules. Conflicts between individuals are regarded either as a rupture in the balance between different individuals' rights and responsibilities or because an individual made a 'bad' choice by not following the rules. Disputes are inevitable but it is assumed that they can be resolvable through rational debate that seeks more objectively to apply the appropriate guiding rules and regulations and have individuals accept their responsibilities if they want the right to participate. For example, when children arguing over blocks are reminded of rules to 'use the blocks quietly, respect other people, and give someone else a turn after 5 minutes', it is assumed that consulting the clock and a brief exchange should be enough to have children agree on what rules have been broken and who ought to be in the block corner.

An individual can only have rights within a group when those in authority can expect someone to 'be responsible' in fulfilling their 'duties'. When a child's actions are interpreted as being 'irresponsible' either because they are regarded as being egocentric or because the child is assumed to be incapable of abstract detached universal thinking then their conduct may be excused. However their views, as well as their bodies, can easily be excluded from group activities. If a group norm has been violated then it is easy to justify removing the normal right to be heard or included. No more block play for the child who's pretending to be a dinosaur and knocking them down.

Moral development theory

The examples I used above of adults regulating children are all enshrined in the pervasive cognitive, affective, and moral developmental theories of Piaget (1975; 1962). They are extended, in particular, by Hoffman (2000), and Kohlberg (1984). These researchers privilege autonomous views of the individual who constructs understandings so that he or she becomes more rational, more empathetic, more objective, and more able to think in abstractions as he or she grows older. Despite academic critique and nuanced interpretation of developmental theories (Rest, Narvaez, Bebeau, and Thoma, 1999; Packer and Tappen, 2001), basic developmental assumptions form the skeleton of the framework used by most early childhood teachers and care-givers to judge the rightness of children's behaviors and the goodness of early childhood practice.

Piagetian theory assumes that a young child lacks the capacity to differentiate others' perspectives from their own or at the very least has a deep egocentric bias that ignores others' perspectives (Gibbs, 2003). For example, 'egocentric impulses of aggression' (Selman and Shultz, 1990) and the fact that children focus on the 'here and now' (Flavell et al., 2002) are seen as examples of this inability or resistance to decentre. Piaget's theory of cognitive development in predetermined 'stages' presupposes that it is only as a child learns to decentre that he or she can develop. Similarly, only over time will she or he be able to move from thinking about the concrete to formal thinking about abstract ideas, such as universal objective rules. When adults' relationship with children is clouded by such a framework it can feel quite natural to regard young children as incapable of relating to adults as equals because they're 'just too immature'.

Piaget's moral development theories, as extended by Kohlberg's cognitive and Hoffman's affective approaches, focus on an individual child's ability (or inability) to make right moral judgments and have good empathetic feelings. Kohlberg proposed six inviolable stages of moral development. 'Mature' moral judgment is not expected until later childhood and early adolescence because it can only occur when a child can decentre to think 'formally' about a question like 'How would you wish to be treated?'

Hoffman (2000) similarly proposes that, beginning in middle childhood, a child moves into 'mature' stages of empathy development as he or she feels more than empathetic distress for another and begins to take context into account in their judgment of how another person feels. Eventually individuals have empathy for groups beyond their immediate situation.

Poststructural and feminist theories of ethics

Using Bauman's (1995) chilling example of the Nazi death camps, Dahlberg and Moss illustrate the heart of darkness in a modernist approach to ethics. There is a pervasive danger that the 'ethical becomes the technical' as 'power and responsibility become detached' (2005, p. 70). As Oliner and Oliner put it, 'Ideology, grand vision, or abstract principles may inure [one] to the suffering of real people' (1998, p. 257). The Nazi mass murderer

Rudolf Hoess could thus describe his actions as moral since morality for him was a 'meticulous desire for justice and a fanatical sense of duty' (quoted in Kohn, 1990, p. 259).

The universal theory of ethics masks power relationships. It does not recognize that beliefs about what is 'right' and 'good' are ideologies constructed and then regulated within institutional and relational power structures that most often privilege and benefit some people and not others. Rather, an 'objective' view of ethics assumes instead that the ability of each individual to reason will lead to universally good laws and actions which will be right for the greatest possible number of people. In totalitarian states like those controlled by the Nazis or the Soviets, what was constructed as right for the most people sent millions to their death.

Power is not the simple exercise of force. Power, for Foucault, is always relational and circulates among people in every interaction. People exercise power over others when they control the meaning of actions and events. An example would be what is (or is not) 'normal development' and 'appropriate practices'. Over time, power accumulates within the discourse of institutions and professional fields of study, operates as 'regimes of truth' which are then invoked as 'the authority' used, for example, by teachers to chastise or exclude children.

Foucault's critical analysis of how people are regulated, controlled, and disciplined in institutions like schools, hospitals, and prisons exposed the relationship between power, knowledge, and truth. People use institutional and discursive power to create what counts as truth/knowledge and then regulate those who do not conform. There is no universal meaning for what is 'right' and 'good' because the meaning of such moral terms depends on who has, and has had, the power to control meanings being made, codify those meanings, and decide what behaviors are, and what are not, 'normal'.

Poststructuralists show how the meanings of words are not objective and external or fixed and static but rather shifting, fractured, dispersed, and always incomplete because they are culturally and textually derived. The meanings that people bring to words depend on their cultural background, the texts that they have had access to, and the contradictions that have been examined (Derrida, 1976; 1978). Derrida argued that people should 'deconstruct' texts in order to reveal that the meanings of words have been constructed. He showed how dichotomies and binaries (like work/play and good/bad) as well as those that construct 'identities of difference' (like boy/girl or adult/child) need to be deconstructed. Such deconstruction reveals how practices of inclusion and exclusion use binaries in the practice of 'othering' by creating standards of 'normality' which are then used to control and manage behaviors and emotions.

Though, for Foucault, subjectivity is constituted by discourse circulating in power relations, Foucault (1984; 1985) also argued that individuals can have moral agency. He conceptualized ethics as a mode of self-formation. Actions are ethical, not when they are in conformity to moral norms but rather when people are forming themselves as moral subjects. An individual's concern with ethics determines 'the kind of relationship you ought to have with yourself' (1984, p. 352). Foucault's view of the self in relation to prior discourses sees individuals forming themselves as moral agents when they recognize their ethical obligations toward moral codes and other societal determiners of good behavior. Over time, for example, some children may strive to repress their desires so that they may become more self-controlled and thus better able to follow particular adult rules while others may work to express their emotions more freely in order to meet the expectations of 'good' behavior repeatedly stated by a trusted adult. Foucault's view of self-formation sees individuals as creating themselves in relation to moral norms made apparent in power relations rather than in developing a sense of responsibility toward particular people.

Power and responsibility toward others are reattached by feminist scholars who have emphasized humans' ethical responsibilities for one another when they practice an 'ethic of care' (Gilligan, 1982; Noddings, 1984; Tronto, 1993; Sevenhuijsen, 1998; Butler, 2005). They conceptualize the self as always in relation to other people and exemplified in actions that show the values of love, empathy, compassion, and commitment. As Noddings puts it, 'the very well spring of ethical behavior is human affective response' (1984, p. 3).

Rather than strive for objective rules and abstract detachment, post-tructural and feminist scholars refocus people's attention on their relationships with other people and on the consequences of their actions. Rather than regard the self as individual, autonomous, and acting on the world, they see a situated 'relational self' that changes over time as it interacts with and is affected by others in the world.

A dialogic theory of ethical action

For Bakhtin, 'ethics is a matter not of knowledge but of wisdom' (Morson and Emerson 1990, p. 27). Thus, it matters little what people know about ethical principles if they cannot be wise about their lives and act ethically in the moment. Bakhtin proposes a 'dialogic' theory of ethical action that complements the theories of other poststructuralists and feminist scholars. Foucault exposes how power can be used 'over others' to control and oppress, while Gilligan and Noddings emphasize how power ought to be used 'for others' in nurturing relationships. Complementing Bauman's view that people should take responsibility for others and Levinas' position of respect for the other in the ethics of particular encounters, Bakhtin's theories, I argue, propose a third way to conceptualize people's intersecting stances to power relations. When people intend to make their interactions more dialogic their stance is to use power 'with others'. Such dialogic explorations can lead to the formation of ethical identities.

People cannot assume that they are ethical just because their acts have followed universal principles, legal rules, or moral norms. As Bakhtin puts it, '*everyone* occupies a unique and never-repeatable place, *any* being is once-occurrent' (1993, p. 40). People cannot ethically hide behind other people's principles. For Bakhtin, a person's actions are ethical when they are 'answerable' to anyone who 'addresses' them about the consequences of those particular actions (1990). Being answerable is more than being responsible. Rather than just accepting responsibility for doing something, when people are answerable their ethical understandings are affected and transformed because they allow themselves to be addressed by another person's ideas that dialogically affect and shape the framework they use to make meaning.

People use what Bakhtin (1981) called 'the dialogic imagination' to evaluate their actions from the viewpoints and discourses of others who address them. Imagination is ethically so significant for Bakhtin because people can evaluate the consequences of their particular actions by viewing and understanding them from the different standpoints of people who may or may not be physically present.

> We evaluate ourselves from the standpoint of others, and through others we try to understand and take into account what is transgredient to our own consciousness. Thus, we take into account the value of our outward appearance from the standpoint of the possible impression it may produce upon the other, although for ourselves this value does not exist in any immediate way. We take into account the background behind our back, that is to say, all that which in our surroundings we do not see and do not know directly . . . although it is seen and known by others and has validity for others. . . . In short, we are constantly and intently on the watch for reflections of our own life on the plane of other people's consciousnesses, and, moreover, not just reflections of particular moments of our life but even reflections of the whole of it.
>
> (Bakhtin, 1990, pp. 15–16)

Highly dialogic novels, for Bakhtin, are ethically potent because people can get outside their ideological assumptions as they experience in imagination what characters in novels experience: the dialogic interplay of characters addressing and answering one another. Novels are much more than a collection of characters, plots, and themes. For Bakhtin, characters embody various discourses. Characters address one another and also us as readers. Characters answer one another, and readers, in imagination, can answer characters when they enter into dialogue with them. Discourses are always ideological because characters' actions are always value-laden. Characters embody discourses and enact their beliefs that include their ethical assumptions about how people ought to be treated. As characters interact, their discourses collide and when readers in imagination join in the interactions they too can explore moral complexities in those novels where all characters have valid viewpoints and understandable ethical positions.

What Bakhtin said about novels, I apply to pretend play. 'The action and individual act of a character . . . are essential in order to expose – as well as to test – his [or her] ideological position, his [or her] discourse' (1981, p. 334). The characters in the stories Michael encountered all enacted 'ideological positions' and used discourse as they interacted in the world of the story to make their ethical assumptions visible in actions. Reading for adults and older children requires the solo use of the dialogic imagination, whereas pretend play is interactive and social. Adult readers silently imagine dialogic interactions whereas child–adult players enact and embody dialogue and discourse. As I played with Michael, in imagination we entered into the worlds of narratives that Michael had read or viewed. In doing so we embodied and used the language of multiple ideological positions and discourses that could then be tested as we interacted and ethically evaluated characters' actions as right-and-wrong.

Michael loved pretending to be very strong and noisy, but he also wanted to imagine being weak and quiet. Soon after Michael discovered dinosaurs we introduced him to Beatrix Potter's *The Tale of Peter Rabbit*. Pretending to be Mr McGregor, Michael could yell 'Stop thief!' as he chased me (pretending to be Peter Rabbit) and then pretended to lock Peter Rabbit/me up. As he chased and captured me, Michael was enacting Mr McGregor's ideological discourse that Peter was a thief. Seconds later, he enacted a competing ideological discourse of Peter Rabbit in need of food. He would pretend to be Peter whimpering to McGregor/me as he apologized for taking carrots and then asked for some food to share with his family. As we interacted in and around play worlds, we ethically evaluated characters' actions, their discourses, and their beliefs. As these discourses intermingled, they added to the fabric of ethical exploration that was to continue via our play until Michael became an independent reader.

Our home was filled with narratives that provided Michael with a multitude of characters to embody in pretend play events. We borrowed and purchased some of the books that captivated Michael's attention during our frequent trips to the library and bookshops. Some of the newspapers and magazines that regularly came into our home captured his attention. Though we rarely watched television we did watch children's videotapes with him. As Michael's mother and I used children's literature in our university teaching, books that might appeal to a young child were always

lying around our home. From birth, Michael met, embodied, and interacted with characters from narratives that ranged from canonical children's
books like *The Tale of Peter Rabbit* and *Goodnight Moon*, to popular videotapes
at the time, like *Thomas the Tank Engine* and the Disney version of *Beauty and
the Beast*. Stories about dinosaurs and talking rabbits along with informational books were soon supplemented with tales of world mythology ranging
from picture book versions of *Beowulf* to *Gilgamesh*. Once Michael discovered
horror fiction at the library, Dracula and the Wolfman regularly joined
St George, Perseus, and Medusa in our home.

Ethical selves and identities

Bakhtin's theories of ethics and the self ground my argument that ethical
identities form in and around child–adult play. For Bakhtin, there is no
unitary self that is separated from other people encountered in everyday
life and in narratives. Bakhtin theorized 'dialogic selves' that are always
in relationship with others. In the following chapters I outline how play can
support the creation of ethical identities. Here I propose that people's ethical
identities intersect with (but are not synonymous with) their social and
cultural identities, all of which are formed over time through social interactions as people's different selves interact.

Adults' discursive and relational power at home and in early childhood
institutions are used to regulate the environment and activities as well as
evaluate actions. This power not only shapes young people's social identities as 'children' and their gender identities as 'boys' and as 'girls' but also,
I argue, affects how children ethically identify with the 'good' (or 'bad')
actions of others.

In contrast with the dominant modernist assumption that identity is
an individual's unitary, coherent, and fixed essence of the self (Best and
Kellner, 1991), feminist poststructuralist theorists (Davies, 1989; 1993;
Lloyd and Duveen, 1993) have redefined selves and identities as multiple,
dynamic, relational, negotiated, emotional as well as cognitive, and (in
different contexts) potentially contradictory. Though people are surrounded
by institutional, material, and structural constraints, they also can have
agency to actively negotiate, construct, and reconstruct their own identities
(Hughes and Mac Naughton, 2001; Evans, 2002). Each person has multiple
everyday selves that act, interact, and interpret situations in relation with
others. I am a different 'I' when I interact with different people. 'Who I
am and how I feel is not just about me in a vacuum. It is about me in relationship to others, and them in relationship to me' (Evans, 2002, p. 3). I talk
and play with my children as my father self and with my spouse as my
husband self, yet when I see my siblings I become my brother self. And when
I am in university contexts I write, and teach, and interact as my professor

self. These selves are not fixed social roles. Though my selves have become stable over time they also change as I interact, and in doing so I change how I identify with groups of other people.

My intersecting and sometimes conflicting social and cultural identities (male, father, spouse, academic, Ohio State University 'Buckeye', White, middle class, Irish-British-American, human, son, brother, fiddle-player, bicycler, Quaker etc.) are markers not only for my multiple acting selves in different social situations but also for my historical and evolving relationships with others in the interconnected social and cultural groups with which I have identified in the past, look forward to continue to identify with in the future, as well as those I seek to maintain in the present. How I identify with others and act in the present is interrelated with how I have acted, been identified, and identified myself with others in the past, as well as with how I hope to act and identify with people in the future. As Norton puts it, identities are 'how people understand their relationship to the world, how that relationship is constructed across space and time, and how people understand their possibilities for the future' (1997, p. 410).

I argue that people's ethical identities are how they frame their relationships to the world in terms of malleable frameworks which can guide both the daily actions of an ethical self and their evaluations of their own and others' deeds in terms of their 'rightness' and 'goodness'. People's ethical identities intersect and overlap with their social and cultural identities. My socio-cultural frameworks connect me with others socially and culturally across many different groups of people. My ethical framework connects me with people in terms of how I identify with their ethical viewpoint and their actions. My ethical self answers those who address me and allows me to critique people's actions and the assumptions of particular groups. For example, my ethical identity intersects with my male identity to create an assumption of gender equality. Interacting as a male self in a group of men, I would question sexist language or assumptions that imply that women are inferior to men. People's ethical identities create ethical frameworks for evaluating how they ought to identify with other people and act in the world. It's my ethical identity that both tells me sexist jokes are wrong because they are oppressive practices, and propels my ethical self into action to say that I don't find the jokes funny.

My ethical identity is the framework I use to evaluate the rightness or goodness of any action. My ethical identity provides me with beliefs about the rightness (and wrongness) of my own and others' actions and is a pattern woven into the fabric of my socio-cultural identities. It connects me with the ethical stances and actions of religious leaders like the Dalai Lama as much as professional colleagues like bell hooks (2003) and Parker Palmer (2004). My ethical identity intertwines with my understanding of the deeds of historical figures like Martin Luther King and Ghandi in terms of their resistance to oppression in an institutionally racist United States, in colonial India, and throughout the world.

The words of Mairéad Corrigan Maguire capture much of my conceptualization of ethical identities as core strands round which other identities weave. The Nobel Peace Laureate from Northern Ireland has worked for peace and reconciliation since she co-founded the Peace People in 1976 after her two young nephews and niece along with her sister had been violently killed on the streets of Belfast. She believes that, 'It is fine to celebrate our diversity and our roots, but we must also rise above those ideas that divide us to understand our most basic identity, our common membership in the human family' (1999, p. 52).

Maguire's beliefs echo Kristen Monroe's (1996) conclusions to her empirical and critical research on altruism. Maguire argues that human beings have what she calls a 'core identity' which 'includes our innermost sense of who we are and what ties and obligations we believe we have to others' (1999, p. 219). Though I now identify as a Quaker, I was born into a family where I was identified as a male Protestant Presbyterian in Northern Ireland whereas Maguire was born a female Roman Catholic. Thus, I cannot identify with her along lines of gender or religious identity. Yet I do identify with her in terms of her commitment to social justice for all people and her non-violent action. My connection with her parallels my identification with other present-day peace witnesses like those in the US-Canadian-UK Christian Peacemaker Team who were taken hostage in Iraq in 2005. Like them I believe in 'the power of love and the courage of nonviolence' and in the light of an ethical identity that can 'reveal the way out of fear and grief and war' (2006).

Authoring ethical identities

Bakhtin argues that, like the writers of stories, people should become authors of their actions and of their identities. Holland et al. (1998) connect Bakhtin's metaphor of authoring with the concept of agency. They argue that when people have agency they choose action from possibilities that take into account other viewpoints. Thus when people author their lives they intentionally and reflectively exercise power in relation to others. They remake their social world as well as their selves and, over time, their identities.

As Holland shows, authoring or agency requires people to improvise responses in social situations by selectively using the cultural resources available to them to address whatever concerns or problems they face. In addition to people's life experiences, their cultural resources include all the narratives they have explored and made their own.

When children play they have very high agency because they continually improvise in their interactions. As Vygotsky stressed, when children play, meaning and intention come to the fore. Together they have to create what-ever imagined world they want to explore. In pretend play, children can improvise freely with their cultural resources much more than they can in everyday life. Everyday experiences as well as imagined experiences from stories or other narratives are transformed in play. From pretending to use the phone to imagining an attack by a T-Rex or taking vegetables from a garden, children can enact and evaluate events that in everyday life could be considered socially inappropriate or bizarre as well as those that would be socially acceptable or expected.

When people play together as they make meaning they can co-author possible selves and over time possible ethical identities. Along with the deeds of their everyday selves, the actions of the possible selves that children (and adults) explore in pretend play create the fabric of their identities. And when children are answerable for their imagined actions they are forming their ethical identities.

There is an inherent academic tension between the fact that identities can be considered to be both historically produced and constituted daily in the power relationships of people's lives that are always 'raced', 'classed', 'gendered' etc. As the sociologist Etienne Wenger notes, 'Identification is a process that is at once both relational and experiential, subjective and collective . . . something we do to ourselves and something we do to each other' (1998, p. 191). Holland et al. (1998) situate this tension in competing academic discourses from the fields of anthropology and social psychology and they locate agency and authoring in this nexus.

Whereas anthropologists tend to see a person's identities as culturally determined over time, social psychologists regard identities as socially constructed in particular interactions. Holland argues that both can be true at the same time. People accept and seek the identifications that groups assume about them – they want to belong and be accepted by groups. People regard themselves as like others and they develop shared narratives that include their selves in social groups. For example, Michael never resisted accepting his identification as a 'boy' or that he was a 'preschooler' and he liked to hear the family stories that we retold on demand. At the same time, people can actively shape their identifications in discursive relational interactions – in particular interactions they resist being socially positioned by others to act or think in certain ways or they position themselves rela-tive to others in new ways. People's identities are tied up with their relative power, status, and privilege and how they use those discursively to position others. For example, Michael once wanted to negotiate with his teacher about wearing his black and red cape to school.

Authoring ethical identities in play

We can author selves and identities when we play. Gee, in his analysis of playing video games, proposes a tripartite view of identities. My 'real world identity' is the person who is playing a video game. My virtual identity is as 'a virtual character in a virtual world' that I imagine I am. In acting as if I am someone else I 'project my values and desires' unto the virtual character with my 'projective identity'. Gee argues that in my projective identity not only do I direct a virtual character, I also 'worry about what sort of "person" I want [the character] to be'. He argues that I experience my projective identity as a projection of my values and desires into the actions and reactions of imagined people or creatures in a created world. Further, he argues that a 'good' video game both requires me to 'have to think reflectively and critically' about the virtual character and it 'makes me think new thoughts about what I value and what I do not' (2003, pp. 52–56).

I make a similar argument for pretend play. Our agency when we play is located in an authoring self that includes an ethical self when I am answerable to others for my actions. Whereas Gee conflates selves and identities I want to separate them: selves act in the moment whereas identities reflectively connect me with my own and others' actions across time and space.

In everyday life we act as our selves and identify with others. When we play we can project and explore possible selves (including possible ethical selves) in imagined worlds. Over time, in and around our play, we can create possible identities (including ethical identities). Just as Gee argues that in playing video games people can contemplate their values, I argue that in pretend play people similarly create space-times where through evaluation of the deeds of possible selves they form and shape their ethical identities.

Child–adult pretend play is significantly different from playing video games in two important respects. First, children can draw on and play with whatever cultural resources they have and are not limited to those of the game designer. Second, they are not abandoned to think reflectively and critically on their own.

In the following chapters I show how Michael's ethical identity formed as he drew on and used cultural resources, especially the narratives we explored as we played. At the same time I show how our ethical identities were co-authored through our dialogic interactions.

Not a conclusion

The Michael I played with as a little boy has grown up into a young man of seventeen at the time of this writing. This book does not attempt to draw simplistic conclusions or direct correlations between our past play and

Michael's present ethical identities. It does, however, develop an argument that our daily play then was as highly significant in the formation of ethical sensibilities as our daily conversations are now about matters of importance to Michael. In the intervening years since we played almost daily, his schooling, relationships with other people, reading, and experiences all have contributed to the formation of his possible ethical selves and ethical identity.

Before you read more about Michael aged three, I close this opening chapter by giving you a glimpse of a future older Michael who, I would argue, was being ethical in a moment that was not playful. When Michael was thirteen he joined me on a visit to the office of our Congresswoman organized by Quakers and other peace activists. The 2003 Iraq War was about to begin. As we waited in the lobby of the Federal Building in the city where we live he read several pages of background information that I had downloaded from the web. The meeting with our Representative's aide was to ask her to support diplomatic moves that could avoid an invasion. About thirty people, including Michael and two other younger children, crowded into the room where we were politely received and in turn asked by the aide to speak. When all adults had spoken the aide began to respond. She had not called on the children to speak. Michael looked at me, and recognizing that he wanted to speak, I interrupted her to point out that she had not heard from everyone. She realized that he had something to say. Her tone changed to be slightly condescending as she asked him how he had got out of school. He replied that I had brought him and I added that I wanted him to see democracy in action. Michael spoke for about a minute. He focused on two things that had not been said by anyone else and that were not repeated from the information sheets he had read. First, he wanted our Representative to imagine speaking to the families of the people who would be killed in an invasion that would include innocent Iraqi civilians. Second, he said that the decision to go to war was more complex than the President was making it sound. He said 'It's not as simple as that. There are always other ways to think about it.' He was asking her, our representative, and the President, to all be answerable to people whose lives were almost entirely absent from the political debate and the media coverage but which in imagination he saw and heard as the voices of real people who addressed and called out to him.

Chapter 2

Mythic and everyday play

Figure 2.1 Calvin/Wolfman and his father

Like Calvin's father, once I could only see my son as a little boy. I was sometimes as shocked as he was with Calvin's behavior when between the ages of about three and seven, his mother and I had to put up with the sudden appearance of werewolves in our home. We grew to expect the arrival of vampires, zombies, mummies, giants, witches, dragons, demons, and hunchbacks. In addition we became acquainted with various creatures that appeared from swamps, caves, forests, outer space, black lagoons, and mad scientists' laboratories.

As Michael began to read independently, the monsters and heroes that fascinated him disappeared inside the covers of books, lurked in the hard drive of our computer, and shrank on to miniature battle fields. By the time Michael was twelve, instead of actually meeting disturbing creatures on a daily basis we could expect to encounter Edgar Allan Poe, H.P. Lovecraft, or Stephen King on a bookshelf, Star Craft on the computer screen, or *Warhammer* figures on the dining room table.

Knowing that Favat (1977) had reported how young children much prefer fairy tales to realistic stories, I was not surprised that Michael by age three loved *The Tale of Peter Rabbit* and the story of *Jack and the Beanstalk*. However, I had not anticipated, and was not ready for, his soon-to-come intense relationship with picture-book versions of tales like *Beowulf* and with movies like *Dracula*.

Calvin's father sees no value in Calvin pretending to be a werewolf. It never occurs to him to enter the mythic worlds of werewolves and other monsters where Calvin, usually as Spaceman Spiff, does battle. And because Calvin's parents and teacher never join Calvin in his play worlds they are never privy to the philosophical questions raised and ideas explored in the conversations Calvin has with his tiger playmate, Hobbes.

For me, it was not until I began to frame much of Michael's play as mythic that my understanding of its significance changed. I anticipated Michael's everyday play as he pretended to drive our car. I had not expected his depictions of gruesome or violent deeds. As I brought a positive interpretation to play events when Michael wanted to imagine he was a monster, I began to embrace and value play about which I had previously felt ambivalent or resistant. I came to understand our play as mythic when it arose from the many mythic narratives that Michael explored and which he demanded I share with him over and over again.

Mythic narratives

Marina Warner, in one of her many books that critically analyses myth, describes myths as 'stories that inquire into everyday realities, projected unto an eternal and supernatural horizon' (Warner, 2003, p. vi). Though the term myth is sometimes used to describe lies or half-truths, in contrast with facts, I use the term as cultural anthropologists use it. Myths are narratives set in landscapes likely to be populated with monsters, heroes, and gods as well as people any one of whom may perform magical deeds. Myths are stories that examine human truths about aspects of the realities of life and death experienced by people in all cultures.

Though myths are in a sense the product of specific cultures they nevertheless have timeless cross-cultural similarities (Campbell, 1972; Lévi-Strauss, 1978; 1996). Readers and listeners can identify with the deeds and life experiences of people and creatures across time and space in often fantastical worlds that are quite different from our everyday lives. The myths from Homer's Greece, the Grimm brothers' Germany, or the India of *The Ramayana*, can still speak to people today. Like the heroes and people in tales hundreds or thousands of years old, people still face violence, encounter rejection, seek love, and finally meet death irrespective of their particular social circumstances and cultural background. As the mythologist Wendy Doniger stresses, 'Myths raise certain basic questions of human meaning . . . myths are about the human experiences that we all share – birth, love, hate, death, . . .' (1995, 1).

As Coustineau argues, mythic narratives can be contemporary creations as well as ancient stories. 'Stories become mythic when they evoke eternal concerns, whether on a stone tablet in the sands of ancient Sumer or on the flickering screen at your local Odeon [movie theatre]. . . . Myths seize the imagination because they take on questions – love and war, birth and death, good and evil – that otherwise cannot be answered' (2001, p. 19). Twentieth-century stories like *Star Wars*, *The Lord of the Rings*, or the Harry Potter novels are epic confrontations between good and evil as much as the Anglo-Saxon saga of Beowulf and Gendel.

Narratives can be said to be mythic in two interrelated ways. The *form* of a story is mythic when its landscape and population are non-naturalistic and clearly separated from everyday reality. The *content* of a story is mythic when it inquires into questions about the realities of being human rather than less momentous concerns. For example, the story of *Saint George and the Dragon* has a mythic form not only because it is set in a long ago time when there were knights and in a far away place where there were castles but also because it is populated by dragons and fairies. The story has mythic content because it raises timeless questions and provides enacted answers about how to rescue people from terror and imminent death.

Narratives may be more mythic in their form than in their content and vice versa. On the one hand, tales of monsters and heroes, like many of the television cartoons made for children, may not consider questions about the meaning of life or death. On the other hand, stories with historical or more contemporary settings and characters, like the novels of Victor Hugo or Charles Dickens, focus on life-and-death issues or good-and-evil confrontations. Other narratives combine mythic and everyday elements in both their form and content. Stephen King's novels, R.L. Stine stories, the Harry Potter series, and the television show *Buffy the Vampire Slayer*, all raise mythic as well as more mundane everyday questions in settings that are at the same time both timeless and modern.

When I use the terms myth or mythic narratives, I refer to stories that engaged Michael with their mythic form and/or content rather than with their everyday concerns or other elements. Non-mythic elements of stories include such aspects as characters and settings that we might encounter every day as well as a focus on factual information, historical events, psychological analysis, social relationships, cultural differences, or literary structure. The more avid a reader Michael became, the more interest he showed in the other elements of narratives. Between the ages of about three and seven Michael wanted to devour one myth after another and in play enter the world of those narratives with me.

Rather than attempt to make a rigid distinction between mythic and non-mythic narratives I find it more useful to conceptualize stories as being more or less mythic in terms of what a reader or audience pays attention to. The story of *Saint George and the Dragon* depicts and is concerned with the historical everyday lives of medieval people in England. Yet when reading Hodges' and Hyman's (1984) picture book version of the story, Michael (at age four) was interested in neither a king's castle nor in the relationships between a monarch, his daughter, and his serfs. Michael was fascinated with the mythic power of a dragon who could burn fields and houses with one breath and who could grasp a knight on horseback in his paw to fly high above the castle. Michael wanted to explore how we might stop the dragon's destruction. At fourteen when he revisited the narrative in a literature class Michael's interests had broadened. During this reading he paid attention to the poetic qualities of the language and raised questions about the status of women in European feudal societies. He was still captivated by the fire-breathing dragon but he now identified it as a symbol of oppression.

Mythic stories are tales for people of all ages. Readers and listeners can identify with mythic deeds with only a minimal need to imagine characters' lives, social encounters, or cultural concerns beyond the particular events enacted in the narrative. Myths are filled with events concerned with life-and-death experiences, but they present those realities more visibly and starkly than realistic or historical fiction does. Mythic narratives have deeds that are mostly uncluttered with subplots, subsidiary relationships, or extra-neous people, places, and objects. They are more focused and accessible than more complex stories of present or past everyday life. The story of *Saint George and the Dragon* shows the dragon's trail of destruction but does not give details of the dragon's psychic state or upbringing. The Red Cross Knight has been raised by fairies and does not even gain his name until the middle of the tale. Una does not debate with her father her position in a patriarchal culture before tending to the injured knight. Critical readers can of course ask psychological, social, and cultural questions about myths and such questions did concern Michael and formed the basis of discussions with him when he was older. However, when he first encountered tales of monsters and heroes Michael was captivated by their mythic elements.

The life-and-death concerns, questions, and inquiries that mythic narra-tives explore have ethical dimensions. Myths not only depict the actions that heroes, monsters, and people *could* perform but also represent for readers or listeners how people *should* use their powers to act in response to, for example, violent monsters, people who need nurture, and those facing death. George, the Red Cross Knight, struggles for three days to defeat the dragon. Una, the king's daughter, tends to his wounds each night, and George faces the dragon each day despite facing death in every encounter. The myth of St George and the dragon is a depiction and ethical exploration of courage and support when confronting evil; it was not (for Michael aged four) a debate about whether or not to confront an evil that has devastated the land and killed scores of people.

Mythic understanding

Michael's passionate attachment to mythic narratives would not have been surprising to educator and philosopher Kieran Egan. Egan argues that myths are psychologically very suited to young children. What he characterizes as 'mythic understanding' develops in early childhood (from around the age of two or three until about the age of seven or eight). In this 'mythic phase' of life 'mythic understanding becomes a permanent constitutive element of our later understanding' (1997, p. 36). Egan is highly critical of Piagetian developmentalist views which tend to over-emphasize children's use of physical objects and understanding of familiar situations. He argues passionately and convincingly in favour of the use of mythic narratives in early childhood education despite their lack of use by educators who tend to read tales of domestic life in safe and socially familiar situations.

Mythic narratives contextualize core aspects of life (and death) in the stories of people whose lives are often in the balance between life and death. Because myths provide people with a sense of the whole, Egan argues that as adults working with children, 'we would do better to begin with general accounts of the world, its place in the cosmos, the variety of forms of life, and so on, than with the routines of the local world' (ibid., 60).

Egan relies on Donald's analysis that 'every aspect of life is permeated by myth'. Myths are 'a comprehensive modeling of the entire universe', covering causal explanation, prediction, and control. Myths are not just primal or contemporary stories, because for Donald, 'myth is the prototypal, fundamental, and integrative mind-tool' (Donald, 1991, pp. 214–215). People use whatever mythic narratives they have access to as core conceptual tools for making sense of past, present, and anticipated future experiences.

Egan takes a structuralist approach to show how conceptual 'binary opposites' are at the core of myths. Through their deeds, characters in myths embody binary opposites like good/bad, love/hate, happy/sad, security/fear, brave/cowardly, permitted/forbidden, knowledge/ignorance, or freedom/oppression. Myths are so important, he argues, because binaries are essential not only to mythic narratives but also to human thought and language as well as to how children learn. Egan combines the social psychology of Vygotsky (1986) who recognized the importance for young children developing categories to recognize contrast with the structural analysis of myths by Lévi-Strauss (1996, 1978) who regarded binary structuring as basic to all myths. Additionally, he notes Bettelheim's psychological analysis that children bring order to their experience by dividing the world into opposites like good/bad, love/hate, and security/fear (1976, p. 74). Folktales provide children with narratives that psychologically reinforce this view because they are structured round binary opposites.

Egan argues that binary opposites provide all people, not only children, with orientations to complex phenomena because binaries allow people to bring new experiences under their conceptual control. Young children form their prototypical understanding of hot and cold from their earliest experiences as they name their physical experiences of being hotter and colder than usual. Similarly, an adult struggling to learn a language that is foreign to her is likely to initially learn words and gestures that are opposites: yes/no, like/don't like, me/you, or here/there.

The myth of St George and the dragon can be seen as having structural binaries like good/evil, love/hate, and freedom/oppression. The dragon oppresses the people and the Red Cross Knight fights for their freedom. The evil dragon's ruthless disregard for others' lives is contrasted with the good knight and the loving Una's nurture of St George. Reading, listening to (and I argue playing with) the myth provides people with imagined, contextualized experiences of abstract concepts like good and evil, love and hate, freedom and oppression that Egan argues are then available as 'mind-tools'.

Oppositional positions

I prefer to use the term 'oppositional positions' (rather than binary opposites) to describe the relationship between St George and the dragon, or Beowulf and Grendel etc. As Egan himself notes, feminist and post-structural scholars have heavily critiqued the term binary. When language privileges one term over another it sets up binary thinking. For example, a male/female binary presupposes that male is 'normal', 'dominant', and 'better'. A narrative like *Saint George and the Dragon* can be critiqued as privileging the male knight as the active partner with the woman being more passive. The knight is also privileged as good and better than the dragon who is evil and bad.

In contrast to Egan's structuralist view I take a post-structural Bakhtinian approach to making meaning of narratives. Meaning is constructed out of competing views and is always open to further interpretation. A post-structural perspective destabilizes notions that narratives need not be critiqued, that meaning resides in a text, or that understanding can be delivered by people with superior knowledge.

Meaning can be regarded as made in a dialogic interplay among the positions of characters and readers on the meaning of a particular event. The dragon, the knight, the lady, the people, and different readers of the story all have different and competing interpretations of the events in the St George narrative. Rather than being in binary opposition they are, in Holquist's phrase, in 'reciprocal simultaneity that yokes each of these pairings in dialogue not only with each other, but with other categories as well' (1990, p. xxvii).

The anthropologist Victor Turner argued that myths often represent struggles between individuality and society. They depict ethical struggles between what Turner calls the 'open morality of the individual' and the 'closed morality of the [social] person'.

> [Myths are] a confrontation between that domain that pertains to the person that is the social structure and cultural order, and that which belongs to the individual that is, the critical and potentially creative destructuration of that order.
>
> (1992, p. 159)

The knight and the lady represent the forces of order positioned in dialogic opposition to the extreme individuality of the dragon. The dragon wants to go wherever he wants and eat whatever he desires. The knight and lady confront this egotism with the needs of all the people who are oppressed by his actions.

Characters in every narrative have particular social positions in relation to the other characters and how each views and interprets an encounter. Characters in myths tend to position each other oppositionally. The dragon and the knight are trying to kill each other. So are Beowulf and Grendel, Jack and the giant up the beanstalk, Perseus and the Minotaur, as well as Luke Skywalker and Darth Vader. The dragon is a remorseless, armoured, killing machine who is unstoppable until he encounters the knight and the lady. The people are terrified and powerless to stop the dragon. The monarch's daughter journeys far from home to seek out a hero whom she sustains when he nearly dies twice. The knight has a sword, courage, and a determination to stop evil do-ers.

When he was fourteen, Michael critiqued implied binaries in the *Saint George and the Dragon* narrative. Couldn't the women or the people have come up with a plan to stop the dragon? And having read John Gardner's novel *Grendel* which tells the saga of Beowulf from the monster's point of view, Michael similarly wondered what the dragon's history might have been in relation to the people. Maybe the dragon had been displaced by people moving in to where he lived?

At age four, Michael was not interested in critiquing implied binaries. Nor did he want me to tell him the meaning of a tale or merely re-enact stories. We engaged in dialogue as we played in mythic worlds while Michael took up oppositional positions. When we played in the world of St George, Michael improvised words and deeds as we enacted battles between the dragon and the knight as well as nurturing by the lady. At different times we each pretended to be all three main characters and thus took up their competing, and oppositional, positions on the events.

Living with mythic narratives

Michael had long-term relationships with many mythic narratives. His engagement with many mythic stories extended beyond our shared reading and play. Michael would look closely at the illustrations of the books we read, carry stories around, and pretend that he was characters from the tales. He coveted stacks of paper, was delighted when he was given a ream for his fourth birthday, and loved to create meticulous drawings of battling monsters that could sometimes be friendly.

Trina Schart Hyman had met and played with Michael when he was a one-year-old child. Michael's mother and I had met the Caldecott Medal-winning illustrator of *Saint George and the Dragon* at the end of a Children's Literature conference when she signed and wrote in our copy of the book, 'To Michael, the brave and beautiful, with love'. Soon after he turned four, Michael discovered the book. Within minutes he was poring over the illustrations that perfectly complement Margaret Hodges' poetic retelling of the tale from Spenser's *Faerie Queene*. I began to summarize the plot and was amazed that as I read extracts he listened intently while examining the illustrations closely. As we returned to the book again and again over the coming months, Michael would beg me to re-read sections. He especially enjoyed hearing the descriptions of the battles.

by Michael

Figure 2.2 A montage of monsters

St. George was the first sword-wielding armored medieval knight that Michael encountered and the dragon was his first flying, fire-breathing, sky-darkening, land-terrorizing, people-eating monster. They were not the last. Rather, they were soon to be joined by many others in an expanding pantheon of heroes and monsters that might appear at almost any moment.

And as can be surmised from the following photographs, mythic narratives as well as other more sedate stories, were readily available to be shared with who ever enjoyed reading and playing with them. Michael aged five-and-a-half is showing his one-year-old sister Zoë Trina Shart Hyman's illustrations while reciting some of his favourite words from Margaret Hodges' text – the dragon was 'throwing forth flames of fire from his nostrils'.

Mythic play

Mythic play arose whenever Michael and I pretended to interact as the characters in mythic narratives that captivated him. At four, it was obvious what captured Michael's attention in the story of *Saint George and the Dragon*. As with all books that really engaged him, he paid close attention to drawings as well as words. He studied the illustrations, asked me questions, and had me re-read parts of lengthy descriptions like the following extract.

> Once more the Red Cross Knight mounted and attacked the dragon. Once more in vain. Yet the beast had never before felt such a mighty stroke from the hand of any man, and he was furious for revenge. With his waving wings spread wide, he lifted himself high from the ground, then, stooping low, snatched up both horse and man to carry them away. High above the plain he bore them as far as a bow can shoot an arrow, but even then the knight still struggled until the monster was forced to lower his paws so that both horse and rider fought free. With the strength of three men, again the knight struck. The spear glanced off the scaly neck, but it pieced the dragon's left wing, spread broad above him, and the beast roared like a raging sea in a winter storm. Furious, he snatched the spear in his claws and broke it off, throwing forth flames of fire from his nostrils. Then he hurled his hideous tail about and wrapped it around the legs of the horse, until, striving to loose the knot, the horse threw its rider to the ground.
>
> Quickly, the knight rose. He drew his sharp sword and struck the dragon's head so fiercely that it seemed nothing could withstand the blow. The dragon's crest was too hard to take a cut, but he wanted no more such blows. He tried to fly away and could not because of this wounded wing.
>
> Loudly, he bellowed – the like was never heard before – and from his body, like a wide devouring oven, sent a flame of fire that scorched

Figures 2.3–2.6 Michael and Zoë reading *Saint George and the Dragon*

the knight's face and heated his armor red-hot. Faint, wary, sore, burning with head and wounds, the knight fell to the ground, ready to die and the dragon clapped his iron wings in victory, while the lady, watching from afar, fell to her knees. She thought that the champion had lost the battle.

(Hodges, 1986, unnumbered pages)

Michael was totally engaged with the battle between knight and dragon. It was obvious every time he jumped down from my lap and ran flapping his arms, baring his teeth, and breathing heavily like the dragon swooping down to breathe fire on people. Invariably he would want me to pretend too. Sometimes I was the knight. At other times he needed me to be the dragon or Una.

Michael would often return to illustrations to ask questions, as well as to show and tell me what to do. For example, Michael wanted to know if the dragon's breath would burn you. I re-read part of the text, explained 'scorched', connected it with touching our oven, and reminded Michael of the red-hot irons he had seen in a fire. I pretended to breathe on him as if I were the dragon speaking in a rasping voice and making a sneer, 'I'll scorch you with a flame of fire'. Michael cried out as if in pain, yelling, 'Stop burning people'. Looking again at the picture he wanted me to grasp him with both hands and hold him up in the air while he pretended to stab me with a spear. I had to pretend to breathe fire and roar as we proceeded to do battle.

Over the next several months Michael had us pretending to be all the characters. Initially Michael was insistent that the basic oppositional positions of the characters remained unchanged, but he soon began to improvise. The dragon was a destroying killer who would not listen to reason. The knight was ready to go on fighting to resist evil, no matter his injuries. The lady nurtured the knight for as long as was necessary for him to be restored to strength. At other times we would try out some alternatives. Our dialogue could create a dragon and a knight with different positions.

'Stop eating people!' yells Michael.
'But I'm hungry. I like people,' I reply.
'You can eat deer in the forest.'
'I don't know where they are.'
'I'll show you.'
'I like eating people though.'
'No people. We don't want to be eaten.'
'Do the deer want to be eaten?'
'Eat vegetables then.'
'OK, I'll try them.'
'Here. Have a carrot.'

Mythic and everyday play

Just as narratives can be regarded as more or less mythic, so can play. Depending on children's attitudes, the same play events can become more mythic for one child and more domestic or everyday for another. Around the Hallowe'en when Michael was four-and-a-half I joined in as he played in the leaves with his friend Mary who was nearly a year younger. They both giggled as they lifted leaves. However, while he pretended to dig up Dracula, she pretended to look for pumpkins. Her play was in an imagined everyday or domestic territory that arose from life narratives and included our previous activity carving pumpkins. Michael's play was in a mythic landscape that was sustained by vampire narratives from movies and books that he had been devouring for several months. As I played with both children I moved between the two imagined worlds.

Aged two, Michael wanted to play alone as much as he did with me. His play grew out of his everyday experiences. After seeing a backhoe digger, he often pretended to be one. At a park we often visited there was a metal toy backhoe in a sandpit that he liked to use. However, he was just as happy using his whole body to scoop up sand as he made the sounds of the machine. Sometimes we would actually pick up plastic toys that I would talk about as if they were rocks or building materials. When Michael imagined that he was a backhoe, pretended to answer the phone, or played at cooking, his play occurred in imagined everyday or domestic spaces where he could experience and explore, sometimes with me, aspects of what it was like to dig, communicate, and make food.

When he was three, Michael's play most often arose from the stories we had shared with him via books and videotapes. In the notebook that I kept over the two-month period immediately before and after Michael's third birthday I noted all the narratives that Michael used to focus our play. Many stories did not captivate his interest including many Grimm Fairy Tales. Those narratives that did engage him all led to recurring play events that I note in the approximate order in which they were most dominant.

- one story from each of the *Thomas the Tank Engine* video tapes that we had watched several times: 'Terence gets rescued' and 'Toby gets stuck'; the stories were also reproduced in book format which he liked to look at;
- two *Winnie-the-Pooh* stories, one from a Disney video tape, 'Pooh goes visiting,' the other told from a pop-up collection, 'Piglet is entirely surrounded by water';
- the folktale *Jack and the Beanstalk* from several versions we had read and about thirty minutes from one video tape of a movie version;
- the Christmas Nativity story that we had told Michael;

- four tales of Peter Rabbit from a set of six books (*The Tale of Peter Rabbit*, *The Tale of Jemima Puddleduck*, *The Tale of Mr Jeremy Fisher*, and *The Tale of the Bad Rabbit*) as well as a videotape of a musical version of *The Tale of Peter Rabbit*; I had noted in September 1992 when Michael was 2:8 that he already loved me to read two of those tales: *The Tale of Peter Rabbit* and *The Tale of Jemima Puddleduck*;
- Kevin Henkes' story *Sheila Rae the Brave* from several readings;
- the story of Santa Claus bringing Christmas presents that we had told Michael;
- pretending to wrap and give birthday presents;
- being covered by sand in the sandpit, pretending to be Piggy from an illustration in a lift-the-flap picture book, *Piggy at the Wheel*;
- shooting with a super soaker water gun from no known narrative;
- *Beauty and the Beast* from one viewing of the Disney video version and one picture-book version that we looked at several times;
- *Caps for Sale* from repeated readings of the picture book;
- *The Little Mermaid* from about ten minutes of the Disney video version and a retelling based on the original Anderson tale;
- *The Jungle Book* from about thirty minutes viewing of the Disney video version;
- *Prospero's Books* from about ten minutes of a video tape that he watched as I viewed it.

Michael never enacted the whole of a story. Rather, he would repeat particular encounters. For example, he loved running away and hiding from me (as Jack, Peter Rabbit, or the monkeys in *Caps for Sale*) as I pretended not to be able to catch or find him (as the giant up the beanstalk, Mr McGregor, or the peddlar). When we played with his *Thomas the Tank Engine* trains he would like to pretend to be Terence or Toby stuck with me rescuing him as Thomas, or vice versa. After watching five minutes of the postmodern movie *Prospero's Books* he pretended to be Ariel stuck in the tree.

Playing at the everyday event of gift-giving in the domestic world of Christmas-time had a mythic purpose for Michael. He used this story to make meaning about expressing love through exchanging gifts.

Michael is rummaging. It is the day after Christmas. From the trash can he pulls out a piece of crumpled Christmas paper. He sits down and tries to wrap the colored paper around the toy cement mixer truck, that he had opened with glee the previous day. The paper covers little more than the wheels. 'There must be a larger piece of paper here somewhere,' I say as I look around. Michael does not respond. His gaze is on the half-covered truck that he grasps in his hands. He beams as he says, 'It's my bir'day.' He will be three years old within two weeks. As he starts to sing, 'Hap Bir'day to meee', I join in and we sing the 'Happy Birthday' song together. As he pulls away the paper, his mouth and eyes open up and his whole body seems surprised and joyful. He looks even more delighted than he did the previous morning.

As I watch and listen to how he pulls and then tears at the paper I see Michael a year younger being initially less interested in a board book we had diligently wrapped than in rustling and crunching up the shiny paper that had covered the gift. As he grasps the yellow plastic truck I remember the look and feel of the red metal tricycle that I had received one Christmas. As I coast down the slope on the driveway of my childhood, and feel the cool breeze on cheeks that are older than those on his bright face, I anticipate future gifts for Michael.

He picks up the torn paper and gives it to me. I move toward the trash can but Michael is pushing the cement mixer toward me as he says, 'Now you be Michael and I'll be daddy.' Together we try to cover the truck. I'm still wondering where there might be another piece of paper when Michael beams at me and says, 'Happy Birday. I love you.' I feel a surge of joy when Michael hugs and kisses me. I feel a hint of surprise as I pull off the paper, lift up my hands, and open up my face and arms just as he did. Now Michael wants me to give him the cement mixer and tells me to say 'Happy birthday. I love you'. Again he is joyful, says he loves me, and feigns surprise.

I'm mystified when Michael gives me the truck again saying, 'Now Daddy, you're a sheep.' He hasn't put the paper round the wheels this time. As I kneel down on all fours I ask him who he's pretending to be. When he says that he's Mary I realize that he means Mary, the mother of Jesus. We had told him the story of the Nativity the day before. I bleat, 'Thank you,' as I nuzzle first the truck and then Michael who bleats as he hugs me again.

After his third birthday Michael was introduced to the story of *Beauty and the Beast*. He ignored the birthday scene in the story as he focused on the mythic scene of the dying beast who is restored to life by Beauty. For months afterward when sitting in his car seat or lying down to go to sleep he pretended to be the dying Beast. I would tell him how much I loved him, beg him not to die, and transform him into the prince with a kiss.

Mythic play worlds

Like Calvin, Michael at age five-and-a-half eagerly entered the world of werewolves where a wolfman could bring death to a victim with one swipe of his clawed hand. Unlike Calvin's father, I followed Michael's gaze and imagined with him a mythic world where the full moon was rising.

Michael becomes a werewolf as he watches the full moon rise. He howls and snarls as he drops to all fours. In one leap he has ripped out my throat and left me for dead. As he turns to search for another victim his torn blood-stained shirt reveals the animal fur on his chest. With the setting moon, the werewolf transforms back into Larry Talbot. The man who has terrorized as a wolf is remorseful. 'I don't want to kill the ones I love,' he wails. He speaks to me. I'm the scientist who has reconstructed Dr Frankenstein's machine having found its design in the ruins of his laboratory. He begs me to tie him down to the machine that gave life to dead bodies. He knows that if the machine's power is reversed it will take life from him and he will die. He looks me in the eye as he says in all seriousness that there is no other way to stop him turning into a werewolf by the light of the moon. I hug him and then he lies down. Reluctantly I tighten the straps and turn on the power. He shudders more violently as I increase the voltage. As I decrease the power his previously gruesome face is relaxed. As the sound of the machine subsides he lies still. The tormented werewolf is at peace in death.

Seconds later, Michael leaps up. His gruesome face and body have disappeared. He wants to watch the movie of *Frankenstein Meets the Wolfman* for the third time in as many days. We've just been enacting a scene that Michael loves to watch again and again. His smiles contrast with his ripped werewolf shirt. That morning, after reading and looking at movie stills of the Wolfman and other monsters in the Universal Studios books that we have borrowed from the library, Michael had put on the specially torn shirt with red paint and sewn-on pieces of fur that his mother and I recently made him.

As I look for the video tape I see one of Michael's many daily pencil drawings on the table. This one has faces, hands, and feet in sequences that show increasingly more hair, teeth, and claws. It's his depiction of the transformation of a human into a wolf.

I find the tape and put it in the rewinder. As we wait, Michael picks up the tape cover as he asks me, 'Daddy, why did Dr Frankenstein not use his power to do good?' Through our play we've been exploring the mythic and sometimes overlapping worlds of Frankenstein, the Wolfman, and other 'monsters' from the black and white Universal Studio movies mostly from the 1950s. We've reread many times the books, illustrated with stills from the movies, that retell the movie plots. Michael has been fascinated by Dr Frankenstein's invention of a life-giving machine that created a living being. We've made and just used in play our own cardboard machine complete with wires, knobs, and dials attached. In contrast with the merciful use of the machine on the Wolfman, Michael knows that having given life to a corpse, Frankenstein abandoned his creature and then set out to kill him.

As I respond to his question Michael looks at the tape cover showing Frankenstein's creature and the Wolfman about to fight. 'Dr Frankenstein was really mean wasn't he', I say. 'I think he wanted to kill the creature because he thought it was evil. But he only looked on the outside and he didn't look on the inside did he?' I've been thinking about the importance of our play. I add, 'I think he didn't find out what it was like to be mean in his play. He wanted to do it in real life. Though of course, that's only a story.'

Michael stiffens his body, lengthens his neck, his eyes go glassy, he turns to look at me. He's become Dr Frankenstein's creature.

'Don't kill me,' he says.

'You're hideous. You're ugly,' I reply.

'I'm not a monster. I'm nice.'

'You killed that little girl.'

'I didn't mean to.'

'You're so strong you might kill again.'

'I wouldn't kill you.'

'I created you so I can destroy you.'

'I'll be your friend. I'll help you.'

'If only Dr Frankenstein had talked with the creature.' I say as myself. 'He might have realized that he wasn't really a monster. He could have taught him.'

The movie has rewound and we settle down to watch.

In a myth, life-and-death events are enacted in landscapes that are at the horizon of our everyday world. Like the ancient maps with 'Here there be dragons' written at the edges, myths are populated by dragons, monsters, and other creatures we would never expect to actually encounter and who, in contrast with most everyday life experiences, use powers in ways that make the territories of myths unpredictable, dangerous, and often deadly. Sometimes the creatures are not what they seem. A werewolf can also become a man. A monster may only look monstrous but be kind in his heart and misunderstood by his creator. A dragon can be hungry rather than evil.

I was initially uncomfortable thinking about such creatures. However, as I came to embrace mythic narratives as cultural resources, I felt much more relaxed as we entered these mythic worlds of forests, caves, labyrinths, castles, cathedrals, lagoons, oceans, and islands. I became more comfortable imagining disturbing encounters with monsters and dealing with the

Figures 2.7–2.9 Michael/Wolfman and Brian/scientist

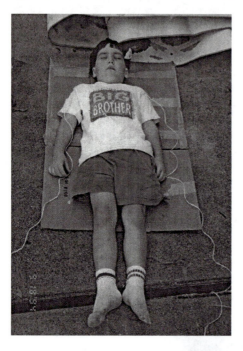

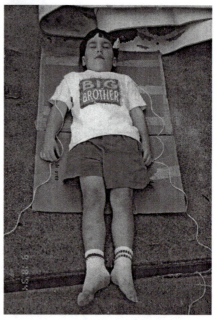

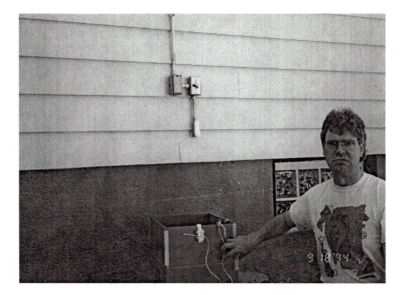

limits of our human powers in life-and-death situations. Though I wanted Michael to be physically and emotionally safe as we played, I didn't want him to stop imagining the deeds of monsters or start pretending to cook, run an office, or dress up as a football player.

As Michael turned three we were introducing him to a wide variety of literature and movies. The Cretaceous and Jurassic worlds of dinosaurs soon swamped the moralizing world of *Thomas the Tank Engine*. Domestic stories with mythic elements, especially those of Peter Rabbit and his friends, remained popular. Michael also continued to imagine the mythic world of the traditional folktale, *Jack and the Beanstalk*. Though I showed Michael picture books of many other well-known Grimm, Perrault, and European folktales from *Cinderella* to *Sleeping Beauty*, only *Beauty and the Beast* continued to captivate him and it was only the story of *Baba Yaga* that he returned to more than once.

Within a year dinosaurs, folktales, and domestic stories had been largely replaced by world mythology. Though illustrations were key, supporting language also captivated Michael. On the heels of his knowledge of the mythic medieval life of St George, four-and-a-half-year old Michael, loved to look at the picture of the dragon Smaug, from an illustrated edition of J.R.R. Tolkein's *The Hobbit*. One afternoon he sat on the porch and listened to all six audio tapes of the epic tale. At the same time Michael watched video tapes for longer periods of time. He tended not to want to watch entire movies though, he most often focused on particular episodes. At this

Figure 2.10 Heroes can transform into monsters (and transform back again)

age Michael was also introduced to the mythic narratives in horror litera-
ture. Soon he was reading books and watching extracts from the Universal
Studios classic movies of the 1950s. One day we went to the library because
Michael wanted some more 'monster scary books'. I took him to the folktale
section and we pulled out a dozen new picture books that he'd not seen.
None captivated him. 'Let's ask the librarian,' I suggested. She beamed at
Michael, got down on her knees, and asked him what he wanted. 'More
monster scary books.' I volunteered that we couldn't find any books in the
folktale section that he liked. I was shocked and speechless when she said,
'Do you like horror stories?' When Michael looked confused she said, 'I'll
show you.' I had been enjoying sharing world mythology and folktales with
Michael. I could justify him pretending to be monsters because he was also
discovering great literature. But horror stories? For a four-year-old?!

Within two minutes Michael was asking me who Dracula was. The
librarian had deposited him in the movie section. Michael was sitting on the
floor looking at a still picture of Bela Lugosi in a children's book that retold
the tale of the Universal Studios movie with accompanying photographs
from the film. He wanted to borrow all the books in the series. We agreed
to leave some for other people and left the library that day with half-a-dozen
slim orange-and-black hardback books that we would borrow again and
again over the following year.

That was the day Michael began his still-continuing relationship with
horror. Our lives were changed by those who stepped or sprang out of those
books: vampires, werewolves, mummies returning from the dead, zombies,
and creatures from lagoons, outer space, or those created by obsessed scientists like Frankenstein and Dr Jekyll. Michael was fascinated not only by
terrorizing creatures but also by those people misjudged as monsters.
However, he was not interested in the more popular cultural superheroes
at this time. After he got a Power Ranger action doll at a birthday party,
he exhibited a short-lived interest that disappeared a day or two after the
party. He returned instead to the more classic Frankenstein's creature, King
Kong, and Quasimodo, the hunchback of Notre Dame.

A year later aged five-and-a-half Michael was reading his first full-length
stories. When he was browsing at a bookstore one day he was drawn to the
gruesome illustrations of the pulp fiction series by R.L. Stine. Over the next
few years he read and re-read more than two dozen books by Stine and
his contemporaries. Initially he read them with me and eventually he read
them alone. Favorite titles included *The Haunted Mask*, *Don't Go Down in the
Basement*, and *Night of the Living Dummy*. Over time I also introduced Michael
to other literature I considered to be of a higher literary quality. He was
drawn to well-crafted language when it described monstrous or heroic
deeds. Though he liked the abridged versions of the stories of H.G. Wells
that I read him (*The Invisible Man* and *The War of the Worlds*), he returned

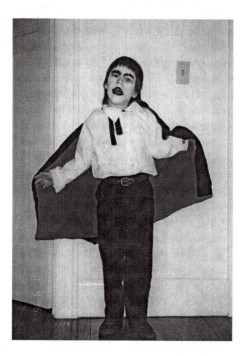

Figure 2.11 Michael/Dracula

Figure 2.12
Michael/Wolfman

Figure 2.13 The Dracula family at Hallowe'en

much more often to illustrated classic horror tales and ghost stories like those of Edgar Allan Poe.

I list below the landscapes of the mythic worlds that I entered with Michael in approximately the order in which he began to explore them. I also note the powers that Michael pretended to have as we played.

Table 2.1 Books that evoked mythic landscapes for Michael, aged 3–8

Mythic world	Landscapes	Inhabitants' powers
Beatrix Potter's Edwardian England of *Peter Rabbit* *Jemima Puddleduck*, *Jeremy Fisher*, and other talking animals	Rural landscapes with fields, ponds, woods, and vegetable gardens	Escaping as Peter. Catching Peter as Mr McGregor. Peter convincing Mr McGregor to let him go.
A world of giants in the sky with *Jack and the Beanstalk*	Giant castle reached by a beanstalk strong enough to hold a child	Giant who can eat children; hen that lays gold eggs; singing harp. Giant's mother who feeds Jack. Giant counting money. Jack helping giant to count money. Jack hiding from and tricking giant. Jack escaping and killing the giant.
European medieval world of *Beauty and the Beast* where a prince has been enchanted as a beast	Enchanted castle, forest	Physically powerful Beast. Wolves chasing Gaston. Dying beast. Nurturing Beauty.
Historical world of Cretaceous and Jurassic Dinosaurs	Plains, seas, swamps, and volcanoes	T-Rex, Dynonychus, and velociraptors with razor-sharp teeth and claws and powerful bodies that attack and kill herbivores. Herbivores that are killed or escape.
Baba Yaga's Russian Forest	Dark and impenetrable forest with village at the edge	Witch who can cast spells on children. Children who escape.
The medieval England of *Saint George and the Dragon*	Rural landscape with villages and castles	Flying dragon who breathes fire, burns buildings, and kills people. Knight who fights for three days. Una who nurtures knight. People who are terrified and then celebrate.
The Anglo-Saxon world of the warrior *Beowulf* and the monster Grendel	Rural landscape with mead halls, seas, boats, fens, forests, and lakes	Grendel who eats warriors. Grendel's mother who also kills warriors. Beowulf who can rip off Grendel's arm and dive down to find Grendel's mother.

Table 2.1 continued

Mythic world	Landscapes	Inhabitants' powers
Homer's ancient Greece	Mediterranean land with enchanted islands, caves and labyrinths hiding monsters	Medusa who can turn you to stone with a glance. The goddess Athena who gives Perseus gifts of winged sandals and mirrored shield. Perseus who cuts off Medusa's head and puts it in a sack. A half-man-half bull Minotaur who eats people. Theseus who defeats the Minotaur. A giant Cyclops who eats people. The sea god Poseidon who brings storms. Odysseus who tricks the Cyclops. The god Zeus who can strike with thunder bolts.
India of *The Ramayana*	Tropical land of palaces, villages, mountains and islands	Ravana the hundred-headed Demon king leading an army of demons. Hannuman, the half-man half-monkey king who can leap to the island of Lanka. Rama the blue skinned prince who defeats Rama.
Gilgamesh's Mesopotemia	Subtropical land of a great city under construction, a forest, and the land of the dead	King Gilgamesh who commands a wall to be built. His friend Enkidu who rescues Gilgamesh when he falls and later dies fighting a monster. A flying goddess.
Tolkein's Middle Earth	Rural landscape with villages, caves, and mountains	Smaug, a fire-breathing dragon sitting on a treasure. Bilbo Babbins, the hobbit, who sneaks past the dragon to steal a key. Savage Orcs who kill people.
The *Star Wars* universe	Other planets and spaceships	Luke Skywalker, Obiwan-Kenobi and other Jedi warriors with light-sabres and the force. Darth

continued

Table 2.1 continued

Mythic world	Landscapes	Inhabitants' powers
The *Star Wars* universe continued		Vader destroying a planet. Darth Vader dying. Luke lifting off his helmet. The emperor's use of the dark force to torment seen as electricity coming from his hands. Luke throwing the emperor into the vortex.
War of the Worlds with Martians on Earth	Martians from their inhabited planet launching an attack on Earth	Martian tripod machines with ray guns.
A world with an *Invisible Man*	A man who is invisible without clothes but visible in the snow and when covered	A man who can move and not be seen. Meeting his childhood friend Kemp.
Power Rangers world where Lord Zed plans to rule the Earth	Fights on Earth	Six Power Rangers using arm and leg kicks to fight Lord Zed's putties on Earth.
Dracula's world of vampires	Dracula's castle and anywhere his coffin goes or where he goes at night	Vampire power to turn someone whose blood they suck into another vampire. Power to kill a vampire by pounding a stake through the heart.
Frankenstein's world where the dead can be brought to life	Dr Frankenstein's laboratory and anywhere he or his creature go	The power to bring the dead to life.
A world of werewolves, like the *Wolfman*	Any night when the full moon rises	The power to turn into a savage werewolf and kill.
The Victorian world of Dr Jekyll who turns himself into Mr Hyde	Jekyll's laboratory and home. The home of his friend Dr Utterson. The streets of nineteenth century London	The power to isolate one's evil nature in another man. The guns of police officers.
The 19th century French world of *The Hunchback of Notre Dame*	The bell tower of the cathedral of Notre Dame. The stocks. The streets of 19th century Paris	Quasimodo's great physical power in a deformed body that others abhore. A whipper who beats him. Esmerelda,

Table 2.1 continued

Mythic world	Landscapes	Inhabitants' powers
The 19th century French world of *The Hunchback of Notre Dame* continued		a woman who brings him water and helps him escape despite risking her own safety.
The 1940s world of *Creature from the Black Lagoon* where a fishlike human creature is discovered in the Amazon	A lagoon and the land beside it	A creature that comes out of the water and attacks.
The 1950s world of *The Fly* where a man and a fly exchange places	Two boxes	A machine that has the power to make a person and a fly exchange bodies.
The Victorian age of a returning to life *Mummy*	An ancient Egyptian tomb	An ancient body wrapped in cloth and placed in a sarcophagus that returns to life when its tomb is disturbed by explorers.
The 1930s world of the giant gorilla, *King Kong*	The island and the streets of 20th century New York City including the Empire State Building	A giant gorilla who is feared but who seeks love. Explorers who capture him.
R.L. Stine's contemporary worlds of horror e.g. *The Haunted Mask*	A home and town in contemporary USA	A hideous mask that sticks to the face and takes over the person with its violent personality.
Raymond Briggs' world of a tiny *Man*	A boy's room and home in contemporary UK	A tiny man who asks a boy to look after him
Worlds with ghosts, e.g. *Mostly Ghostly*	A haunted castle	People who have died but whose ghosts are still present.
The 1960s world with zombies in the *Night of the Living Dead*	A graveyard and a home where the people barricade themselves	Zombies who return to life as the undead without feeling but who kill whoever they meet.
The 1980s nightmare world of *Nightmare on Elm Street*	A bed where a person sleeps	A man who has been disfigured and killed and returns via a nightmare to seek revenge and kill his murderer.

Michael invariably followed the same pattern when his play focused on a new narrative. At first, his embodiment of events resembled how particular oppressive and nurturing encounters were depicted in the book or movie. For example, the dragon Michael first pretended to be was like the one that St George and Una first encountered in Hodges' and Hyman's depiction of a terrorizing destructive killing monster. Michael would switch between pretending to be the dragon and St George, occasionally imagining that he was Una. As needed, I took the part of oppressor, oppressed, and nurturer. At first, if as the dragon I tried to negotiate with Michael, for example for food or a home, he would say something like, 'No talking. This dragon only wants to kill.' Michael was only ready to improvise having already established relationships as they were depicted in the narratives.

Mythic play purposes

'Every culture on earth has required myths to inquire into life and death and to try to explain their mysteries', stresses Marina Warner (2003, xiii). Myths offer explanations of mysteries by telling stories that show how people have acted and reacted in life-and-death situations. Myths can embody abstractions like the power of death or the power to create life in the characters and actions of people, monsters, heroes, and gods. The powers of life and death are less mysterious when they are captured in deeds depicted in the narrative worlds of myths.

As we imagine the world of a myth we can author dialogic meaning about the events with which we identify. Through mythic play children and adults can inquire into questions they ask or imply about the events in different mythic stories. Playing in different narrative worlds gave Michael and me increasingly complex answers. Is death the end of life? Not in the world of zombies. Yes, and no, if you are Dr Frankenstein. Is love stronger than hate? Yes, if you love the Beast as Beauty did. No, if Mr Hyde kills you. Can good defeat evil? Yes, if you 'use the force' in the world of *Star Wars*. Maybe, if you can't kill a murderous zombie.

As we interpret the events in myths we can do so for ethical, as well as social, cultural, psychological, and physical purposes. Myths can show us how people in narrative worlds have faced and understood the mythic issues that concern us as both individuals and groups. For example, in the world of Dr Jekyll and Mr Hyde the police enforce cultural rules to imprison murderers and shoot escaping suspects. Additionally, Jekyll's physical transformation into Hyde can be regarded as a depiction of the two sides of a split personality. As I explore in the next chapters, myths have an ethical function when they suggest how in the future we ought to act and react to people like Jekyll/Hyde.

A society's living myths are those narratives that most people turn to for explanations of life and death. As Coustineau notes, a culture's myths will be either living or dead (2001, p. 10). The ancient Greeks shared tales of gods and heroes as explanations of the life-and-death relationships between divine, natural, and human powers. Today most people regard those narratives as 'just stories'. In order to explain life in the physical world and our part in it, most people in Western cultures rely on the folk versions of dominant scientific narratives like the 'survival of the fittest' gloss on the theory of evolution. The Greeks told stories that illustrated the capricious powers over mortals of the thunderbolt-wielding Zeus and his pantheon of gods. We have narratives that show the powers of natural selection favoring the development of the human capacity to compete with other species. Death is not the end of life when seen as integral to the evolution of a species.

People also interpret non-scientific narratives to understand the mysteries of life. Children who desire to engage in mythic play are doing what we do as adults when we embrace narratives from religious, philosophical, family, literary, movie, and other mass media texts to seek explanations. As human beings, whatever our age, we have an ongoing innate desire to understand more of how and why people live and die, love and hate, or are judged as good or evil. We can seek answers to our mythic questions in narrative texts as diverse as those promoted by a religion or by a movie producer, by a collection of literature or by tales told at home. The Anglo-Saxon epic tale of *Beowulf* is potentially as useful as the movie *Alien* is for understanding how to face an unknown creature with unpredictable strength that kills whoever it encounters.

In our home we made multiple narratives available to Michael that he could turn to as cultural resources. Michael could explore some of his domestic concerns through narratives, like Winnie-the-Pooh stories that had characters with powers very like his own, living in settings similar to ours. When we went for walks in the woods near us, we sometimes pretended to get lost as Pooh and Rabbit did.

Michael was most captivated by stories that had both mythic form and mythic content. He returned to them again and again in order to explore and understand life-and-death, love-and-hate, good-and-evil. Michael and I both made meaning as we read, viewed, and played in multiple mythic worlds. He did not simply adopt the views of the narratives but rather made inquiries into his questions about mysteries of life and death. Sometimes he asked direct questions. 'Why did Dr Frankenstein not use his power to do good?' Mostly, Michael resonated with inquiry questions that were posed tacitly within the encounters that fascinated him, like 'How could you stop someone who wants to kill?'

Encounters in mythic worlds provided a focused and intense context for Michael's inquiries into life-and-death questions that he wanted to explore.

He could not examine these questions in more domestic narrative worlds. For example, Michael liked to pretend that he was Pooh stuck in Rabbit's door, floating with a balloon, or following tracks in the snow with me as Piglet. But in the world of Winnie-the-Pooh Michael could never face death or violent oppression. Whereas people can face creatures in mythic worlds that can kill them, on his adventures Pooh only faces difficulties like the bossiness of Rabbit, the exuberance of Tigger, and the timidity of Piglet. In one story, tiny Piglet has nightmares about being chased by gigantic heffalumps and, though Pooh reassures him and becomes worried as they follow tracks in the snow, they never have to face a creature that could actually harm him.

So it was through mythic narratives showing people facing powerful dangerous foes that Michael came to understand how power could be used. This understanding was extended and made increasingly more complex over the next four years as we explored multiple mythic worlds.

Engagement and protection

> I'm not scared of monsters because we play with them. I know that they're pretend. I feel a little bit scared, but I like feeling I want to be scared.
>
> Michael, aged four-and-a-half

Protection in play

Children choose to play, know that they're playing, and understand that whatever events they pretend are happening are not actually occurring. For instance, pretending to kill is quite different from actually killing. Imagining I am dying does not mean that I am about to die or that the person who pretended to kill me should be arrested. The experience of being both engaged in another imagined world and present in the everyday world provides physical and emotional protection for children.

Playing is an ongoing choice. At any moment children may choose to start or stop pretending. An imagined world could appear or vanish, sometimes to be replaced by another, as Michael chose to pretend that he was elsewhere or stopped pretending. In the Wolfman example, Michael chose to sustain our play in Dr Frankenstein's laboratory for over 20 minutes. As we waited for the video tape to rewind we played for 20 seconds in the parallel world when Dr Frankenstein was still alive. Sometimes Michael would shift in and out of a play world or focus on an everyday issue like an untied shoe.

When people play, the actual physical and emotional consequences of their actions are intended and desired or accepted when unanticipated. Michael and I engaged in noisy and apparently violent 'rough and tumble play' as we would chase one another or roll on the ground pretending to fight. But there was never any intention to hurt one another physically. If one of us said 'Stop' or if I said something like, 'Wait a moment. I have to answer the phone', then the play world disappeared, at least for me.

Michael's words at the beginning of this section show how he desired and accepted the emotional consequences of our pretend play. 'I'm not scared of monsters because we play with them. I know that they're pretend. I feel a little bit scared, but I like feeling I want to be scared.' As Vygotsky puts it, using the example of children playing doctor and patient, 'The child weeps in play as a patient but revels as a player' (1967, p. 549).

Though Michael was clearly always aware that he was playing, occasionally he would check that I was playing. When we first encountered werewolves Michael kept asking me, 'You're not going to turn into a wolf-man, are you, daddy?' Play became more predictable as we returned again and again to the same mythic worlds. Similarly, when Michael and I played with other children I often had to make a more formal agreement to give all children the power to exit from a socially imagined world. Some children had to be reminded that, 'Everyone has to be having fun, not just you. So if anyone says "Stop" you have to stop. OK?' Knowing they are physically and emotionally safe as they play, children are able to feel deeply about imagined events that in everyday life would be so violent, horrific, or traumatic that they would have difficulty contemplating their significance.

Identification with imagined events

When Michael identified with imagined events he did so physically, emotionally, and intellectually without reservation. By feeling protected he could project himself into the consciousnesses of all of the main characters. He did not act in a self-conscious sense but rather embodied one consciousness after another. As a werewolf he contorted his whole body. He hunched his shoulders, his eyes bulged, he exposed his teeth, and he grasped with claw-like hands. His snarls looked and sounded vicious, and his howls were blood-curdling. Yet when he became the scientist starting up Dr Frankenstein's machine he was a poised focused serious adult. One moment I imagined hair on a hideous face, the next moment I could see a white coat framing a concerned expression.

My presence, my shifts in and out of play mode, and our ongoing negotiations both within and outside our play worlds continually reminded Michael that we were pretending. Further, by interacting with me he could shift from one consciousness to another and thereby get outside one projection to contemplate and evaluate events.

Monster scary and people scary worlds

Michael aged four-and-a-half was clear that 'Monsters are in monster world'. One day he pretended to be a Power Ranger after watching a video of one of the television programs about the superheroes' fight with Lord Zed. I asked Michael how scary the world of Power Rangers was. He used his hands to show the width of his body. Then I asked him how scary Dracula was. This time he stretched out his arms as wide as he possibly could. Grendel? He was as scary as the whole room. What's the scariest story you know? Mary Poppins.

Michael protected himself from emotionally upsetting fictional experiences. When he saw police officers run into a house, knock things off the walls, and chase chimney sweeps in *Mary Poppins* he immediately switched off the video. In similarly abrupt ways he exited other seemingly innocuous narrative worlds we introduced to him expecting that he would like them. When Michael (aged three-and-a-half) saw children throwing stones at the boy with the balloon in the French movie of *The Red Balloon* he asked why they had done that and never chose to view the movie again. At a children's production of Shakespeare's *Romeo and Juliet* I whispered an explanation to Michael (aged five-and-a-half) that Romeo kills himself when he thinks that Juliet is dead and Michael got up and made me take him outside. In contrast, Michael emotionally immersed himself in, and never seemed satiated by, stories about werewolves, vampires, zombies, hideous creatures, and all manner of monsters that we were concerned might scare him. Michael explained he loved 'monster scary' worlds. However, he did not want to imagine 'people scary' worlds like those of Mary Poppins, the Red Balloon, and Romeo and Juliet.

Werewolves who attacked and could kill along with the people who could use silver bullets to kill them were among those who populated mythic worlds that were emotionally safe for Michael. Children who threw stones at a boy with a balloon and ran away laughing were part of an everyday world that felt emotionally unsafe for him. When Michael felt emotionally upset by a movie, no amount of rational discussion would persuade him to watch the video again. He protected himself.

The limits of experience

In our mythic play, Michael stretched the limits of what might be scary: Giants? Dinosaurs? Dragons? Vampires? Werewolves? Mummies? Zombies? Ghosts? Nightmares? Michael pushed himself to experience the emotional limits of mythic narratives. Though he eagerly sought out more and more scary stories he studiously avoided realistic violence. He would often ask adults he met what was the scariest story or movie that they knew.

Though they might be taken aback by the question, many did respond with a reference to what was invariably a horror tale. When pressed, despite doubtful looks from one of his parents, some visitors narrated events from the stories. Michael would frequently seek out these narratives on our regular trips to the library, bookshops, and video stores. Often he was content to look at a book or video tape cover. While he could borrow any book he wanted to from the library we limited the movies he watched. We did not have a television receiver until Michael was about seven. When we watched videos we always gave Michael the video controller and either sat with him or were in a nearby room. We were open to talking about whatever he watched. He occasionally fast-forwarded or stopped a movie and often rewound to watch favorite scenes again. Pat (Michael's mother) and I agreed to limit his viewing to G or PG movies in addition to the 'classic' unrated Universal Studios monster movies mostly made in the 1950s. Though he once pointed out that *Mary Poppins* had a G rating, he broadly accepted the authority of the rating system when we explained it. He also listened and accepted when I told him that I didn't want to carry around some violent images in my mind, set in places that were familiar to me. In effect, I was telling him that I wanted the protection of imagining more mythic worlds.

The movie that became a benchmark for scariness in our family was *Night of the Living Dead*. One week when Pat was away I succumbed and agreed to rent the movie that I had not seen but that had intrigued me for many years. Later she and I disagreed about whether or not we should have watched it. On the one hand it was a monster movie, but on the other hand its violence was more realistic than that of others he had watched. The movie had been a departure from the tone of previous monster movies made by Universal Studios. We trusted Michael's ability to emotionally self-censor, yet part of our responsibility as adults was to set limits on his experiences. How and why the movie is scary remained a topic of discussion with Michael into his early adolescence. It came up years later when we debated whether or not he should watch other violent mythic movies, like *Alien* and *The Matrix*.

Though Michael aged six had seen movie stills and drawings of zombies, and had pretended to be a zombie, this was the first and last zombie movie that we watched. The mythic undead zombies who in the movie emerge from a graveyard at dusk inhabit a largely non-mythic world of the 1960s. Michael was captivated by the zombies' walk, as well as by their outstretched arms, staring faces, and relentless determination to kill people who were then turned into zombies. I told Michael how emotionally unsettling I found the scene when a girl, who has been turned into a zombie, kills her mother. Though Michael listened intently, he watched the entire movie without fast-forwarding or stopping. He also wanted to pretend to be zombies immediately after it was over.

Fear in everyday life

Michael was not afraid of the mythic monsters he read about in books or viewed in movies. On the contrary, when he pretended that he was a powerful creature he was unafraid of whatever the creature could have power over. Once when he was aged nearly five, Michael wanted to go sledding at night with an old friend. Kamyar asked Michael if he was afraid of the dark. Michael, who was wearing his cape, said calmly, 'I'm Count Dracula. I'm not afraid of the dark.' Michael has rarely had nightmares in his life, although about a year after first watching *Night of the Living Dead* he did have a nightmare of a zombie chasing him.

However, he was afraid of tornados. After completing his first tornado drill at preschool, Michael aged nearly five was fearful that a tornado might hit our home. He was dismayed that we did not have a basement as he had been told that was the safest place in a house. He was much less worried once I pretended with him that a tornado was coming and we crouched down inside our closet under the stairs. Fortunately we never had to cope with an actual tornado sighting. However, if Michael was home for the testing of the sirens on Fridays at noon he was always a little agitated until we showed him a clock and assured him that there was no tornado.

At about the same time, Michael was terrified by a story his cousin Halley told him. Halley is four years older than he and knew that he loved monsters. One weekend when we visited Michael's cousins who lived in the country, on a walk outside she told him with a serious face that a monster lived near by. As we walked around the shed and the fields she said she had seen the monster. Michael became frightened and fearful that the monster might attack us. Even when I, and then his cousin Halley and her brother Thorne, who is two years older than Michael, said that she had only told him a pretend story, he remained scared. He wanted me to carry him and take him inside. Halley had confused him into thinking she was describing a people scary world rather than a monster scary world.

Only as we played did Michael begin to be in control of his fear that day. I asked him what he thought the monster might look like. As he described its teeth and claws, I moved my face and hands and asked him if I was doing it right. Then I suggested that I pretend to be the monster and he chase me. He wanted me to hide and he decided that he would have a sword. I played with Michael for about five minutes. I hid behind the swing set, a wall, and a tree as Michael found me, chased me, and used the sword to kill me six or seven times. Then Halley and Thorne joined in and we played together. First they helped Michael chase me. Then he pretended to be the monster and we all chased him. After about ten minutes we climbed a tree, played on the swing set, and went for a walk to the river, seeing and chasing several other monsters on the way.

Playing with the powers that the monsters, heroes, and people had in the narratives with which he identified gave Michael power in everyday life as well as in fictional worlds. Rather than feeling overwhelmed by images of the most powerful creatures he could imagine, Michael relished pretending to be those creatures. As we played, he could imagine facing any situation imaginable. With the powers of those creatures and people, as we played he could face everyday fears both as they were embodied in fictional narratives and in stories that brought fear closer to home.

Dominant beliefs about mythic play

In valuing mythic play, I found myself at odds with many of the negative or neutral judgments made by some teachers and academics about what is most often termed superhero play, as well as weapons play, violent play, and war play. This teacher is unambiguous about her opposition to play that depicts violence.

> I think that allowing children to engage in war play undermines all the values we want to teach them. . . . Do we want to raise children who learn that we kill people when they are bad or when we don't agree with them? I want to teach children to use words and express their feelings when there's conflict; to try to see the other person's point of view in a disagreement. I want to teach children to resolve differences in a non-violent way and in a caring way. I don't believe it is okay to pretend that someone is getting hurt. I believe that society is promoting the kind of play in children that develops a war mentality, and as teachers we have a responsibility to sabotage it.
>
> (a teacher quoted in Carlsson-Paige and Levin 1987, p. 5)

I absolutely agree with the wishes expressed by the teacher that children learn to use words, express feelings, and try to see other people's points of view in disagreements. I can understand why she would want to sabotage children's desires to pretend to kill, but in this book I speak on behalf of those children, especially boys like Calvin and Michael, as well as their parents and teachers who want to pretend that they are in the worlds of savage monsters and questing heroes.

Adults like the teacher quoted above want to ban superhero play because they assume that if children pretend to be violent they will become violent. The recent trend that has extended a zero-tolerance of violence in schools to banning war, weapon, and superhero play in early childhood settings is rooted in this assumption (Carlsson-Paige and Levin, 1990; Cupit, 1996; Holland, 1999; 2000). However, Holland (2003), Jones (2002), Katch

(2001), Paley (1986), and others, all suggest that adults need to re-examine and question this assumption.

Penny Holland is highly critical of such a blanket ban. Violent play is an under-researched and under-theorized aspect of early childhood. Her intention for her theoretical analysis of action-research studies of children's play is to open up dialogue. She notes the irony of adults using their power over children to impose bans in order to promote peaceful relationships. 'Zero tolerance relies on the use of adult power in the real world to enforce a moral and behavioral imperative against powerless children operating in a fantasy world' (2003, p. 99). She suggests instead that adults should consider the need to model negotiations with children. She concludes with a quotation from Paley:

> If I have not yet learned to love Darth Vadar, I have at least made some useful discoveries while watching him at play. As I interrupt less, it becomes clear that boys' play is serious drama, not morbid mischief. Its rhythms and images are often discordant to me, but I must try to make sense of a style that, after all, belongs to half the population of the classroom.
>
> (1984, p. xii).

After highly publicized incidents of violence by children or young people, like the Columbine shootings, inevitably a media storm erupts finding culprits in the violence of television or video games. Gerard Jones is a journalist who makes a compelling argument for the value of making media images of violence available to children. The title of his book aptly summarizes its content: *Killing monsters: Why children need fantasy, superheroes, and make-believe violence*. He makes detailed reference to an extensive array of academic literature and interviews with authors that collectively belie causal links between images of violence and emotionally, psychologically, or socially damaged children.

Rather than make assumptions about whether or not images of violence are bad for children in general, he advises us to pay attention to the lives of the particular children that we care for. 'Children want to be strong, secure, and happy. Their fantasies will tell us what they feel they need to attain, if we pay attention. But we need to look beyond our adult expectations and interpretations and see them through our children's eyes' (2002, p. 21).

After over a dozen years of thinking about my play with Michael I can now argue that mythic play, especially when an adult joins in, can actually promote all the values we would want children to learn. Paradoxically, through pretending to be violent, I was able to promote a non-violent critique of war: by imagining monsters' attacks Michael learned to work against being monstrous in everyday life, and by imagining suffering and death he gained a more caring attitude to life.

Freudian theoretical framework

Though pretending to be monsters has largely been ignored in the literature, it has been argued that it is emotionally and socially healthy for children to imagine they are war-like superheroes because they are acting out, and gaining control over, their aggressive and domineering impulses.

'Children have a lot of aggressive feelings which this type of play allows them to express safely.' Carlsson-Paige and Levin quote a teacher to explain why they value children pretending to be 'superheroes' or people with weapons (1987, p. 5). They elucidate that when children imagine they are fighting they 'feel very strong and in control . . . they are able to express feelings of hostility toward imaginary foes, and to gain control over these feelings within themselves'.

These limited views of the value of mythic play are firmly located in Freudian theories that have been applied and extended for a century. Freud's ideas are pervasive not only among academics and teachers but also within the wider culture as 'common sense'.

A Freudian theoretical framework interprets play literally or analogously rather than metaphorically, regarding playing in general as escapist, essentially unreal, and thus often in need of adult control. Though Freudian beliefs are useful, I have found them inadequate for understanding my play with Michael.

Drawing on Indian philosophy, Richard Schechner takes a radically different view of playing as part of life. In doing so he supports those academics noted in the previous chapter who view playing as a mode and play as an attitude toward any activity (Garvey, 1977; Bruner et al. 1976; Lurker, 1991). They are all at odds with the dominant theoretical Freudian framework that sets play apart from reality by dichotomizing activities into play or non-play, play or work, serious or frivolous, real or not-real.

Schechner argues not only that playing is an ever-present possibility in all activities, but that 'ordinary life is netted out of playing'. We are 'at play' during any interaction whenever we recognize that our 'relationships are provisional' (1988, p. 11). We are playing when we see the world as dynamic and changing, we are not playing when we see the world as fixed and static. Play is like a net through which we can sieve our experience. Over time, our social and cultural realities have been, and continue to be, 'netted out of play'. What we regard as socio-cultural reality is in fact less stable than we may assume. What is viewed as socially acceptable behavior changes both over time and across cultures. What we consider to be appropriate practice in one situation can change across time as people play with rules, question assumptions, and try out alternatives. Some new ways of interacting are overlooked whereas others are gradually accepted. Changes in everything from dress codes to teenage behavior, from voting rights to a child's right to childhood, can be viewed as having been netted out of people's play-fulness. Pretending with children can be regarded as a way of tapping into playing that is 'the underlying always-there continuum of experience' (ibid., p. 17).

Freud, like Piaget, contrasted play with reality. As Freud insisted, 'The opposite of play is not what is serious, but what is real' (quoted in Morson and Emerson, 1990, p. 187). Their views of play are quite different from those of Vygotsky and Bakhtin. Whereas Freud drew a sharp distinction between the 'reality' of everyday experiences and the escapist 'fantasy' of play, art, daydreams, and dreams, Vygotsky saw play as thought and imagination in action. Bakhtin theorized that we make meaning in aesthetic, as opposed to everyday, spaces. And I've argued that child–adult play can be aesthetic activities in which children experience real feelings and thoughts and in which they author understanding.

Freud theorized that the motivation of play (as with dreams, daydreams, and art) was a person's lack of something. Thus play, for Freudians is 'the fulfillment of a wish, a correction of unsatisfied reality' (quoted in Morson and Emerson, 1990, p. 187). I find this aspect of Freud's theory useful. Michael wished that he had more power. He must have felt very powerful indeed when he imagined that he was a dinosaur, a dragon, a knight, or a werewolf.

Freudian theory stresses the value of play from therapeutic and socializing standpoints. Helen Schwartzman summarizes Freud's two core assumptions. First, 'in play, children act out and repeat problematic life situations in order to master them.' Second, 'in achieving mastery children project their own anxious hostile feelings into other individuals or objects' (1978, p. 175).

Michael did on occasion use play for mastery of feelings when he was young. He was certainly aware of this function of play aged thirteen when he talked with me about why he liked participating with friends in live action role playing games like 'Vampire'.

> If I'm feeling frustrated or mad and I just want to hurt something or do something evil, I can wait until Saturday until I get it out in the game. It doesn't have repercussions in real life. It still gets the feeling out but no one gets hurt. On recess I play games with my friends that also let me do that, not as much as Vampire [the role playing game] does that but it helps. Knowing that I get that all out on Saturday or on recess really helps me deal with anger and frustration. . . . Also I can feel good feelings and experience the good things that happen to the characters [in books and fantasy games]. I also feel good. I like it when the character faces evil and he gets through it and it's good. And it's fun!

He also talked about how he could use reading in a similar way.

> If I'm frustrated or whatever I can go into another place or world and I don't have to be frustrated or angry. I can feel whatever the character is feeling even though I have to do what I have to do in this world – do my best and learn and all that good stuff – I don't have to do that in the 'reading world'. I think it does me good.

Freud regarded play as important for reducing anxiety. Freudian psychologists, such as Bettelheim (1976), have shown the use of play as therapy because children can learn to cope with and master their fears and antisocial tendencies as they play. Scholars who have extended Freud's theories, most notably Erik Erikson, have also stressed a corollary – the social growth enhancing qualities of play that has no overt therapeutic aim. Erikson suggested that 'the child's play is the infantile form of the human ability to deal with experience by creating model situations and to master reality by experiment and planning' (1963, p. 222).

Freudian theory is clearly useful and relevant for understanding aspects of children's play. In one sense Michael must have mastered his fears as we played. He clearly did so the day his cousin scared him. We also used play to learn pro-social behavior, for example when I pretended to be a car running into him so that he would not run out into the road or when he pretended to be a gentleman at the table. However, as Michael played he was doing more than coping with fears and learning to be safe or polite. Our mythic play rarely created what people would consider model social situations.

Applying Freudian theory to understand mythic play, without extending it with Bakhtin's and Vygotsky's theories, can promote a negative view of play in three interrelated ways. First, the significance of play (especially play involving imagined violent actions) can easily be dismissed (as not real), diminished (as mere wish fulfillment), or pathologized (as an expression of hostile feelings). Second, Freudian theory interprets play events analogously rather than metaphorically. Adults are regarded as being able to interpret a play event, like a dream, as a 'window' into the psyche or a 'mirror' of a person's feelings. Play is seen as a message from a child which we can attempt to decode for its meaning. Children at play are regarded as acting out their particular fears and hopes, and specific feelings of anger or pleasure. Freudian approaches assume that children project these feelings about particular everyday events on to objects and other people. When children pretend to be silly, or imagine that they are, for example, parents in the home, or firefighters at work, then a Freudian interpretation can view such play as an expression of future wishes, and as promoting affective and social growth. However, when children pretend to be hateful or violent (for example as werewolves, dragons, or superheroes), a Freudian interpretation makes it quite reasonable to view such play as a disturbing view of previously hidden inner (or 'unconscious') feelings of anger or fear about particular people and prior events. Third, such play can be interpreted as dangerous, as an expression of feelings that are likely to get 'out of control', and as promoting antisocial growth.

Whereas Bakhtin theorizes the self as dialogically engaged in ongoing internal and external social conversations with struggles for meaning among competing positions, Freud theorized a divided view of an individual self. Central to Freud's theory is a conflict between what an individual is 'conscious' of and what is 'unconscious'. For Freud, there is an ongoing battle between the rational conscious and the irrational unconscious. My unconscious is seen as an unruly realm of feelings, fears, complexes, and repressions which influence my thoughts and actions but which are largely unknown and only glimpsed through dreams, hints like 'Freudian' slips – and play. Further, there is a clear hierarchy – the unconscious must be controlled and mastered by the will of the conscious ego. Though people need to 'express feelings', Freudian approaches argue that they must also learn to 'control impulses' because these can easily get 'out of control'. The pervasiveness of Freudian theory is suggested in common phrases like 'Don't bottle it up', 'Let your anger out', 'Get a grip on yourself', or even 'What dark corner did that idea crawl out of?'

Adult control of mythic play

Adult control of mythic play, including adult repression, can be justified as necessary from a common sense (and Freudian) approach to play. If children are perceived to be out of control or exhibiting antisocial behavior, then it is reasonable for adults to sense a need to exert control. A Freudian view of maturity is conceptualized as mastery and control of impulsive emotional outbursts. Thus, children's play is valued when children are perceived to be learning 'impulse control' because they are 'learning to control feelings' of anger or aggression toward people that they are pretending to be (Erikson, 1963; Schwartzman, 1978; Bredekamp, 1987; Reynolds and Jones, 1997).

At first, I unknowingly followed this common sense approach. I interpreted Michael's actions in play as impulsive manifestations of specific fears or aggressive tendencies and as verging on being out of control. I felt a need to control Michael's actions so that when we played he would act in more socially acceptable ways. However, as I recognized that he would always stop playing when requested, was very rarely intentionally aggressive with other children, never seemed scared by our play, and identified with multiple positions, I began to feel more comfortable with his play.

I accepted that his actions as we played were rarely external manifestations of particular inner fears but rather were explorations with me of how the world might be.

Vivian Gussin Paley during her thirty-plus years of experience in the preschool and kindergarten classroom was similarly drawn to control mythic play. Paley's controls did not remove mythic play. For years she attempted to censor such violent aspects of children's play as pretending to shoot one another with weapons. She made her opposition to weapons clear. However, even when children had 'agreed' to a 'no guns, no play shooting' rule and did not bring toy guns to school, the boys still pretended to be superheroes who would shoot at each other. Most worrying for Paley was her realization that children who otherwise were observant of rules were learning to deceive adults.

> Few of the boys have guns at home. In our community, social pressure weighs heavily against guns. Superhero paraphernalia is purchased but not guns. It is a prohibition however that has no effect on play. Even in nursery school, the boys pick up any loose item and shoot. The euphemism is accepted and the children learn how to negotiate with the teacher. By kindergarten they are masters of guile.
>
> 'This isn't a gun,' Andrew tells me even before I ask.
> 'It looks like a gun,' I say.
> 'It's an invention.'
> 'What does it do?'
> 'It X-rays people.'

In the end, Paley was emphatic in her conclusion that despite any adult reservations and attempts to contain it, mythic play cannot be repressed. 'There is no way to prevent superhero drama. The images will not go away' (1984, p. 70).

Gisela Wegner-Spöhring sheds light on both children's fascination with the content of mythic play and adults' frequent antipathy toward it. Mythic play explores 'themes and subjects that they [children] do not usually encounter in [everyday] reality, yet that preoccupy and disturb them: death, injury, fighting and war, violence, fear, being left alone, "If Dad and Mom were dead . . ."' (1994, 107). She quotes Brian Sutton-Smith's (1987) observation that play is 'the sphere in which the unspoken finds expression . . . and unrecognized desires [are] satisfied'. However, she makes the powerful observation that 'As adults and educators, we have always had difficulty with this idea' (ibid., 109).

Paley agrees. 'The fantasies of young boys are little tolerated in school these days. The perception of increased real violence in the country has created an inhospitable setting for the pretend stuff that has led most teachers to ban pretend weapons and pretend fighting' (2001, p. ix).

Teachers, like Paley, who see value in mythic play have controlled play so that children do not physically or emotionally hurt themselves or one another. Jane Katch, after a year of observation in her kindergarten/first grade classroom, recognized that children showed as much affection as anger in their play. She concluded that there is a clear distinction between pretending to be violent and actually hurting others.

> One thing I have learned is making a clear distinction between pretend violence and behavior that truly hurts or frightens children. Pretend violence, like pointing a finger and saying 'bang' while your friend falls on the ground, does not hurt anyone, and the rules can be negotiated by everyone involved in the game. Real violence hurts bodies or feelings, is frightening, and is often closely connected with exclusion.
>
> (2001, pp. 129–130)

Katch realized that it was exclusion from play, not the content of play, that provoked violence among children. She concluded that 'exclusion and violence seemed to be inextricably intertwined. Excluding someone from the group seemed to justify violence, both by the excluded child and by those excluding him' (ibid., 130).

I found it very supportive to read Katch's honest analysis of her own feelings about the children's violent play and to recognize that I was not alone (as her mentor Bettelheim had pointed out to her) in discovering that a tendency 'to avoid our most difficult feelings is always present' (ibid., 129).

Katch, Paley, and Holland, along with many other academics, promote control of play through honest discussion with children about the content and actual consequences of their play for others. They also value sharing with children our difficult feelings as well as our positive emotions. Such talk is significant from a Bakhtinian viewpoint because talk can begin to create an aesthetic dialogic space in which understanding can be authored with children. However, the value of talk alone can be limited when it is not accompanied by other multi-modal ways of making meaning, which include drawing, and the movement that accompanies pretending.

As I applied the theories of Bakhtin and Vygotsky to our mythic play, I began to recognize Michael's words and actions as struggles between different consciousnesses ranging between altruistic heroic voices and egotistical monstrous voices. I began to recognize that rather than attempt to control his actions via censorship or evasion, I could be most influential by engaging in conversations with him as we played – conversations that interpreted mythic events metaphorically.

Play and metaphorical interpretation

> Fairy tales are more than true: not because they tell us that dragons exist,
> but because they tell us that dragons can be beaten.
>
> G.K. Chesterton

Play events can be interpreted metaphorically, analogously, or literally. Like all young children, Michael wanted literal explanations of the world that extended to some of the facts of life and death. For example, he was interested in how bullets kill and what coffins are made of. But when Michael asked me, 'Daddy, why did Dr Frankenstein not use his power to do good?' he was not asking me to interpret Dr Frankenstein's actions literally to explain the power of electricity. Nor did he expect me to interpret Dr Frankenstein's actions analogously connecting Dr Frankenstein's desire to kill the creature that he had created as a parallel for when he or I might have felt angry enough to hurt or kill. Rather than seeking literal explanations or analogous one-to-one correlations between the events we had depicted in the lives of Frankenstein and the Wolfman and those in our lives, Michael wanted to interpret our play encounters in the way that as adults we most often interpret literature, movies, plays, and the other arts – as metaphors. When we interpret metaphorically we can each draw many *possible* imaginative connections between our lives and events from a life depicted in an aesthetic space.

Play events themselves were largely metaphorical interpretations of narrative events. As we interacted in play we rarely replicated events from everyday life or fictional stories. Michael had minimal literal concerns as we played and only occasionally had a strong analogous focus on events from his everyday life. When Michael was nearly three we had a minor but traumatic car accident when our car driven by Pat, and carrying me, Michael, and his cousin Halley, slid off the road going round a bend in newly fallen snow. Michael initiated play focused on this event off-and-on for nearly a year. Initially our play resembled what happened on that day. Michael imagined being the driver as well as being a passenger. As we talked about what might have happened, Michael soon added alternative scenarios to our play that ranged from us all being rescued by an ambulance helicopter to Pat and me at Michael's funeral. He was interested in literal details like why cars slip in the snow. Initially he was interested in replaying the events. Later he transformed them into alternative possibilities. His play could initially have been interpreted almost entirely as an analogy for what had happened but soon play events no longer had a direct correspondence to actual events. When he pretended to scream he was echoing his cousin Halley's scream on that day, but when he pretended to fly a helicopter I metaphorically interpreted this event as an example of Michael's expectation of being rescued from danger that intersected with his fears of being killed.

In the spaces of play created in imagination we embodied and interpreted possible actions in various social and cultural relationships. Play
with each mythic narrative provided various interpretations of the possible
ways that people can relate to one another. Mythic play depicted actions
at the extremes of possibility. Dr Frankenstein's hateful attitude toward
his creature contrasted with the scientist's compassion for the Wolfman. At
other times, we imagined both that Dr Frankenstein loved his creature
and that, as a werewolf, the Wolfman killed the scientist. As we played, we
embodied actions that for Michael could range from the mundane to the
mysterious. As Larry Talbot watched the full moon rise, he changed into a
powerful killer, and as Dr Frankenstein turned knobs to operate his machine
he brought a dead body to life.

Michael interpreted our play actions metaphorically. Across multiple
narratives he was aware of an array of possibilities of how characters could
use their powers. He authored multiple metaphorical interpretations of
narrative events rather than single analogous interpretations of how depicted
actions might relate to our everyday lives.

To interpret Michael's words and deeds when we played I had to regard
Dr Frankenstein's actions metaphorically as more than the literal deeds
of a nineteenth-century scientist in a world first created by Mary Shelley.
And when Michael used phrases like 'I don't want to kill the ones I
love', I had to resist drawing a particular analogy between the Wolfman's
despair and feelings that Michael might have at times of wanting to kill
me. In responding to a question like the one Michael asked about why Dr
Frankenstein did not use his power to do good, I had to seek out various
possible connections between events in the imagined mythic world and how
we might use our powers in our relationships with other people in our
everyday lives.

When I said that, 'he only looked on the outside and he didn't look on
the inside', I offered one metaphorical interpretation of Dr Frankenstein's
desire to kill. I connected with previous narrative events that we had
embodied and interpreted from stories ranging from those of Dracula to
Quasimodo that showed how a person's external appearance can mask
an inner reality. I suggested another metaphorical interpretation when
I compared what Dr Frankenstein did with how I valued our play by saying, 'I think he didn't find out what it was like to be mean in his play. He
wanted to do it in real life.' Finally, I emphasized that both of my suggestions
were interpretations of fictional events when I added, 'of course, that's only
a story'.

Play as aesthetic activity supporting ethical action

Bakhtin (1990) advocated an aesthetic approach to life. He did not separate art, or any aesthetic activities, from life. I argue that this idea can be extended to child–adult play. Bakhtin stressed the connection between aesthetic activities and ethical actions. Aesthetic events start to become ethical when a person contemplates and evaluates how their own actions affect others. In the next chapter I consider in detail how ethical identities can be authored in play. In this chapter I consider how ethical actions grow out of aesthetic activities when I view actions from the standpoint of how my acts might affect others.

Aesthetic activities are authored

Aesthetic activities are value-laden creative acts of seeing, feeling, and intentional response that create form. People are authors in aesthetic activities. Readers as well as writers are authors when they create images of people (or other beings), each with a consciousness different from their own. Bakhtin (1990) described all such fictional people as 'heroes'. For Bakhtin, people need fictional heroes to be able to contemplate how they might act in the world. In the world of St George, Una and the knight are heroes and the dragon could be thought of as an anti-hero.

As Bakhtin puts it, 'An aesthetic event can only take place when there are two participants present; it presupposes two non-coinciding consciousnesses' (ibid., p. 22). Holquist summarizes Bakhtin: 'aesthetics is the struggle to achieve a whole' the meaning of which is 'always a negotiated relation between two [paired] powers . . . and two value systems . . . in a state of intense and essential axiological interaction' (1990, p. xxvii). Bakhtin also uses the metaphor of competing 'voices' that Morris describes in this way: 'a voice will always have a particular "intonation" or "accentuation" which reflects the values behind the consciousness which speaks' (1994, p. 251).

Any reader of the story of St George and the dragon will perceive the tale both as a whole aesthetic world, bracketed off from everyday life, and as a struggle within that world between knight and dragon. The dragon and knight have different irreconcilable consciousnesses, alternative views of the world that are oppositional positions in the myth – those of oppression and resistance to oppression. The lady's consciousness is closer to that of the knight in that they are united in their desire to defeat the dragon, yet her viewpoint is different from his. She watches, waits, hopes, and nurtures.

In addition to non-coinciding consciousnesses within an authored world, Bakhtin proposes that the most basic of the paired powers in aesthetic activities are an authoring shaping 'self' and an imaged created 'other'.

Authoring is not only an act of imagination, it is also the forming of value-laden images of life as events in an aesthetic space-time that are contemplated for meaning. Authoring can create ethical understanding. The particular images of battling between knight and dragon are 'other' than the authoring self, and are value-laden because they represent a struggle between two different value systems. The dragon believes he should be able to eat whatever and whomever he wants. The knight believes he should not attack and kill people or destroy their homes. Reading is authoring. For Bakhtin, reading is similar to writing. Both require people to create and contemplate images that are other than self. To be able to read or write requires the ability to imagine and create images of people who view the world differently from self. Michael was doing this as we read and talked about narratives. Playing is authoring. Michael created and contemplated other selves when he made faces and sounds, changed his body shape, dressed up, moved, and spoke in other consciousnesses. He was creating and contemplating when he drew pictures, wrote words, and made structures out of cardboard that became incorporated into and transformed in our play.

Life can be experienced aesthetically to create opportunities for ethical action. Bakhtin gives the example of encountering a suffering person. One person may cognitively understand the situation but remain outside the person's experience while another person may become emotionally entangled in the other's fate. Neither can author a response. An aesthetic response is action that is authored from both projection into, and contemplation of, another person's experience. A cry in an aesthetic experience of an everyday event is 'not a cry of pain but a word of consolation or an act of assistance' as a first act toward completing a response to the person's particular situation that might culminate in giving the person something or taking them somewhere (1990, p. 26). People's responsive actions are ethical acts, for Bakhtin, when they result from their projection and contemplation. Their actions answer those who address them. Though life can be experienced aesthetically, art always is. Child–adult play is also an aesthetic experience.

The three facets of aesthetic activities and ethical actions

For Bakhtin, fundamental to aesthetic activity and ethical action, is 'co-experiencing of the inner state of an object or the inner activity of contemplating an object' (1990, p. 62). 'When we empathise we "in-feel" our own inner state into an object, we still experience this state not as immediately our own but as a state of contemplating the object i.e. we co-experience with the object' (ibid., p. 61). There are three intersecting facets, then, to all aesthetic activities and ethical actions. Using Bakhtin's terms, these are projection, outsideness, and consummation or finalization. They may occur consecutively and/or simultaneously.

First, I empathise or imaginatively project into another's consciousness. I project myself into another in order to experience his life from within him, from his life-horizon. As I put myself in his place, in effect I coincide with him. To do this I must detach myself from what is inconsistent with his consciousness. This is harder in life than in play, especially for consciousnesses that are monstrous or heroic.

Second, I move outside the other's consciousness into my own consciousness. As Bakhtin puts it, 'I must return into myself, a return to my own place outside the other person' so that I can be 'outside' the other consciousness. Returning to myself is supported for children in child–adult play through interactions with the adult.

Third, I form and consummate action that provisionally finalizes my response. From my position outside the other person I see, feel, and value the world differently. As I experience the world as she does, I can shape and author a response that is unique both to me and to her particular situation and person. As Bakhtin also describes it, I am being 'addressed' by the other person. My action is ethical when I make an intentional response that 'answers' the other and changes the situation for the person. My intention is to 'consummate' or move toward 'finalizing' the situation in some way, through an act of completion, fulfillment, or conclusion.

Young children find it easy to project themselves into the possible selves that are depicted in other narratives of the world, especially as they play. Most adults find it harder. Children look but see a situation other than the one they are actually in, they listen but hear in another space, they move as they feel in another time. Adults often assume that staying in their own consciousness is sufficient. However, as Bakhtin stresses, for an activity to be aesthetic, and an action ethical, I must experience inside as well as outside the consciousness of another. Ironically, children are likely to be able to do this more easily than adults.

Michael himself did this often and daily as we played. One example comes from our Wolfman play, when Michael asked me, 'Daddy, why did Dr Frankenstein not use his power to do good?' as we waited for the movie to rewind. He was now outside the consciousness of Dr Frankenstein. In asking his question he was referring back both to play we'd just finished and to play from several days earlier. On those occasions he had projected into the consciousness of Dr Frankenstein and the 'monster' as well as the wolfman as we had enacted several encounters from the Universal Studios movies *Frankenstein Meets the Wolfman* and *Frankenstein*. Michael had wanted to be the creature coming to life. He had wanted me to pretend to be Dr Frankenstein turning on the machine, making its noises, and using the words from the movie about bringing him to life, 'He's alive! He's alive!' After reading the story, Michael had known that Dr Frankenstein had wanted to kill the 'monster' that he had created. As we talked about the story I had said that I wasn't sure if the monster was a 'monster'. What should we call him, I wondered. I started to say 'Frankenstein's . . .' and paused. He's 'Frankenstein's' said Michael definitively. And that name was what we usually called him.

> Michael stiffens his body, lengthens his neck, his eyes go glassy, he turns to look at me. He's become Dr Frankenstein's creature.
> 'Don't kill me,' he says.
> 'You're hideous. You're ugly,' I reply.
> 'I'm not a monster. I'm nice.'
> 'You killed that little girl.'
> 'I didn't mean to.'
> 'You're so strong you might kill again.'
> 'I wouldn't kill you.'
> 'I created you so I can destroy you.'
> 'I'll be your friend. I'll help you.'
> 'If only Dr Frankenstein had talked with the creature.' I say as myself. 'He might have realized that he wasn't really a monster. He could have taught him.'

I argue that this brief play encounter was an aesthetic event, as was our brief conversation in response to Michael's question. The conversation referred back to previous play events as Michael made ethical meaning in contemplating them. In the play event Michael took ethical action. He projected into the consciousness of Frankenstein's to contextualize his question in an encounter with the person that he knew wanted to kill the creature. Michael was outside the consciousness of Dr Frankenstein, but had previously been inside it. He responded and answered him, not from his everyday consciousness but from within the consciousness of Frankenstein's. His talk of being 'nice', of friendship, and of 'helping' posed an alternative way to complete, or finalize, their relationship. This talk was ethical action because Michael/Frankenstein's was answering the address of Dr Frankenstein.

The aesthetic potential of play

Bakhtin was ambivalent about the aesthetic potential of play. I doubt that he had played much with children. He did not recognize that play needs to be seen not as isolated events but as a mode of interacting across relationships. Nor did he consider the potential of child–adult play. When we shift in and out of play with children, we support and assist them as they project into different ways to look at the world, contemplate possible action, and suggest alternative ways of relating to others. As I explore in the next chapter, talking, interacting, and playing with children allows us to explore possible selves and over time to author ethical identities.

Bakhtin regarded play as an example of 'expressive aesthetics'. It is 'self-experiencing without any reference to the other as such' (1990, p. 64). 'In playing I experience another life without exceeding the bounds of my own self-experience and self-consciousness and without having anything to do with the other as such ... I experience another life, while remaining myself' (ibid., 63). He believed that aesthetic contemplation is mostly absent in play. 'I contemplate my partner with the eyes of a participant not a spectator. All the feelings that are possible in relation to the other as such are excluded here, yet what one actually experiences is another life' (ibid., 64).

Bakhtin contrasts imagining with imaging. 'Play images nothing – it merely imagines' (ibid., 74). He gives the example of boys pretending to be robber chieftains. They only desire 'to take part in that event, to experience that life as one of its participants ... his relationship to life as a desire to experience it himself is not an aesthetic relationship to life' (ibid., 74). He compares playing to day-dreaming or the artless reading of novels where under the guidance of an author 'we "identify" with the main character in order to experience – in the category of "I" – his existence and his fascinating life' (ibid., 74).

Bakhtin must have observed children engaged in largely 'parallel' play where each is projecting into their own fantasy world. Like Piaget, he assumed both that play largely replicates or imitates and that little is happening socially. Play can be highly imitative. However, I soon realized Michael was often authoring and exploring subtle alternatives even in play that seemed highly repetitive. Though the machine that he wanted me to hook him up to as the Wolfman remained the same, before he lay down to die he would say different things. Once he dictated words to be put on his tombstone. 'Here lies Larry Talbot. He didn't want to hurt people.' On another occasion he told what he wanted to happen to his possessions. 'I leave my cane to the nurses in the hospital.' Playing has similarities to reading and writing in terms of authoring. However, a child's authoring as he or she plays with other children or adults is quite different from reading or writing alone. As was illustrated in our brief exchange as we waited for the movie to rewind, meaning can be negotiated among competing viewpoints when we play, just as when we converse in everyday life.

Bakhtin recognized that playing begins to approach art – as dramatic action – with the presence of a spectator. 'This imagined life becomes an imaged life only in the active and creative contemplation of a spectator' (p. 75). He assumed this only happened with an external audience. Paley (1986), Dyson (1997), and Gallas (2003) have documented, for example, how playing can easily become performance as stories are performed to an appreciative audience of peers or adults. However, turning playing into a play makes it into something else. Preparing and performing for an audience that is outside the imagined world changes the improvisatory nature of the children's playing. The spectator stance is essential but it does not have to come from applause. When playing is viewed across time and events children can move into a spectator stance whenever they reflect on what had gone before. This frequently occurs in child–adult play. Michael was a spectator on previous events when he pretended to be Frankenstein's creature asking Dr Frankenstein why he wanted to kill him, reinterpreting what happened to the little girl, and suggesting friendship rather than aggression.

Play as a workshop for life

In chapter one I proposed that play can be regarded as a workshop for life. This chapter has examined how children can explore life in mythic as well as everyday play.

A functional view of play as a rehearsal for life encourages and validates play that explores social roles and domestic pursuits. The dominant view is that play is only productive when it 'pictures and re-enacts the experiences children have had and can imagine having in the *real* world, within the safety of the *small* world of play that the child has created' (Erikson, 1950, cited in Reynolds and Jones, 1997, p. 3; my emphasis). Imagined actions are assumed to resemble or reflect experiences of everyday life. However, imagined actions are often neither small nor replicas of everyday experiences. Rather, play worlds often substantially enlarge and distort experiences children encounter in life and literature. When children play, imaged realities predominate over actual physical laws, socially accepted norms, and cultural constraints. Possibilities can take mythic as well as domestic form.

Play that is a workshop for life needs to embrace landscapes on the mythic horizon as well as those nearer home. Mythic play explores the limits of how people relate to one other and the world in events where people act in heroic or monstrous ways. Mythic play protects children so that they may experience with intensity, and explore with emotional depth, aspects of the human realities of life and death, love and hate, fear and safety, etc. in encounters that are experientially close yet also feel far away from everyday life.

In contrast to a Freudian view of play as a 'window' into the psyche or a 'mirror' of psychological states, I suggest that play events are like various lenses that children can use to examine aspects of life. Play lenses magnify or focus children's (and adults') concerns about the world to make them more visible and subject to interaction.

Rather than interpret his actions as a view into a psyche that might be troubled, I came to recognize our play most often as lenses on life which Michael held up and which we looked through together. As I learned to interpret our play metaphorically, I could value it more as shared inquiry into human questions. In doing so I critiqued some of the dominant beliefs about play, especially about the need to control children's play that depicts violence.

What Coustineau says of myth can be applied to mythic play. 'Myth is Janus-faced: one face turned to the . . . world of heroes and monsters; the other face turned inward, personal, soulful' (2001, p. 7). I would add that this doubled-view also gives children perspectives on social and cultural life when pushed to human limits.

By projecting into the viewpoints and actions of the heroes, monsters, and people in whatever narratives engage them, children inquire about those aspects of life that are difficult to examine in the everyday world. How do you experience and contemplate the power to kill, the power to heal, or the power to love? How do you discover what might happen if you really hurt someone, without actually hurting? How do you know how to respond to violence without being in danger? Mythic play allows you to do so through the protection of pretending to be in other worlds. In mythic play children can explore answers to implicit questions like: 'What if I, or you, had the powers of a dinosaur, a giant, a knight, a dragon, or a werewolf? What could we do if we encountered those people or creatures? How might we respond? How ought we to react?' Mythic play allowed Michael to experience, and author understanding about, how people could act in the world. Mythic worlds showed him the best and worst of deeds at the extremes of behavior. He had mythic purposes when he inquired into understanding about life-and-death questions. As we pretended to be the monsters, heroes, and people in mythic worlds, we explored the extremities of how power could be used. Michael explored fear and other emotions as we played. Over the time that we engaged in mythic play Michael also authored understanding about life and death. Finally, he did not confine his meaning making to interpretations of the mythic tales. In the next chapter I examine how, as Michael explored possible selves, he also authored ethical identities.

One evening when Michael was nearly seven he wanted to sit with me when I told him I was about to watch the first episode of a television documentary about World War One, called *The Great War*. Though I told him that it might be scary because it would show people being killed and dying, he stayed to watch. Michael was captivated for over an hour. He was jubilant at the story of the fraternizing in Christmas 1914 between some German and Allied troops who played games and exchanged gifts, but devastated that the war had begun again the next day. He was insistent in his demand to know why people had volunteered to fight. I tried to explain how people believed that they were heroes doing the right thing for their country. I connected with mythic narratives that he knew by saying they felt they were like Beowulf or St George. As he watched men signing up and heard the recording of a military band playing a jingoistic tune he spoke both to me and to the new recruits on the screen.

> The monsters are in your brain, upstairs in your brain. You're not the hero, Beowulf or St George. You're really the monster. Monsters are really the ones who want to go off and fight. St George fought because he wanted to save the city. He wanted to live a quiet life. He didn't want to go off and fight and be ra ra ra [cheering for victory]. He didn't want to go off and fight and cut off dragons' tails and stab them in the throat. He just wanted to live a quiet life.

Chapter 3

Playing with possible selves and authoring identities

Selves and identities

How do I know how to act ethically – to do what's right in a situation? Should I do what others tell me would be moral behavior, or should I just do what I believe is right? Bakhtin offers a third viewpoint: people ought to be answerable to one another for their actions. In effect, to be ethical we should do the best thing we can live with in a particular situation. To contextualize an exploration of Bakhtin's theories, I turn first to a work of literature before applying the ideas to child–adult play.

On the one hand, to show me what is right, other people can give me advice or point me to a moral code. But, ethical rules have to be interpreted and may not have a clear application in a particular situation. Though the opinions of others are important, only I can live my life and I have to live with the consequences of my actions. On the other hand, if I turn to my beliefs or thoughts or feelings, how do I know which ones I ought to follow?

'Who am I?' asks Jean Valjean, a central character in Victor Hugo's nineteenth-century novel, *Les Miserables*, as he struggles with how to act. His question probes his sense of self and how he identifies himself ethically. A man, now in chains in the courtroom near the small French town where he is mayor, has been wrongly identified as Valjean. If he identifies himself as a convict who has broken parole, Valjean faces return to the galleys where he had previously spent nineteen years. He knows what that hell is like. If he just walks into the courtroom as the mayor and factory owner he has become, he will be safe but he will have to watch the man be condemned in his place.

'I am Jean Valjean,' he finally declares in answer to his question as he strides into the courtroom. His deed is an ethical action performed by his ethical self. But at the same time it is an act of identification with one social group and an erasure of his identity as a member of another cultural group. As he enters the court, Valjean identifies himself as the former convict, and reveals that his identity as the mayor has been built on a lie.

This ethical action has not arisen merely in response to particular thoughts and feelings, nor has he followed a moral rule. Rather, Valjean acts in answer to the silent plea from the man in the courtroom. That plea resonates with other inner voices that the musical version of the story makes visible in song. He answers his question 'Who am I?' by saying to the man in the courtroom, 'We are ethically connected.'

In imagination, Valjean has projected into the fate that awaits the man if Valjean does not speak up. He contemplates this certainty in relation to the inner voices of conscience that tell him to remain silent or speak out. If he does not speak he remains mayor. As mayor he has been able to help many people, including a sexually abused young woman with a child for whom he cares. If he does speak he returns to being a convict. As a convict he had served nineteen years in the galleys as punishment for stealing bread for his starving family. On his release he remained branded a criminal for life. His humiliation continued until the day he met a bishop who protected him from the police, gave him the silver candlesticks he had stolen so he could get started in honest work, and restored his dignity by treating him as a human being. Then to avoid being always judged as a law-breaker he had changed his identity and stopped reporting to the police. The voice of the bishop has continued to speak to him internally during the past nine years. It resonates with the voices of all those people whom Valjean has helped since the day the bishop had compassion for him. The bishop had forgiven him and answered his need by giving him a way to make another life for himself. His struggle is between different identities. As mayor and a factory owner his cultural identity provides him with social status, respect, a comfortable life, and the means to help others. As a convict he would be stripped of his possessions, locked up, and identified as an unworthy social outcast.

Yet his inner conflict is located not only in social and cultural identities but also in what I describe as his ethical identity. Taking an ethical focus on his predicament, he contemplates two possible futures in these words, 'If I speak I am condemned. If I stay silent I am damned'. In speaking he would be condemned to return to being identified as a convict. But to stay silent would mean that he could not live with himself. He would judge his actions as immoral.

Socio-cultural and ethical identities

To ask, 'Who am I?' is both an intimate and a public question of identity and sense of self. Trying to identify who I am is at the same time both a socio-cultural and an individual issue. The answers refer to how my relation-ships with other people past, present, and future make a difference in how I relate to myself. To ask, 'Who am I?' is also an ethical question because it raises questions about how I believe I ought to live my life and act in the world.

Holland et al. propose that 'Identity is one way of naming the dense interconnection between the intimate and public venues of social practices' (1998, p. 270), which Hall regards as 'points of identification and attachment' with different cultural groups (1996, p. 5). My identities are not static social markers. My sense of myself as a member of various communities with shared experiences provides me with structures and practices that make a difference in how I live my life. As Evans realized in the conclusion to her study of identity formation, identities are not just about what people do with others to sense that they belong to a group. They are also about the consequences of individual actions and how one person's actions affect other people. 'Perhaps part of flourishing as humans involves working toward an ongoing awareness of the possible multiple (emotional) effects of our actions, as we engage in the emotional work of becoming in relation to others' (2002, p. 35).

In bringing together scholarship from the fields of cultural studies and social constructivism, Holland et al. (1998) argue that identities are formed in two complementary and intersecting ways that can be grouped together as people's socio-cultural identities. On the one hand, from a cultural viewpoint, identities are determined by the narratives and practices that particular groups share and that people identify with when they regard themselves as members of that group. On the other hand, from a social constructivist viewpoint identities are formed as people consistently position others with more or less power, authority, and status. For example, families can be considered to be cultural groups while at the same time being regarded as a collection of intersecting social relationships. Children learn how to behave in general ways and in specific situations both because of their identification as a member of a particular family and because of their identities as a child relative to adults or siblings.

A 'narrativized' or 'figured' identity creates a framework for viewing, interpreting, and acting in one particular community and relating to other communities (each of which is a culturally constructed or 'figured world'). Every group tells stories about itself that carry shared meanings and values. People's ongoing figured identity formation, especially when shared in visible cultural practices or the use of symbolic objects, evokes in every participating member a sense of self and of appropriate action that is consistent with a particular identification with a social community. As Holland et al. note, 'the signs or markers of culturally constructed identity, whether they be the display of particular skills, the enactment of certain motives, the cultivation of ways of speaking etc. . . . especially if objectified in the figured world, means to evoke one's own sense of who one is and so organize one's behavior' (1998, pp. 281–282). Over time people also develop perspectives on the world as part of their 'positional' or 'relational identities' because of how they are socially positioned in relation to other people. Relational identities, like 'son' or 'sister', are 'a set of dispositions toward themselves in relation to where they can enter, what they can say, what emotions they can have, and what they can do in a given situation' (ibid., 143).

Valjean acquired socio-cultural identities and related dispositions as a member of at least two social groupings: convicts and middle-class property owners. On the galleys Valjean had learned the shared language, practices, and ideology of thievery as a member of a socially ostracized cultural group. At the same time, having been persistently positioned in degrading ways as unworthy of humane treatment, he had acquired a disposition of acting without humanity toward others. On being released he acted in accordance with this convict identity when he stole the candlesticks one night after being given shelter in a bishop's home.

When he began to participate in middle-class culture, Valjean's cultural practices and social positionings were quite different. He learned how to run a business, make money, and look out for his own interests so successfully that he became mayor. His emerging bourgeois identity superceded but could never entirely displace his convict identity. Though his convict identity might have seemed to him to be in the past, the framework he developed over twenty-plus years could still affect his views even though others would only see the mayor at work.

Though these socio-cultural identities created frameworks for acting both in and on the world, as Valjean stood in contemplation outside the courthouse he could use neither of these conflicting viewpoints to 'organize' his behavior. As he entered the courtroom, Valjean's action can be regarded as consistent with his ethical identity. He identified with the practices and positionings of other people in a way that can be seen as cutting across and intersecting with his socio-cultural identities. Nine years earlier, Valjean had significantly been positioned as an equal by the compassionate bishop who treated him with respect and showed a belief in his humanity and ability to make a life of social and spiritual service. This way of being positioned had been in stark contrast with his dehumanizing experience as a convict. It was how he must have wished people would treat one another. Valjean had identified with the bishop neither as a member of the clergy nor as someone in his congregation but as a person whose actions had been compassionate, loving, and trusting. Though they had never seen each other again, Valjean continued to have inner conversations with the bishop that guided him when he acted with compassion toward others and mitigated the inhumanity he experienced in the world. Over time he created a community of people with whom he identified not just socially or culturally, but ethically. Now he could still identify with former convicts but not with their brutal behavior, just as he could identify with his fellow business owners but not with their capitalist practices. His ethical identity allowed him to identify with them through whatever deeds of kindness and support they might have performed.

Valjean ethically identified with the future life of the man in the courtroom even though they had never met. He could not abandon him because he related to him through his evolving ethical framework. He saw another human being like himself who did not deserve the inhumane treatment that awaited him but who should be treated with compassion.

Authoring selves and identities

Drawing on Bakhtin's theories of authorship and the self, Vygotsky's theories of development and mediation, and Bourdieu's (1977) theories of culture and agency, Holland et al. (1998) argue that people have agency in relation to the development of their identities. Authoring selves that act, as opposed to reactive selves that behave, over time will change and to an extent author identities. An authoring self is unique since it acts from a position in time and space that no other person occupies or will ever be in again. As Bakhtin puts it, 'everyone occupies a unique and never-repeatable place, *any* being is once-occurrent' (1993, p. 40). And as Morson and Emerson clarify, 'Ethical action is born of a sense that each act is unrepeatable and responsibility is nontransferable. What can be accomplished by me cannot be accomplished by anyone else, ever' (1990, p. 179).

There is a space for authorship between how identities are culturally determined and how they are the product of social positioning. People are authors when they improvise responses to particular events that affect their position in the social situation. 'Agency lies in the improvisations that people create in response to particular situations, mediated by [their] senses and sensitivities. They opportunistically use whatever is at hand to affect their position in the cultural game in the experience of which they have formed . . . sets of dispositions' (ibid., 279).

When authoring socio-cultural identities is a 'cultural game', then people can jostle to alter their social positions so that over time their identification with a group changes as well as their dispositions toward the group. Though the interactions that people engage in would be entirely understandable from a socio-cultural viewpoint, they could be highly questionable from an ethical standpoint. People on the galleys could become more powerful through the strategic use of violence. People in a factory could acquire more power through tactical moves to have someone else dismissed. Adopting an ethical framework, because improvisation both affects other people's social positions and is part of a process that actually affects one's own and others' identities, people should consider the ethical dimension of their actions.

The bishop had improvised on the night when Valjean, having been caught with the silver candlesticks that he had stolen, was brought to him by the police. The bishop had told the police officers that he had given Valjean the candlesticks. His word could not be questioned by the police officers and so Valjean had been protected from the wrath of the law. Publicly the bishop's actions had positioned the police officers with less authority than he had to determine guilt. Privately, his actions had positioned Valjean as a man in need, not a thief. In their subsequent conversation, the bishop positioned Valjean as a man who could be an agent of his own destiny. In the years following, Valjean not only changed his socio-cultural identities but also changed the ethical dimension of his identities. I argue that those changes formed an ethical identity that intersects with but is not congruent with any one socio-cultural identity.

Valjean turned the bishop's actions on that night into a significant image, or 'sign'. Over time he could improvise actions with reference to it. In imagination he revisited the event in order to make ethical meaning about past deeds and possible future actions. For Holland et al. he was using the sign as a 'heuristic device'. He would have evaluated this event ethically as 'good' and 'right' because he had been treated with compassion, respect, and trust in ways that he wanted to repeat. By returning to that momentous encounter heuristically, the significance of that event deepened, bred, and intersected with other events all of which he could evaluate as ethical. Over time he heuristically authored and developed an evolving ethical identity.

Like all identities, Valjean's ethical identity provided him with a way of relating to other people via social practices, feeling membership in a group, and dispositions toward others. The people he connected with were both physically present but also accessible through imagination as inner voices. For Valjean, he developed an ethical alternative to his largely immoral or amoral socio-cultural identities.

He used his ethical framework to answer his question, 'Who am I?' In declaring, 'I am Jean Valjean', he identified himself with the actions of the bishop, with his own ethical deeds in the intervening years, and with the person he wanted to become. His ethical action as he entered the courtroom accepted his past, acknowledged the present moment, and embraced one particular way of being in the world. Using Bakhtin's term, Valjean was being wholly 'answerable'.

Answerability and integrity

As Valjean entered the courtroom and stood unsure of what to do, he could easily project into the consciousness of the man in the courtroom to empathise with him and contemplate both the man's future and his own. He considered two parallel but starkly contrasting futures. Either the man would be condemned in his place and Valjean's current social life would go on as before, or Valjean would reveal his past life but destroy the world he had constructed over the past nine years. When he entered the courtroom one of those possible futures would be finalized by his deed.

As Valjean entered the courtroom he was 'answering' his understanding of the situation 'with his whole life' (Bakhtin, 1990, p. 1). For Bakhtin, aesthetics and ethics meet in my ethical self when I answer those who address me. In a sense, rather than knowing 'the right thing' to do, being ethical is doing the 'best' thing in the situation, while answering those who address me.

As I outlined in the previous chapter, an aesthetic stance on both life and art that supports possible ethical action has three intersecting aspects that may be experienced concurrently or consecutively: I project into another consciousness, I return to my own consciousness to contemplate the other consciousness from outside it, and I perform an action that provisionally completes or finalizes the situation.

Valjean was engaged in an internal struggle as he contemplated his possible action. In the musical version of the story his inner conflict is made visible through song in a 'dialogue of conscience' (Morson and Emerson, 1990, p. 225). As Morson and Emerson put it, 'Bakhtin imagines the self as a conversation, often a struggle, of discrepant voices with each other, voices and words speaking from different positions and invested with different degrees and kinds of authority' (1990, p. 218).

At this moment different inner voices are struggling for dominance in his consciousness. In addition to the voice of the man in the courtroom, he hears the voices of those from his past life in the galleys, the voices of those in his comfortable current life, as well as the voice of the bishop. He does not separate one part of his life from another. Rather he listens to and accepts all of his inner voices, allowing them to interpenetrate each other. Heard through his socio-cultural framework, the voices that told him to stay silent would have been strongest. But heard through the framework of his ethical identity, those that resonated with the bishop's were more powerful.

Valjean acted with integrity. Integrity for Bakhtin means that 'The individual must become answerable through and through: all of his constituent moments must not only fit next to each other in the temporal sequence of his life, but must also interpenetrate each other in the unity of guilt and answerability' (1990, p. 2). The more the voices of all those who address us are answered, the more integrity an act has. In choosing how to act, Valjean answered his inner voices with his whole life, past, present, and future. He was wholly answerable in this moment. Emerson clarifies why it was so arduous. 'The most difficult work I face is creating a self whose integrity I can stand behind, which I can love and respect' (1997, p. 238).

This was a fateful moment for Valjean. It transformed his entire life and reshaped who he was psychically, socially, culturally, and ethically.

When Valjean accepted his personal and legal guilt, as a parole breaker, he did not excuse his actions or pass the consequences to someone else. He would not allow an innocent person to take the blame for the consequences of his past actions. Using another of Bakhtin's (1993) ethical terms, he did not look to another person to be an 'alibi for Being'. As Bocharov clarifies, 'a human being has no right to an alibi – to an evasion of that unique answerability which is constituted by his actualization of his own unique, never repeatable "place" in Being; he has no right to an evasion of that once-occurent "answerable act or deed" which his whole life must constitute' (1999, p. xxii).

Actions are never independent. Actions are always a reaction to other acts, or as Bakhtin puts it, an authored action is always answering another action in an ongoing dialogue. Acts not only are intentional deeds. They are also words, thoughts, and any physical, social, or cultural product formed from thoughts, words, and deeds. They can take forms ranging from letters to novels, and from painting to child raising. Ethical acts contrast with amoral behaviors that are unintended and not performed in answer to feeling addressed.

Valjean's authoring actions form a moral axis for the musical that make his ethical identity visible. He has acted with a high degree of integrity before he ever advances into the courtroom. As mayor he saves the life of a man who is being crushed by a cart, though by doing so he makes others suspicious of his background by betraying the great strength he developed in the galleys. He rescues and protects a woman from sexual abuse despite angering one of his socially powerful employees. He finds, adopts, and raises as his own the woman's daughter after the woman's death. He rescues the man who loves his daughter from certain death during the crushing of a revolution. And near the end of the story he faces with compassion Javert, the chief of police, who has relentlessly pursued him since the day he skipped parole.

Of course, people are rarely placed in positions where they feel that they have to be wholly answerable with their lives. Yet Bakhtin argues that to act with integrity people cannot be selective about which inner voices they ignore and which they listen to as they contemplate action. Disregarding, or silencing, inner voices are psychically destructive acts that have ethical consequences.

The self as self-others

We dialogically author our selves, and over time, our identities. Freud looked within to find a decontextualized relatively stable individual self. He regarded each person as having a separate consciousness and saw relationships as having psychic effects on individuals. In contrast, Bakhtin's view of the self is always in dynamic relationship with others.

Whenever I encounter another person, if I am answerable to the person, I attempt to project into the viewpoint of their consciousness, allowing their voice to affect my previous views and thus my awareness of what my understanding now is. As Bakhtin's collaborator Volosinov puts it, 'In becoming aware of myself, I attempt to look at myself, as it were, through the eyes of another person' either in the moment of interaction or in relation to a cultural group (1987/1927, quoted in Morris, 1994, p. 45).

Another way to conceptualize the self is to use Bakhtin's image of the tripartite self: I-for-myself, I-for-the-other, the-other-for-me. How I view a particular action in relation to myself is different from how I view it in relation to another person, which is different again from how others view it and me as the person acting. Across time, my interactions with others change how I view the world. If in imagination I attempt to see the world from others' viewpoints, to bring their consciousnesses within me, then 'I' am always in relationship with people, past as well as present. I am never an individual separated from others' views and deeds. I have many I–you consciousnesses. Consciousness, for Bakhtin, is always contextualized and relational.

It is in these senses that Bakhtin conceptualizes the self as distributed among many different self-others. Every long-term or casual relationship is a different self–other experience from which I can learn and author 'my self'. Over time, self-others come together, or are brought together by me, in varied combinations to form and shape my evolving consciousness of the world and my place in it. As Morson and Emerson stress, 'Selfhood is not a particular voice within, but a particular way of combining many voices within' (1990, p. 221).

As Valjean does, in new situations I can pay attention to my inner conversations as well as to any outer conversation. I can attempt to author my actions, and shape my consciousness, by listening to the combination of voices that represents my ethical identity and/or my socio-cultural identities. However, some voices will be louder and more insistent than others. As Morson and Emerson make clear, 'Consciousness takes shape, and never stops taking shape, as a process of interaction among authoritative and innerly persuasive discourses' (1998, p. 221).

Authoritative and internally persuasive discourses

Bakhtin used different broadly parallel terms to theorize that, in both face-to-face and inner conversations, different consciousnesses, voices, or discourses are in dialogue with one another. Each of these has different degrees of authority over me. These voices are more or less authoritative, and thus are heard and when followed affect my actions despite prior views that would suggest a different response. They are also more or less persuasive, and thus open to interpretation and debate. Some internal voices seem to be clearly telling us what to do, whereas others seem to make suggestions or just give a quiet nudge.

When Valjean was on the galleys he could not question the authoritarian words or deeds of his overseers who had more power than merely that of their individual authority. These jailers may have been conscious of the power of others, or had a sense of social superiority, or moral judgment. In their dealings with inmates their discourse will often refer to these powers and views. The more closed a jailer is in his views, the more authoritarian his discourse. This is apparent, for example, in yelled commands or threats of punishment. The more open he is, the more internally persuasive the discourse. For example, such a jailer would give people choices.

In the musical, Javert illustrates a consciousness inhabited by powerful authoritarian discourses. Bakhtin refers to such discourse as 'monologic' in contrast with internally persuasive discourses that are dialogic. Javert never questions the authority of the law or the people who apply the law. His moral judgments come only from fixed bureaucratic and inhumane monologic discourses. Liapanov would interpret Javert's ethics as 'desolated'. For him the ethical has been reduced to applying rules rather than generating values (in Bakhtin, 1993, p. 84). Javert relies on a legal code to predetermine his relationship with Valjean and any other people who have broken the law. The law determines his professional behavior. His position could be seen as amoral. His views are so rigid that he hears no inner voices questioning his actions. He does not believe he needs to think about Valjean's life since he ran away, or listen to Valjean's pleas to let him help the mother and child he has been caring for. Further, for Javert, anyone's life is irrelevant in matters of morality.

How I respond to and answer voices changes the degree of authority they hold over me. Javert is consistent in his disposition toward Valjean, treating him like any other lawbreaker. For Javert, his monologic discourse remains unchanged until a moment in the story when he does respond differently. Then the authority of the legalistic or monologic viewpoint suddenly collapses. Javert commits suicide rather than live without the certainty of a fixed legalistic moral order.

In the galleys and on the day he stole the candlesticks, Valjean was reactive, behaving rather than choosing to act. He was using a preexisting consciousness and an oppressive monologic discourse that saw the world and everyone in it as an object to be hated, despised, and ignored. But in answering the bishop's actions with an authoring self that chose to act, Valjean began to undermine the authority of that discourse so that nine years later, though he could hear its voice, it held little sway with him. As he stands outside the courthouse his consciousness is a chorus of voices attempting to persuade him. Different discourses are in a dialogic relationship with one another. None is monologically drowning out any other.

We watch Valjean in a dialogic authoring event as he struggles to make sense of the moment. As we watch the characters answer when they are addressed by others and by the world, we can create meaning about our lives as well as watch characters find (or in Javert's case, lose) meaning in theirs. And on a rereading of the text or a return to the theatre to watch another performance we can author more meaning about their world and our own.

Reading books, watching movies, going to the theater and aesthetically contemplating other works of art, we are addressed by the voices and discourses of the fictional lives of the characters. If we feel addressed by art, and by life, and choose to be answerable, we are authoring meaning not only about a book or play, but also about ourselves. The monologic discourse of a fixed moralistic message will close down meaning; a dialogue with the characters from a text will open it up. As Morris puts it, 'To mean is to respond constantly and open-endedly to one's addressivity in the world, as all human beings must. Meaning is always becoming, an absolute potential in an absolute future. Bakhtin is fundamentally opposed to any notion of meaning as fixed in time or space' (1994, p. 249).

When we are open to new meaning, then literature, life, and (I argue) playing with children, can open up new ideas about life and death. Literature and play also have a way of destabilizing monologic 'truths' or apparently stable moral certainties. For as Bakhtin stresses, "'Truth" is relativized by its dialogical contact with another social discourse, another view of the world' (1981, p. 279).

Children's selves and identities

'Who am I?' is a question young children ask implicitly as soon as they begin to communicate and observe the world around them. They form answers as they begin to feel connected to other people and start to develop a sense of their own individuality. Whereas adults have a well-developed sense of self and many diverse and intersecting identities, the younger children are, the more embryonic their identities and developing sense of self. How these develop depends on what sort of relationships they have with the adults in their lives.

Following the synthesis of Holland et al. (1998), children's identities and related senses of self form in two complementary and overlapping ways: identities are the result of children's participation in the practices and discourses of figured cultural worlds and are produced as they are positioned in social interactions. Through improvisation, children have agency to co-author with adults, identities and selves that, as I have argued, include ethical identities; running through children's developing socio-cultural identities is an ethical strand. Adult evaluations of practices and events, family stories, combined with how children are positioned over time, and how meaning is negotiated with children in pretend play, collectively explore and clarify the social rightness and wrongness of actions.

Cultural dimensions of children's identities

Young children's primary cultural identity is being a member of their family and, for most at a later time, being a member of a child-care group or preschool classroom. Though children form ad hoc groups when they play together, unless children, with or without adults, gather regularly for similar experiences, no culture will develop in Geertz's sense of people who publicly negotiate 'socially established structures of meaning' (1973, p. 12).

The structures and practices of a family, or child-care group, grow through the countless shared activities that adults and children engage in. A child's identity with a family or group, including gender groups, becomes narrativized in whatever stories are told and retold as well as in the explanations that accompany them. Barrie Thorne (1993) for example shows how children become gendered by the way adults and peers treat them as well as when adults accept ways of being with others as normal rather than questioning those norms. Children's identifications are 'figured' as it becomes clear to them what the social and ethical norms are that underlie 'how we do things' and 'why we do this'. Parents impose cultural norms when they dress infant girls in pink and boys in blue, give them different gender-differentiated names and toys, and expect them to act differently.

> Teachers frequently give boys more classroom attention than girls. Children pick up the gender stereotypes that pervade books, songs, advertisements, television programs, and movies. And peer groups, steeped in cultural ideas about what it is to be a girl or a boy, also perpetuate gender-typed play and interaction. In short, if boys and girls are different, they are not born but *made* that way.
>
> (ibid., p. 2)

As parents of a boy (and then a girl) we were very aware of the power of gender assumptions and positionings outlined by scholars like Thorne. Thus, for Michael (and later for Zoë) his clothes were all colors and we made all sorts of toys and narratives available to him. We were particularly aware of the need to critique gender and other socio-cultural, as well as ethical, assumptions that Michael might have accepted without question. Comments that ranged from the colors of infants' clothes to the jobs women performed undermined the normalizing influences that surround all children. Through critique and dialogue we wanted our children to be aware of choice not only in their actions but also in their understanding of social life.

Until he was four, Michael didn't have to deal with many cultural differences. For instance, he didn't have to accommodate to different cultural practices and norms. As a baby, we had in-home care for him. As a young child, we arranged for care in other loving family homes with adults who nurtured Michael and created kind, socially supportive family communities consistent with our values. If Michael was safe and happy when he was with others then we were pleased.

When Michael was two-and-a-half we moved for two years to a university international housing complex. Though the physical layout encouraged social interactions among many families, the children engaged in more shared activities and extensive interactions than the adults did. Whereas Michael wanted to run around, dig in the sand, or climb with children who spoke no English, most parents maintained polite social and cultural distance even when they shared space while walking, sitting, or eating outside. But this did not mean that Michael had to identify differently with the children he played with. What was much more important for him than any ethnic differences was a cross-cultural practice with an ethical edge that permeated his life: he cared most about sharing.

Michael identified any other child as a 'friend' if they shared space and toys with him in the communal grassy areas, climbing frames, or walkways. He and other young children easily fell into and out of friendship and sought one another out to play based largely on whether or not they shared. At the same time I noticed how some children, from any culture, could control others by restricting their access to toys that were 'special' or by insisting on which video would be watched on a visit to their home. For these reasons I promoted a family value of sharing. I was insistent that Michael would not truncate sharing by declaring that an object was 'mine'. My other reason was that I had grown up in a household where we rarely shared. I did not want our children to exclude others or feel left out from activities that could become more collaborative.

When Michael was about two I first negotiated with him about those few things that he could refuse to share. One possession that was clearly his was a beloved blanket that as 'blankie' had comforted him since he had been a baby and which he always held when he went to sleep. All objects he did not identify by his actions as 'his' were, by default, shareable. Linguistically I was careful to refer consistently to these and other objects as 'ours' and to talk about what 'we' did when referring to family activities and practices. 'We need to clear the table and then we can read one of our books'. I'd also use phrases like, 'Can you pass me the pen, please' or 'Are you using that cup?' rather than refer to 'my pen' or 'your cup'. I was repeatedly addressing Michael from an ideological viewpoint of sharing. In responding with phrases like, 'Thanks for sharing', I was evaluating actions as 'right' when they were consistent with that value. One phrase that I used repeatedly was, 'We love to share'. In later years the phrase became a family joke, but when our children were little it was a useful evaluative sign to bind together prior experiences of sharing with a present event.

My view of community extended beyond the walls of the house and our family group. I would insist that Michael (and later his sister Zoë) share whatever toys they brought outside. They had to take them inside if they did not want to share them. I was equally insistent that they shared space and objects with children who visited our home and took turns with them just as they did with one another.

Shifting among cultures and adjusting to different social expectations is one way in which norms become more visible and their socially constructed nature becomes clearer. It was not until he went to preschool aged three-and-a-half that Michael experienced a cultural shift and had to consistently act differently and thus develop another figured identity. At this time we were in need of child care and because Michael liked Anna's home and her many toys and books when we visited we agreed to enroll him. Anna's in-home preschool accommodated six children whom she daily ferried around in her van on very engaging field trips. She had routines and procedures that Michael was unused to, but which he accepted immediately. One such was eating snacks at a table in the same way that lunch was eaten communally. The biggest cultural change for Michael was that Anna did not want him, or any of the children, to pretend to be violent. This was a problem because Michael spent much of his life pretending to be monsters and heroes. However, this was a non-negotiable condition of joining her family care. She said she believed violent play might scare the other children. I now realize that her cultural early childhood practices and beliefs were located among the dominant discourses I discussed in the previous chapter. She seemed to believe that children would become violent if they pretended to be violent. We talked with Michael. He wanted to return to Anna's home to use her slide and he agreed that he'd not pretend that he was a mythic character when he was with her.

Invariably as we drove to drop off Michael at Anna's home he was pretending to be a knight, the Beast from *Beauty and the Beast*, or some other monster or hero. Before we got out of the car we would negotiate a cultural change. 'I need to talk to Michael,' I'd begin. 'Can you leave the monsters and heroes in the car, please. OK?' And as I lifted him out of the car seat I'd usually say, 'Let's say goodbye to the Beast' (or whoever he was pretending to be). 'He'll be there when we pick you up again.'

What Anna did not appreciate was that play allows children to participate in and explore new cultures. As Holland et al. stress, 'the play worlds that children create are akin to the more complex culturally constructed or figured worlds that they enter into as they grow older' (1998, p. 280). Children can enter those cultural worlds to engage in practices with very different norms, without having to negotiate and reach the sort of agreements Michael had to in order to join Anna's preschool. The only agreement necessary is that we're pretending. Once that is set, all actions are appropriate when they are consistent with the culture of the figured world.

Narratives are figured worlds that children can step into as they play. Like the everyday cultural worlds of home, preschool, restaurants etc., play worlds 'carry dispositions, social identifications, and even personification just as surely as they carry meaning' (ibid., p. 271). When Michael pretended to be a vampire his disposition was to bite people's necks and drink their blood. He identified with vampires as a group, wanting me to be a vampire too so that we could find our coffins to lie in together. He personified Dracula when he wore his black and red cape, painted his face white, and used words and gestures from the movie *Dracula*. He even talked like Dracula when he addressed me as the famous actor Bella Lugosi does with a half-smile, an ambiguous look in his eye, and a Transylvanian accent, 'I bid you welcome. I am Dracula.'

Vygotsky (1986) realized that children's play is consistent with different social rules, but he didn't recognize that those rules could be very different from everyday life, especially in mythic play. Play worlds are 'liminal' spaces in Victor Turner's (1974) use of the term, when play is perceived as being at the edge of what is 'normal' or 'ordered'. James et al. argue that adults believe children in general 'have to be constrained into social order' because they 'represent a potential challenge to social norms by virtue of their constant promise of liminality'. When seen as liminal, mythic play seems particularly abnormal and often disorderly. It appears to provide adults with disturbing 'living exemplars of the very margins of [social] order, of its volatility and, in fact, its fragility' (1998, p. 198).

Robert Coles, the well-known psychiatrist, provides a very different view of children. He has shown how children can show moral leadership in his documentation of the courage and wisdom of children from cultures in crisis situations all over the world (1986). In a more recent book he discusses how children develop what he calls their moral intelligence (1997). He shows the importance of the ongoing everyday interactions and conversations among adults and children for developing the desire to be moral as well as an understanding of what ethical action looks like.

Coles argues that children learn how to be moral by observation and through 'moral companionship' with adults who are ready to examine the morality of their own and their children's daily lives as well as the ethical dimensions of other people's actions. His belief parallels Bakhtin's view that people must be answerable when they are addressed. 'We become the people we are, morally – through experiences and our responses to them and to one another as we go through them' (1997, p. 9).

Being moral and recognizing ethical action, for Coles, is not sophisticated. Children don't have to wait until they're older to know that we're moral when we're good. We're moral, not when we talk about ethics or engage in moral reasoning, but in our everyday ethical deeds. And to know how to be good we need look no further than the Golden Rule. People all over the world understand in their bodies as well as their minds why the standard for treating others should be the way they want to be treated.

Coles gives as an example of being good, the 'high character and great humanity' of a seasoned pediatrician he met as a young doctor. The elder man had 'respect for other people as well as himself, the deep awareness he acknowledged of our human connectedness' that guided his work with children and their parents. Though a 'big shot doctor', he was also 'respectful of others no matter their station in life; he was a "good person" – courteous, compassionate, caring, warm-hearted, unpretentious' (ibid., p. 6).

In contrast, 'not-so-good' people are 'bad', for Coles, because they have a 'moral undertow' (ibid. p. 21). This is apparent when people have developed the sort of 'unreflective egoism' that George Eliot portrayed in the character of Casaubon in her novel *Middlemarch*. The not-so-good person pays 'scant attention to the rights of others, not to mention one's own ethical obligations within a family, a classroom, or a community' (ibid., p. 22). 'Bad' people, in Bakhtin's terms, are only minimally answerable. Other people's voices are only on the horizons of their consciousness whereas for 'good' people those voices are loud, up close, listened to, and answered.

Coles is emphatic that children's ethical learning is an adult responsiblity. How an adult is answerable in everyday situations establishes an ethical approach to life.

> We grow morally as a consequence of learning how to be with others, how to behave in this world, a learning prompted by taking to heart what we have seen and heard. The child is a witness: the child is an ever-attentive witness of grown-up morality – or lack thereof; the child looks and looks for clues as to how one ought to behave, and finds them galore as we parents and teachers go about our lives, making choices, addressing people, showing in action our rock-bottom assumptions, desires, and values, and thereby telling those young observers much more than we realize.
>
> (ibid., p. 5)

When adults play with children, what Coles calls their moral companionship accompanies them on the journeys into narrative worlds. In these narrative worlds what he refers to as their moral imagination can develop.

And these narrative worlds can be much more challenging and morally demanding worlds than the everyday world. In these play worlds children watch intently to see adults using their 'grown-up morality' as they struggle alongside them, make choices, and collaboratively try to work out 'how one ought to behave'.

Narratives provide children with access to a vast array of possible human behaviors ranging across the ethical universe, showing deeds ranging from the monstrous to the heroic, from the debauched to the sublime, and depicting, through art, multiple viewpoints on good and evil lives. Adults entering into that universe through the play portal can continue their ethical conversations with children about situations that children find particularly fascinating, though which adults may find ethically challenging.

Positional dimensions of children's identities

Positional identities develop alongside figured identities as children are positioned over and over again as 'children' in relation to adults. Michael was also positioned as a 'boy' in relation to girls. He also developed an identity as 'son', 'grandson', and later as 'brother'. Children tend to be positioned by adults with less power, less privilege, and less status than adults. Adults tend to assume that only they should apply and interpret the norms of behavior. Children are rarely given the authority to contest or negotiate any amendments to adult-imposed rules. Only adults should be able to choose what to eat, where to move, when to go to bed, when to speak, and how to judge actions as socially appropriate or morally right. As James et al. argue, when children are regarded as having to be managed and controlled with very limited agency it is because they are regarded as 'unstable, systematically disruptive and uncontained' (1998, p. 198). From this perspective the whole field of Childhood Studies can be regarded as different ways to 'police the boundaries between the morally acceptable and the morally unacceptable'.

The dominant discourses of early childhood position children in binary opposition to adults. Adults tend to dichotomize their social roles, privileging their adult position over children, and relying on assumptions about how children ought to be in the world rather than on developing social relationships with them as people. On the one hand, children are viewed as simplistic thinkers, ignorant, or primitive, while on the other hand they are viewed as just expressing themselves, or being childishly creative. In any event, it's adults who must take charge, control children, and tell them what to do socially and morally. James et al. bemoan the outcome: childhood is 'dispossessed of intentionality and agency' (ibid., p. 21).

Though adults tend to regard children with the largely fixed positional identities of 'children', Davies and Harré (1990) stress that subject positions are never fixed even though they may seem to be static or rigid. Their theory of positioning provides a dynamic poststructural discourse-based alternative to the well-known sociological concept of 'social role' that perpetuates the notion of stable selves and identities.

Davies and Harré provide a radically different perspective.

> An individual emerges through the processes of social interaction, not as a relatively fixed end product but as one who is constituted and reconstituted through the various discursive practices in which they participate. Accordingly, who one is, that is, what sort of person one is, is always an open question with a shifting answer depending upon the positions made available within one's own and other's discursive practices, and within those practices, the stories through which we make sense of our own and others' lives.
>
> (1999/1990, p. 35)

Change the positioning and you change the positions available to people is their radical argument. Children take up different selves when they are positioned differently. As adults often discover, the child that they thought they knew seems to become a better or worse person with other people or in different settings. This is because positioning is always relative in 'ever-shifting patterns of mutual and contestable rights and obligations of speaking and acting' (Harré and Langenhove, 1999, p. 1). When different people position children with different amount of power to move, talk, and question, the relational self that arises in each case will be different. Thus when children are consistently positioned as competent, knowledgeable, human beings who are able to explore ideas, negotiate, and reach agreements, then they will take up selves, or subject positions, that are exploratory, competent, and open to dialogue.

Positioning theory conceptualizes the self as dispersed among many subject positions, a location from which a particular way of understanding the world can be developed, along with inherent rights, duties, and privileges. Positioning theory can be contrasted with role theory which conceptualizes people as acting fairly predictably within a fixed number of social roles (like 'son' or 'parent').

> Once having taken up a particular position as one's own, a person inevitably sees the world from the vantage point of that position and in terms of the particular images, metaphors, storylines and concepts which are made relevant within the particular discursive practice in which they are positioned.
>
> (Davies and Harré, 1999/1990, p. 35)

The subject positions of young children are less complex than those of older children or adults since they have less understanding of, and less interest in, the sophistication possible in social positioning. Only for older children or adults is a position likely to have all of the following strands: 'a complex cluster of generic personal attributes, structured in various ways, which impinges on the possibilities of interpersonal, intergroup and even intrapersonal action through some assignment of such rights, duties and obligations to an individual as are sustained by the cluster' (Harré and Langenhove, 1999, p. 1).

Following children's desires

What young children want from adults is no different than what all human beings want and need in their hearts: authentic trusting tender relationships. Children desire to be loved, to be cared for, to be heard, and to be treated as an equal deserving of respect. At the core of children's learning to be human is the opportunity to learn about whatever aspects of the world they want to explore. To be able to support children's desires to learn means as adults we must be prepared to follow where children want to lead us.

I followed Michael into fantastic worlds where he was eager to imagine cultural practices and social positionings that were very different from those in everyday life. Through mythic narratives Michael explored the ethical as well as the socio-cultural dimensions of life by socially imagining the words and deeds of the people in those worlds. We explored how people with power and authority ought to behave toward others, as we imagined encounters between St George and the dragon, Luke Skywalker and Darth Vader, or Dr Jekyll and one of Mr Hyde's victims.

Our daughter, Zoë, led me in a different direction. I don't know why Zoë didn't engage with me in play to the extent that Michael did. I was responsive to her desires just as I was to Michael's. I was open to mythic or other fantasy play with her and made available to her all the narratives that Michael had liked. However, my relationship with Zoë developed more through discovery and discussion about the physical and social worlds around her rather than by exploring possible worlds in narratives.

Why was there such a difference? First, though Pat and I spent a great deal of time with both of our children when they were young, Michael had more time with me and Zoë was more often with her mother. Second, as a girl she may have looked more to her mother than her father as a social model. Though Pat would participate in pretend play when asked, she tended to engage in more everyday pursuits. Third, being four-and-a-half years younger than her brother, Zoë inevitably was not as interested in the topics her brother was interested in. Additionally, as more of an observer she had much less control of the created experiences and she would sometimes be frightened. Finally, she has always seemed more focused on physical and social worlds than on worlds of fantasy.

Zoë has always loved finding and making patterns and being physically active. By the age of twelve she was a champion Irish dancer, talented at sports, had a flair for mathematics and music, and strong trusting friendships. At the age when Michael had jumped off my lap pretending to be a dinosaur, Zoë jumped down to lay out the pattern blocks. Zoë would often be on the edge of my play with Michael or engaged in a parallel activity. She always had access to scores of narratives including ones Michael had loved but she preferred stories with domestic themes. She had moments of pretending to be characters when we would address and answer one another during the reading of a book; but on the whole she preferred to read and then talk about stories, analyzing them as ourselves rather than entering into them as if we were other people. And when she played she preferred to do so alone. Whereas Michael had loved to stomp as a giant talking to me as Jack, she delighted in skipping alone as a fairy. Michael had played with toy trucks but Zoë preferred to pretend to use the phone. He had imagined worlds populated with monsters and heroes. Her most fantastic moment of pretend play was when she was four. She drifted across the floor dressed in some of her mother's clothes and announced in a husky voice, 'I am the woman in black and I am going to Australia'.

Authoring selves and identities in play

The story of *Les Miserables* is a cultural representation in two ways. First, within the universe of Victor Hugo, the narrative shows, on the one hand, how people living within socially constructed worlds like those of prisons, public officials, or revolution may be snatched up or discarded. On the other hand, it shows how individuals have choice in their response to the situations they find themselves within. Second, the novel and musical are cultural products that represent aspects of culture for readers or viewers to contemplate and use to make sense of the world. Art can always be interpreted in these two complementary ways: by imagining that we are living a life inside a narrative world and/or by using the fictional world to illuminate our understanding of the world that we live in every day.

Neither aspect of cultural representation is understandable without recognizing the connection between culture and play. Humans create culture through play that is taken seriously. People at play create novelty within their everyday life experiences and part of the experience of living is playing that creates objects depicting aspects of life. As Holland et al. (1998) put it, 'Human life is inexplicable without our abilities to figure worlds, play at them, act them out, and then make them socially, culturally, and thus materially consequential' (p. 280).

As humans we often struggle to understand life (and death). The 'Who am I?' question becomes repeatedly contextualized, sometimes crystallizing relationships in life-changing ways. One question that I now ask on two continents stretches across the events of my whole life: 'Who am I, as a person in this family?' When I was seventeen, I had to ask, 'Who am I, when my parents die?' 'Who am I when I live in a different country?' was a question I asked at eighteen, and again aged thirty-two. Answering all of these questions involved serious play. I could not remain the person I had been because relationships, social situations, and cultural expectations had changed.

The arts, including literature, theater, film, and (I argue), child–adult play, can in different ways all provide us with artifacts to contemplate that can assist us in making sense of the world. As Grayling puts it in discussing literature, 'it educates and extends the moral imagination, affording insights into – and therefore the chance to be more tolerant of – other lives, other ways, other choices, most of which one will probably never directly experience oneself' (2003, p. 229).

In contemplation of imagined events we make meaning. When we represent and evaluate possibilities for how we might choose to live, we may then play with them in our thoughts and conversations. The deaths of King Lear, the salesman Willy Loman, and Darth Vader, all provided me with ways of revisiting my own father's death, to consider my own death, and to talk internally with the fictional characters and my father, about the meaning of parental life in relation to one's children, and vice versa.

The space for authoring selves and, over time, identities, is more intentional, vast, and expansive in child–adult play than is ever possible in everyday life. Play creates spaces where authoring is the norm. When people play they are intentionally making and shaping possible selves and ways of identifying with others. In contrast, in everyday life selves and identities will form whether or not people actively author them. This is particularly the case for young children whose socio-cultural identities are tied up with those of their parents, care-givers, and peers. Play opens up a myriad images in cultural spaces and significant shifts in subject positions. With this play children may author meaning about whichever aspects of the socio-cultural and ethical dimensions of life (and death) intrigue them, as they explore why deeds are good (and evil) as well as right (and wrong).

Playing with possible selves

When children play they author ethical meaning as they choose to act in an imagined world and are answerable for their actions. In the cultures of the different narrative worlds opened up through play, children can explore actions in novel situations.

Pretend play can be conceptualized as taking place in three socio-cultural spaces: everyday spaces, socially imagined pretend play spaces, and projective-evaluative authoring spaces. I propose this, by extending the ideas already developed in this chapter, using in particular Bakhtin's theory of the tripartite self noted above. I also use his theory of aesthetic activity discussed in chapters one and two, along with Gee's idea of tripartite identities also noted in chapter one.

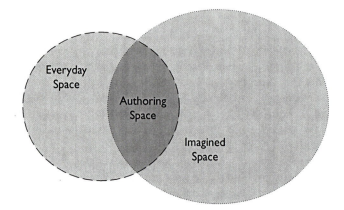

Figure 3.1 The spaces of play

Everyday spaces

People live their lives in everyday socio-cultural spaces. Everyday selves are people's everyday acting consciousnesses in the multiple and intersecting social and cultural worlds of family, school, restaurants, sports teams, work-place, etc. These worlds are figured and narrativized in daily life through participation in cultural activities and through social positioning. A person's developing identities are affected by how he, or she, is socially positioned by other people, as well as by how he or she accepts, opposes, or negotiates this positioning. Young children mostly accept how they are positioned, though, the older children become, the more likely they are to seriously question or resist how adults position them.

Children, like adults, have agency in authoring selves and, over time, identities. They do so by improvising responses to affect their relative position. They opportunistically draw on their cultural resources in response to particular situations, as mediated by their senses and sensitivities. They will co-author selves and identities when they improvise in a situation with an adult. Such improvisation requires an aesthetic approach to life. I argue that everyday authoring occurs in the same aesthetic projective-evaluative space where pretend play is authored.

Socially imagined pretend play spaces

People, like other mammals that play, know that they are playing. The anthropologist Gregory Bateson recognized that communication in play always carries a metacommunicative statement, 'This is play'. Bateson uses an example from animal play to explain this: 'These actions in which we now engage do not denote what these actions for which they stand would denote. . . . The playful nip denotes the bite but it does not denote what would be denoted by the bite' (1972, p. 180). In other words, when people play they are always in effect saying, 'Remember that we're only pretending'.

People begin to create parallel worlds when they play in socially imagined spaces that parallel and overlap with the spaces of everyday life. Though everyday life never disappears, everyday concerns dissipate as social relationships are played at within the socially imagined spaces of an emerging fictional play world. These social relationships can be intensified, inverted, refracted, magnified, diminished, or distorted. Narrative worlds give people access to how social relationships could be very different in other people's lives in parallel with the stability of their everyday social lives. Pretend play gives people social opportunities to play with any of those relationships and thus explore whatever 'what if . . .' situation takes their fancy. When, in playing with other people, we enter narrative worlds we begin to author a parallel universe where we can play with possible selves.

The overlap between everyday and socially imagined pretend play spaces

Everyday and socially imagined spaces always overlap since the latter are built from cultural resources that are transformed in imagination. There is a relative emotional pull between everyday and pretend play spaces that is very different for adults and children. Older and younger people are likely to have different experiences of their relative strength, intensity, and sense of solidity.

Adults have a necessarily deep commitment to everyday realities. This may produce a feeling of not being able to let go of the here-and-now enough to be able to fully enter an imagined space with a child. Adults have literally invested their lives in their everyday practices. Using Lave and Wenger's (1991) term, they are 'old timers' who in repeated participation in shared activities have developed a great deal of experience and expertise in whatever spaces they inhabit from those of daily work to that of a sports team. The figured worlds that continue to be constituted in their daily activities have deep and complex meaning-making structures for them. A play world can easily seem ephemeral, trivial, miniature, and childish by comparison.

Young children, in contrast to adults, have necessarily developed less depth or attachment to whatever social and cultural worlds they inhabit. They just have not been around for as much time as adults nor have they had the same amount or intensity of experiences. Adult worlds can seem complicated, irrelevant, over-powering, and largely incomprehensible in comparison to story worlds that may be entered at will when pretending. As a way of trying to capture a child's experience, I reproduce an extract from a notebook where I tried to imagine Michael's viewpoint aged three.

Life outside the home can be confusing and feel oppressive. When you go to other people's houses to be cared for you can't predict their rules and you can find yourself unexpectedly in trouble. Restaurants are the worst because you have to sit still even though you want to move and do something apart from listen to adults talking about incomprehensible things. Even at home, when you do something different you never know whether your mom and dad will laugh or frown. So often you feel small, insignificant, and powerless – but not when you play.

When you play you can become more powerful than you could ever be in everyday life. As you play you can imagine other possible selves beyond your everyday self. You can be stronger and taller and smarter than any sibling, your friends, and your parents. And you can have weapons – armor, swords, and guns. And you don't have to walk – you can drive or fly at will. And you can go anywhere – up the tallest mountain and into the deepest cave. And you can identify with anyone you want inside the events of whatever stories you know.

Using Lave and Wenger's (1991) terms, as relative 'newcomers' in adult worlds children are continually positioned as 'peripheral participants' in activities that are dominated by predetermined cultural practices and adult ideas that are often not explained to children. Children are often bewildered by the social rules in operation in figured worlds like restaurants and grocery stores or their parents' work places. They may also be confused by the rules at home or in a care setting unless these have been explained in context.

Only as children begin to participate in cultural worlds can they author meaning. As children participate in the daily practices and experiences of everyday home life, from dressing to eating together, its socio-cultural reality becomes more tangible and meaningful. Conversely, dressing a child up in sportswear does not create an experience of being in the world of a sport. Pretending to be famous players does. Going to games, catching a ball, joining a team, and watching games on television with a knowledgeable adult, will all create depth and intensity of experience that gives everyday figured worlds more social solidity and emotional pull. Similarly, as children participate in, and come to understand the purpose for, shared classroom activities, a sense of permanence about preschool life and an investment in it will grow. Further, pretending to be in an everyday space like a school or a restaurant not only allows children to explore their ideas but also provides a sense of reality to what initially may seem to be arbitrary words and movements. As children play they choose which encounters to project into as participants. Within this imagined world they have willed into being, however, the encounters are always contextualized by cultural practices reflecting 'how we do things' because of who we are.

Playing allows children to transform their observations, experiences, and sense of possibilities within everyday life into fantasy worlds where the social rules are always understandable and the events are always under their control. The emotional and physical safety of play worlds provides children with spaces where they can feel competent and capable while choosing to explore whatever aspects of life interest them. At the same time everyday concerns dissipate. Schwartzman (1978) believed that adults had missed much of the potential meaning of play for a child by failing to take a 'sideways glance' at whom children play with. To invert her observation, when children play they only take sideways glances at everyday life.

While participating in more adult-focused everyday social practices the reality of pretend play may have a greater appeal. The younger children are, the more likely it is that play worlds will have a much stronger pull for them than everyday life. When Michael accompanied us to restaurants he was largely disinterested in the events going on around him. He was much more committed to his books, his drawings, and to pretending alone or with me. He also wanted to move. So where possible I would walk round with him, or carry him when he was very young, looking at pictures on display and talking with him about whatever he noticed people were doing as some waited while others served. He invariably drifted into play mode. I can't tell in retrospect which one of us initiated being more playful but certainly Michael was always more responsive and interactive as I played than when I did not, and I was mostly eager to pretend with him. In any event, he would often transform parts of any actual space into a parallel play space that intersected with the physical space. For example he used a wall outside to hide behind as Jack or pretended that climbing into a high chair was going up the beanstalk.

I found that being playful could make abstract purposes and the views of absent people more concrete and obvious. Abstractions like clock time and the views of people not physically present make little sense to children as they move to their own rhythms – they want to eat when they're hungry, go to bed when they are tired, and play until they lose interest. I found that abstract purposes could become more apparent by tapping into the concrete particulars of a briefly entered play space. Michael would sometimes resist putting on clothes that were different from those already in his hand. But then I looked out the window, for example at the snow, and pretended to shiver with cold and put on my gloves. Michael joined in the play event that I had initiated and would invariably start putting on his gloves as well.

Michael would dialogue when activities became more playful. For example, to make negotiations over leaving the house in the morning more dialogic I would pretend to talk to Michael as though I was the bus driver driving the bus and counting down the time to when he'd arrive at our stop. Or I'd be one of Michael's preschool teachers looking through the books to read and asking him which one he would like to see.

Projective-reflective authoring spaces

Authoring occurs in a projective-reflective space. Playing is projecting a possible self into a narrative world and through interactions creating images of a play world. Every narrative, whether from a book, a movie, or a told story, provides people with possible ways of being, acting, and relating to other people. Stories provide us with images of possible selves. Pretending to live in story worlds gives us temporary opportunities to live different lives. Michael lived a thousand lives and died a thousand deaths in the mythic worlds we explored together.

Every imagined relationship is a way to position and be positioned differently. As we played, Michael loved others as he nurtured, rescued, and cared for them. In turn, Michael was loved. I too, as his play partner, loved and was loved in imagined worlds. As we played, Michael also hated. He attacked, killed, mutilated, and humiliated people. In turn, he was hated in a pretend space. I also pretended to hate and become the object of hate when we played. This was sometimes very difficult for me to do, and I discuss such resistance to pretending in detail in the next chapter.

Authoring spaces are reflective as well as projective. There is no aesthetic space for Bakhtin unless we contemplate action as well as act. It's reflection that allows us to get outside our own or others' actions in order to make meaning and understand through a physical and/or verbal act of partial finalization. In doing so we are exploring possible identities. As we contemplate how we ought to act toward others we explore aspects of possible ethical identities.

Exploring possible identities

In everyday life people both reveal and build their socio-cultural and ethical identities through their own actions and as they interpret other people's identities by making assumptions about the purposes of their actions. To be able to function socially and participate in social group interactions or as an observer of others, children must also develop the ability to read people's identifications. They do so by learning the different shared cultural meanings of the signs that people use in daily activities. They have to be able to read the words, gestures, and objects used with particular social meanings that signify membership in particular cultural groups. Over time, as Michael learned how ordering happens in restaurants he could request food that he liked as he engaged in a conversation with a server, used the specialized descriptive language of food preparation, and consulted a menu.

To become an insider in any group, children must learn broad and later subtle distinctions among the actions of individuals within groups as well as between groups. Young children must answer socio-cultural questions that either they raise tacitly or that are raised by adults. Who's a family member? Who's a friend? Who's a teacher? What's socially appropriate behavior here and there? How's it different if I'm with this or that person? Pondering questions like these creates socio-cultural answers to the existential question, 'Who am I?'

Because actions are value based they always have ethical dimensions. Actions reveal people's ethical identities. Interpreting actions evaluates aspects of a person's presumed ethical identity. To be able to read the world ethically, young children must develop answers to ethical questions that they either tacitly ask or that adults ponder with them. Who can be trusted? What activities are safe with this person? What actions should I be cautious of? What is it always wrong to do? What is it always right to do? Are there exceptions? How do I know how to do the right thing, or the best thing, in a particular situation? Questions like these explore the ethical dimensions of the primal question, 'Who am I?' The answers do not exactly match one socio-cultural identity or another but rather intersect across many.

Children need adults' interpretations to be able to make meaning about socio-cultural and ethical identities and their related practices. When Michael was three or four he didn't really care whether he was playing with his cousins or his friends. The important issue for him was whether or not other children wanted to run around with him or share their toys. However, by referring to people in terms of their relationship to us, and by telling him what behavior was appropriate and what was not in different situations, we helped Michael build different identities. Driving to his grandparents' home for family gatherings we would show Michael photographs to remind him of his cousins, uncles, and aunts. Michael would see us enter his grand-parents' home and interact with people in very different ways to how we would act on visiting friends. For instance, when visiting relations we would enter without ringing the doorbell and become intimate very quickly; this was not how we would act when going to a friend's house. However, we also had to make clear to Michael that there were new social limits when we visited his relations. He and his cousins could go almost anywhere inside or out, without asking, but they couldn't sit in their grandfather's chair and didn't have the authority to change the channel on the television. As far as Michael was concerned, though, as his parents we still expected him to share.

My values inform how I interpret the world and make assumptions about other people. Michael learned these implicitly as I would talk about my interactions with other people. Though I interact with relations differently than with strangers, nevertheless I believe in having an open approach to interactions with all people. For example, rather than say something monologic like, 'Never talk to strangers', I tended to initiate conversations with people wherever I met them. Michael would see me talk with people walking past our home, in the playground at the park, on the bus, or at the grocery store check-out. I would often bring Michael into conversations by referring to him or asking him a question. Later I would briefly talk with him about how the other people had acted or what they had said and interpret their behavior as 'nice' or 'kind' or 'confusing' etc. 'Wasn't that nice how he helped us find the way?' 'That girl was really kind to share her ball with you, wasn't she?' 'I wasn't sure what that man was thinking. He seemed upset about something. What did you think?' I wanted Michael to be open with people in general and treat them with respect, but pay attention to how they interacted from an ethical as well as from a social point of view.

Every narrative that children encounter presents them with possible selves. Stories that I, or other people, told Michael were all filled with examples of possible ways of living in the world both as social beings and as ethical ones. Though now, aged seventeen at the time of writing, Michael can discuss people from literary or family narratives in sophisticated ways, a decade earlier, he was not interested in more than brief reflections on events that did not involve physical movement and play.

Playing to create possible worlds from the narratives of actual events allows children to revisit those experiences and play with different ways of being. For example, for several months Michael wanted to play around with different possible selves in response to the car accident that I referred to in chapter two. Michael could be a responsible adult as well as a needy child. He could imagine what a parent might do as well as how a rescuer might act. Similarly, every fictional narrative provides children with additional possible selves. Mythic narratives open up worlds where children can imagine possible ways of responding to crisis situations where the stakes are very high.

Every possible self has socio-cultural identities with intersecting and sometimes overlapping ethical identities. In domestic play like Michael's play around the car accident, possible selves always act as members of

groups and always within an ethical ideology. Just as we always have relations to call on for help, so an ambulance driver always has colleagues
whether or not we actually see them. We should assume that all ambulance
drivers are dedicated to saving lives even to the point of sometimes being
prepared to put their own lives at risk.

Similarly, within any fictional world, each possible self can be regarded
as only one among many such people or creatures with similar ethical viewpoints. Encountering any dragon in a mythic world, to avoid being eaten
we should assume that the dragon identifies with other terrorizing, dangerous, potentially deadly dragons. Anyone ruled by the dark side in the world
of *Star Wars* is sure to be ruthlessly oppressive. Any vampire is going to need
to suck someone's blood to remain undead. Any zombie will kill without
remorse. Conversely, heroes like St George, Una, Beauty, Beowulf, Perseus,
Rama, or Jedi warriors, are all going to act for the good of their community.
They are all prepared to confront and stop the monstrous creatures or
people who are oppressing others in their narrative world.

Positioning in everyday worlds protects into positioning in play worlds

As Heathcote notes in discussing adult responsibility in using imagined
encounters, adults should 'protect children into experiences' (1984). Child–
adult play between a trusting adult and child can be extremely powerful and
effective at supporting children's agency in forming their own discourses
and identities. When a relationship is not a trusting one from the child's
experience, either because of newness or because of unsettling events, then
interactions among adult and child will be less productive.

However, when playing together across time has been collaborative,
mutually supportive, and joyful, a child will be able to experience multiple
ways of being positioned by an adult within play worlds ranging from
the highly oppositional (like the battles between knight and dragon) to the
highly supportive (like the nurturing of the knight by Una).

Adults' reassuring presence signals to children that an experience is
only occurring in an imagined space. This reassurance allows children to
project into many consciousnesses they might avoid in everyday encounters.
Whereas oppositional positioning in everyday life can provoke rejection,
experiences of confrontations in a play world can be relished. When children feel emotionally attacked as 'themselves' because of their actions then
they are likely to be defensive. Attempts by adults to make a child listen and
change may well be resisted. As Bakhtin might say, the child may finalize
in response rather than engage in a dialogue.

However, within the emotional protection of a play world that has been
mutually created among children and adult, any viewpoint, discourse, or

action, no matter how hateful or oppressive it might be judged in everyday life, can be entered into by a child and used to position people within the play world. The viewpoint can then become an object for evaluation by an adult as well as by other children that is provisional because it occurs in an imagined space. Of course, when adult and child switch positions the adult must be able to project into the other viewpoint to become, within the protection of the play world, an object for the child to contemplate and finalize.

Playing as projection into interrelated viewpoints

Confusing 'play' with 'a play', adults can expect playing in a narrative world to be one step away from the play performance of a narrative. Teachers and parents can easily expect and assume that one child will (or should) become only one character. It is more accurate to conceptualize playing as people collectively moving among the viewpoints, consciousnesses, positionings, and actions of the different interrelated people in a narrative. Moving among points of view will not necessarily occur in a single play event. Especially with narrative worlds that children are eager to return to and explore, taking different positions will happen across many play events over a period of weeks or months.

For over six months Michael pretended to be the knight, the dragon, the lady, and the people in the world of St George. So did I. At the same time, he and I also inhabited the consciousnesses of nearly every character in the encounters of the narratives that we read or viewed. Those that he did not care about passed by like people we would see from the car. Those he was attracted to were like the strangers we might talk with on the bus to friends whom we would visit regularly.

Shifting among embodied discourses

As Michael played with me he projected into other consciousnesses by moving among the viewpoints available in a narrative, adopting the language of different people or creatures, and taking action as if we were those people or creatures. In doing so we were entering into the ideology and values of each consciousness. Each of these consciousnesses had its own discourse that was embodied through action. Discourse is the exchange between people as they talk but for Bakhtin it also encompasses much more. Language is ideological; it is more than words with individual and collective decontexualized meaning. Language in use and in context always carries with it a way of viewing, being in, talking about, valuing, and taking action that positions other people and the world. The dragon and the knight may talk to each other but they use entirely different discourses as they adopt oppositional positions.

The dragon's egotistical self-satisfying discourse assumes a privileged position that does not need to hear from humans. This discourse becomes embodied in the dragon's terrorizing actions as he takes food, burns homes, and kills people. The knight's discourse, by contrast, is egoless and rooted in service to the Fairy Queen and the people. He demands that the dragon stop attacking and embodies this discourse in his three-day battle. The discourse of the lady, Una, shares an egoless assumption of service to the people and is embodied in supportive nurturing actions that sustain the knight.

In a sense, the mythic tale of St George, as written, has one overarching discourse composed of other discourse strands in oppositional relationship with one another. It is a story of struggle, love, service, and courage in the face of apparently hopeless and insuperable odds. To internalize aspects of the narrative and to integrate it into my identity, I must enter into an aesthetic relationship with the text and engage in dialogue with all of the discourses contained within it. I cannot project into one while ignoring the others. Of course, when Michael was older discourse could become lengthy discussions, but before he entered school, discourses were mostly embodied in movement appropriate to different characters. As we played in mythic worlds we both engaged in aesthetic activities and created episodes on an ethical quest. By embodying the actions and using the words of each character as they encountered one another, we were repeatedly addressing one consciousness from the point of view of the other consciousnesses and then being answerable from that viewpoint. We were playing with possible selves and exploring possible identities as we projected into the consciousnesses of characters in events from mostly mythic narratives and thereby shifted among the interrelated discourses.

Good-and-evil selves

> What wisdom can there be to choose, what continence to forbear, without knowledge of evil?
>
> Milton, 1644

> Innocence cannot be wise, and wisdom cannot be innocent.
>
> Philip Pullman, 2002

Michael pretended to be evil as well as good when we played. His possible selves at play could be thought of as being good-and-evil. Over the years that we played, Michael attacked as a dragon, cut off the head of Medusa, whipped Quasimodo, the Hunchback of Notre Dame, blew up a building

Figure 3.2 Good-and-evil selves

around the time of the Oklahoma City bombing, turned humans into vampires by sucking their blood, killed without mercy as a zombie, imagined being Dr Jekyll and Mr Hyde, and slashed people as Freddy Kreuger. At the same time he acted to stop the perpetrators of evil when we played. His play was central to a daily life in which he was kind to his baby sister and considerate of other children. When Michael was answerable for the actions of his everyday and possible selves then he was acting ethically. In the authoring spaces of play he was shaping his ethical identity.

Accepting that otherwise nicely behaved children actually choose to pretend to be mean can be difficult for adults. Somehow when children pretend to shoot or attack one another it doesn't seem quite right. It seems wrong to allow them to fill their minds with images of evil and perform deeds we would protect them from in their childhood. Like many of the adults I've informally talked with and observed, I too had initial negative reactions when pretend guns were pointed at me.

Discovering that children are imagining that they are bad can be disquieting and difficult to embrace. Once when Michael was about five he was hiding behind a bush with a friend in the front yard as two mothers passed by with sleeping children in strollers. One parent smiled as she waved and asked the children in a sing-song voice if they were pretending. Michael's friend Robin growled, 'We're bad guys.' The mother quickened her step and drew her hand protectively round her sleeping child as she said, 'Oh, no. We're good guys, aren't we?'

All people have the capacity to do evil deeds

In his ground-breaking study *Evil: Inside human violence and cruelty*, the social psychologist Roy Baumeister (1997) synthesizes research from psychology, criminology, history, anthropology, sociology, and other disciplines in order to understand the psychology of those who commit violent and cruel deeds. Professionals and academics tend to describe, categorize, and analyze undesirable behavior as, for example, anti-social or psychotic. Baumeister uses the term evil because of its common usage. Rejecting any notion of evil being external to people, Baumeister locates evil in how people evaluate the behavior of others. By evil, he means the deliberate infliction of harm by one person (a perpetrator) on another (a victim) who feels a state of personal or social violation (p. 5). Though Baumeister's examples range widely from impulsive reactions and petty cruelties to systematic torture and mass murder, his controversial conclusion is no less applicable to genocide than it is to domestic violence, 'Most people who perpetrate evil do not see what they are doing as evil. Evil exists primarily in the eye of the beholder, especially in the eye of the victim. If there were no victims there would be no evil' (p. 1). Baumeister argues that it is victims who socially determine whether or not an act is evil because perpetrators almost always believe that their acts are justified and are neither evil nor bad. Victims who use the word evil repeatedly refer to the lasting psychological and social effects on them of others' deliberate acts of violence and cruelty.

Andrew Delbanco (1995) in his book *The Death of Satan* argues that people need the concept of evil to connect, for example, the racist genocide of Auschwitz with the social horror of a father who rapes his child. He details a contemporary moral vacuum in which most people have lost their sense of evil in a postmodern rootless 'culture of irony' that is 'without a criterion of wrongness' (ibid., p. 214). If people regard the Jewish Holocaust as an unrepeatable historical event or paternal rapes as deeds perpetrated by evil people who are disconnected from 'us', then this promotes the self-delusion that evil is something done only by others.

Delbanco makes it clear that evil never just 'goes away'. Rather, 'evil has returned . . . as the blameable other – who can always be counted on to spare us the exigencies of examining ourselves' (ibid., p. 234). In other words, evil is externalized and projected on to others who are demonized and dehumanized. In this way we can avoid recognizing our own capacity for evil deeds. In 2003, Saddam Hussein and his supporters became the latest in a long line of blameable others. In the foreign policy narrative presented in speeches and soundbites, President George W. Bush positioned the murderous Iraqi regime, along with the governments of Iran and North Korea, as evil. But during the disastrous occupation of Iraq, with mounting military and civilian deaths and casualties, few, if any, public questions were initiated by the Bush Administration about how American policies and actions might have contributed to the alienation of the population, the insurgency, and the collapse of civil order. Instead, with an air of certainty, blame was heaped on supporters of the former regime. When the abuse and extreme humiliation of Iraqi prisoners became public, only a few soldiers and contracted civilians were added to the list of those to be blamed.

Baumeister believes that 'the hardest part in understanding the nature of evil is to first recognize that you or I could, under certain circumstances, commit [or acquiesce in] many of the acts that the world has come to regard as evil' (ibid., p. viii). Daniel Goldhagen (1996) would agree. In his contentious book *Hitler's Willing Executioners*, he was insistent that it was 'ordinary' Germans who enacted the Jewish Holocaust. It was not only Nazi Party members indoctrinated in the Hitler Youth, but also normally law-abiding decent people who hunted Jews, volunteered for firing squads, and took jobs operating the gas ovens. Germany was not infected by an evil force, nor were people forced to commit evil. Rather, the socio-cultural norms and discourses changed under National Socialism. At first, people were no longer subject to legal sanctions for acts of violence directed at Jews and other 'undesirables'. By the early 1940s people were socially encouraged and could be institutionally rewarded for doing deeds that a decade previously they would have found abhorrent.

Similarly, during the initial occupation of Iraq the ordinary American and British soldiers who were discovered in 2004 to have abused, humiliated, and (by UN standards) tortured Iraqi prisoners in prisons like Abu Ghraib, were not bad or evil people, or inferiors just following orders, or simply people in the wrong place at the wrong time. The soldiers lived and identified with groups that unofficially promoted and rewarded the violent degradation of prisoners. The fact that their actions were against military rules and in contravention of the Geneva Conventions was no deterrent to people committing or condoning such inhuman acts. Likewise the Iraqi interrogators who had tortured prisoners in the very same cells occupied a situation similar to the one that Goldhagen described in Germany because the Baathist regime actively rewarded such actions.

The feminist theologian and scholar Elaine Pagels agrees that we are all capable of performing evil deeds. She stresses that if we want to know ourselves then it is 'essential . . . to "know" one's own potential for evil'. She quotes from the Gnostic gospel of Philip to illustrate that we must know the 'truth' about ourselves which is 'more than an intellectual process'. Rather, 'each one must strive to recognize his or her own inner state, and so to identify acts that spring from the "root of evil," which consists in such destructive emotions as anger, lust, envy, pride, and greed' (1995, p. 174). All of the emotions that Pagels identifies and the actions that spring from them separate perpetrators' experiences from those of victims. Love, compassion, and sharing, all connect people. Hate, anger, and self-justification all divide people.

When I feel compassion I am on the edge of being answerable and acting ethically in response to how another views the world. I am projecting into the consciousness of another person and seeing the world from his or her viewpoint. My words or deeds are ethical when I act in response to the other person's consciousness, having allowed it to enter my own. I finalize the situation when I act to make a difference that is 'good' for the other person as well as for me. But if I am feeling anger or hatred I am locked in my own consciousness. I am not projecting. I have shut down. I have stopped listening to the other's voice. I cannot act ethically. My actions are amoral when I act without hearing and responding to the voices of others. My actions are evil when I hear others' voices opposing my words or deeds but I choose to ignore or silence them.

When Michael was aged fourteen, I talked with him about the fact that many academics, parents, and teachers would be concerned that he'd spent over a decade imagining that he was evil or bad. His earlier pretend play in which he killed or hurt people had transformed into reading Stephen King novels, watching movies like *The Silence of the Lambs* or the thriller *Seven*. He also sought out violent video games such as *Zombie Attack*, and with friends played table-top miniature games, like *Warhammer*. Michael was happy to explain.

> I think that when we play evil, nasty, cruel characters that we get to know that evil part of ourselves. And that because we are exploring that evil part and looking at it and facing it and most importantly accepting it (because everyone has evil inside them) we learn to live

with it and not let it take over our good part because we know it's there. And by knowing it and accepting it we cannot turn away from it, but not let it overwhelm us. And also if you're being evil and nasty in play it's much better to do that than do that in real life. That's basically what I think about that. What do you think?

Michael's articulate response might seem significantly different from his obsession with violence at age four. The perspective of the novelist Susan Cooper is salutary. Her 'Dark is Rising' series of mythic novels for young readers casts children as protagonists in epic struggles with the power of evil. She reminds us that 'People talk about children as if they are a different species. They are not. They are just not wearing this heavy overcoat of time. People are people. There are young people and older people. But we don't suddenly change our species at [any particular] age' (1996).

As for protecting children from experiencing the sort of intensity of evil that became unavoidably visible in Nazi Germany, Aranka Siegal, a Jewish Holocaust survivor, strongly disagrees. 'I believe we all protect children too much. We say, don't tell the children. This is not good, because these [today's] children cannot take anything. They have to grow up in a world where terrible things happen, and if they don't have any experience in over-coming hardship, then they think they won't be able to face it when it does happen to them' (Lehr, 1995, p. 47).

Todorov (1996), in his book *Facing the extreme*, argues that life in the Nazi concentration camps and Soviet slave camps illustrated the nature of good and evil. In addition to the depravity of guards and the bestiality of prisoners who were stripped of their humanity, there were also extraordinary acts of kindness, love, and heroism. No young child should be subjected to the almost incomprehensible horrors of holocaust or genocide. Yet children can encounter and grapple with understanding horror though mythic literature and play.

What Ingebretsen (1996) noted about the benefits of reading and interpreting mythic horror literature is also true of mythic play – it allows 'contemplation of the unspeakable' and thus the possibilities of adopting an ethical relationship with the evil actions in a mythic world. In mythic play children can not only speak what adults often leave 'unspoken', they can also act out and reflect on what is often regarded as 'unactable' – death, birth, hatred, injury, and violence. Pretending to act the unactable and speak the unspeakable can be disturbing for adults who are pleased when children pretend to be altruistic, yet are much more ambivalent about children pretending to do violent actions that we'd consider evil deeds. Playing with children is so important because adults can protect children into productive active experiences with evil and then reflect on those experiences with them.

Children can encounter terrible deeds in mythic narratives where they are not burdened with the complexities of historical events. In mythic play they can experience struggling with and overcoming overwhelming hardship. Delbanco's cultural analysis of the need for mythic narratives illustrates how ethical identities can extend beyond everyday socio-cultural identities to include the extremes of possible deeds that we imagine and interpret but do not actually perform. He stresses that people in all societies need metaphors of evil (as well as metaphors of good) so that we will be able to conceptualize and recognize our own capacity for doing evil as well as doing good. He argues that 'the idea of evil is not just a metaphor that some people find useful; it is a metaphor upon which the health of society depends' (1995, p. 227).

Negative and positive identification

Wenger (1998) stressed that people identify with others in both extremely positive and negative ways, with negative identification being the mirror image of positive identification. Identification is both positive and negative 'in the sense that it includes relations that shape what we are not. It includes what we enjoy being and what we dread. It engenders identities of both participation and non-participation' that includes both what we pride ourselves on being and that of which we would be ashamed (ibid., p. 191). Negative identification can feed ethical desires and actions. For example, I identified so negatively with my oppressive schooling that it sustains my desire to promote democratic, anti-oppressive pedagogy. And my parents' hands-off approach to children's lives in general is ballast whenever I launch the ship of play.

Like Wenger, Stuart Hall conceptualizes identity as being positive and negative. 'It is only through the relation to the Other, the relation to what it is not, to precisely what it lacks, to what has been called its constitutive outside that the "positive" meaning of any term and thus its identity – can be constructed' (1996, p. 5). Hall stresses that identities always categorize people into 'not-us' in relation to those people who are 'us'. He notes that 'identities can function as points of identification and attachment only *because* of their capacity to exclude, to leave out, to render "outside", abjected. Every identity has at its "margin", an excess, something more' (ibid., p. 5).

To know who I am, I must exclude as well as include other people. In forming my socio-cultural identities I construct concepts like 'parent', 'scholar', or 'Irish' by identifying who is 'not-a-parent', 'not-a-scholar', or 'not-Irish'. In forming ethical identities we similarly construct ethical concepts like 'right' and 'wrong', 'respect' and 'disrespect', or 'just' and 'unjust'. In varied situations different people will contrast 'good' deeds with deeds they'd describe as 'bad' or 'evil'. We cannot know what we mean by being a 'good parent', a 'good scholar', or a 'good Irishman' unless we form understanding of 'bad parenting', 'bad scholarship' or an 'evil Irishman'. We cannot understand 'good' actions without understanding 'bad' or 'evil' deeds.

Until I read Baumeister's book on evil I was uncomfortable with using the word evil as extensively as he does. When Michael in everyday life would use the word evil to describe a person I used to say 'People aren't evil. They only do evil things.' I'd also often say something like the following, 'Evil is a really strong word. Can you say anything good about them?' I paid attention to my language and tended to talk about people 'doing bad things' and used the term 'evil' to refer to the deeds of monsters. Because the distinction has always been messy for me, the terms have remained quite open and always contextualized. When I asked Michael, aged thirteen, to explain his thoughts on good and evil and whether people can be evil, this is what he said.

> There's always evil as well as good . . . because without evil there can't be good. There needs to be shadow for there to be light. There needs to be yang for there to be yin. They need each other. If everyone was perfectly good there'd be nothing to define the good or to make it good.

The unavoidable exclusions of other people that socio-cultural identifications create can be used to 'other' the behavior of people in particular contexts. Strangers' norms can be positioned as 'strange' and foreigners' actions regarded as 'foreign' to us. When those contexts promote the sort of cultural and institutional hatred that was pervasive in Nazi Germany, then people who are not-us can be positioned as abnormal 'outsiders' who are not listened to and who can easily be moved outside the protection of 'our' law. Over time, such othering can lead to cultural and legal norms that allow for the treatment of other people as non-human vermin and justify their extermination like rats.

Conflating socio-cultural identities with ethical identities

Though they may not be articulated, there are always ethical dimensions to who 'we' are, and conversely, who we are not within the groups we have been born into, like male or female, and those we acquire, like joining a musical emsemble, or participating in a play group. In other words, we can always assess what the shared values and beliefs of any group are and how those values and beliefs apply to others. From a cultural and ethical point of view, people would often be considered 'good' or 'heroic' when they championed the values of a culture in struggles with people who undermine those values. What those values are will determine the ethical basis of any struggle. For example, in different cultures some people like Martin Luther King have been called heroes in their fight for social justice for all, while others, like Hitler, have been regarded as heroes when they champion racial superiority.

Because identifications unavoidably mean that 'we' regard ourselves as different from those who are 'other' than us, people lay potential ethical minefields as they identify socio-culturally with some people and not with others. If a socio-cultural framework is hierarchical it can carry with it an ethical framework that says only 'we' really know what is right. This is especially true if we negatively identity with others from a superior emotional distance rather than listen to them as equals in interactions. When people appropriate a cultural hierarchical identity based on such a framework they can create relationships with others which evaluate the others as inferior because of what they lack in terms of qualities and values that are at the core of the framework.

A hierarchical socio-cultural identity can meld with an immoral framework to regard others more as objects to be manipulated than as subjects to be heard. Such a framework of superiority was at the root of the sectarianism that permeated the divisive cultural/ethical identity and dispositions I grew up with as a Northern Ireland Protestant. Such a framework fueled hatred in the violent 'Troubles' that erupted in the late 1960s. But Northern Ireland Protestants were not alone in having dominant corrosive socio-cultural/ethical identities that exploded into violence. Many countries have experienced how extreme nationalism, religious fundamentalism, or political fascism has led to the oppression, torture, or death of other people regarded as not one of us. And more stable societies have experienced how daily intolerance and erupting anger is bred in divisive identifications that support racist, sexist, heterosexist, classist, ableist, and adultist attitudes and hateful deeds.

People who have lived in, or are knowledgeable about, any divided or deteriorating society, from racist cultures in America to colonial and then post-colonial situations in African countries like Rwanda, know how people with divisive identifications can begin to demonize those whom they regard as inferior. In such cases they cease to see each other as human beings with rights to be treated with human dignity. When one community has access to cultural resources that include power and authority over another community, there is the potential for creating the social time bomb that I lived in when I was growing up.

At the heart of social and cultural differences that ferment divisions and hatred is an unthinking conflation of socio-cultural and ethical identities so that what is assumed to be culturally right for a group becomes unquestioningly ethically right for everyone in the group. When group norms are regarded as synonymous with moral norms, actions that in different contexts would be judged as evil or wrong can be assumed to be the right thing to do. For example, when I was young I used to love the spectacle of bands of thousands of Orangemen marching round the walls of the city where I grew up. The Orangemen were commemorating seventeenth-century battles when the armies of Protestant William, Prince of Orange, defeated those of the Roman Catholic King James. The marchers' identity as Protestant was tied up with their identity as Orangemen and expressed in the cultural practices surrounding the annual marches. What I did not appreciate as a child was that the marches were also viewed as provocative, sectarian and triumphalist by many people in the Roman Catholic community, especially when policed by a force that was almost entirely Protestant. In advance of the rioting that led to British troops being deployed in Northern Ireland, requests by Catholic community groups to reroute the marches in August 1969 in order to avoid a repeat of violence that had been simmering for months were rejected out-of-hand by Orangemen as threats to 'our heritage' and 'our rights' and not taken seriously by the police. Protestant politicians who raised ethical questions about whether marching was right were positioned as cultural turncoats by Orangemen and other Protestants in authority. The Orangemen were conflating their cultural and ethical identities. Their practice of marching was fused with a belief that marching was right and an assumption that other people's views were largely irrelevant.

Growing up in Northern Ireland, my ethical identity was largely conflated with a British national identity, a Protestant religious identity, and a Unionist political identity. At home, at school, and at church I was presented with a British-Protestant-Unionist view toward the island of Britain culturally and toward the United Kingdom (of Great Britain and Northern Ireland) politically. We not only looked away from our Catholic neighbors in the island of Ireland but also regarded them as 'not us' because they did not share our identifications. Divisive identities were touchstones for what was considered right action. Because 'we' supported the union with Britain, developing Irish cultural ties was implicitly regarded as destructive of our identity. Sympathizing with nationalist political aspirations could even be seen as traitorous.

It was only when I began to distinguish among my ethical identifications and my socio-cultural identities (while still recognizing their interconnections) that I began to have agency over how I identified with others, past and present. Whereas growing up I swam in a sea of either-or assumptions and all-or-nothing rhetoric with a pervasive disposition of intolerance that could easily erupt into prejudice, I now seek to embrace both-and approaches and where possible avoid dichotomous and divisive language and thinking. As an adult, reinterpreting historical and political events from positions of fairness and mutual respect allowed me intellectually and emotionally to understand causes and effects of British colonialism in Ireland on all people. Believing that oppression was wrong, I began to identify with all those people, past and present, who suffered oppression (not only with those who had benefited from using power over others) and with all those who had resisted domination and/or struggled to bring peace to the island of Ireland and in other lands. I began to loosen and become more critical of my identifications with prior social, cultural, and historical events. I began to conceptualize myself as Irish as well as British, as a nationalist as well as someone with a British heritage, and as identifying religiously with aspects of both Protestant and Catholic theologies and rituals as well as with other religious traditions by connecting with spiritual human commonalities like love and compassion.

There may be unexpected and far-reaching consequences for any adult who begins to question a prior congruence between socio-cultural and ethical identities. For example, the first US soldier after a year's active service in Iraq who proclaimed himself to be a conscientious objector faced being called a coward, accused of betraying his men, and charged as a deserter. Conviction by military tribunal could have technically carried a death sentence. Why had he put himself in such a position? Camilo Mejia's explanation was that 'There comes a point when you have to realize there is a difference between being a soldier and being a human being' (Goldenberg, 2004, p. 6)

I wanted Michael to form socio-cultural and ethical identities that were not fused. Knowing that he would tend to accept my beliefs, I also wanted him to be able to question my assumptions and I looked forward to having ethical discussions with him. Our play, and especially our mythic play, provided opportunities for those wishes to be realized.

Good-and-evil possible selves in mythic play

The oppositional positions that children adopt when they pretend to be heroes and monsters can be regarded as good-and-evil selves that in their deeds embody reciprocal positive and negative ethical identities.

Mythic play is so important because it allows children at the same time to identify in intensely negative as well as positive ways. Negative identifications are the yang to the yin of positive identifications. Identifying with monstrous dragons is the shadow side of identifying with heroic knights. As dragons, children can negatively identify with a creature that silences others' objections to its actions. As knights, children can positively identify with a person who voices the views of silenced people and who opposes actions that they experience as oppressive. To ask children to identify only with heroes (and not with monsters) would be to promote an unbalanced and ultimately ethically shallow identification with other ways of being in the world.

The idea of balance is integral to the theories of the psychologist Carl Jung. He used the yin–yang symbol, and others, to illustrate his conceptualization of a unified healthy psyche with an ego or persona in balance with a shadow. The persona is everything that a person wants to be, whereas the shadow is everything the person does not want to be. Jung viewed psychological development as accepting and integrating the powers and energies of our shadow personality into consciousness so that we would become whole. The Jungian psychologist Robert Johnson conceptualizes the persona–shadow psyche as a teeter-totter, or see-saw. 'We must hide the shadow from society generally . . . but we must never try to hide it from our self' (1991, p. 14). Psychologically healthy people use their shadow energy as well as their ego energy. The shadow energy is the socially unacceptable deeds that people intentionally turn away from as they turn toward the socially acceptable.

For Johnson, the location for doing good is at the fulcrum, not on one side or the other of the see-saw psyche. People choose how to act in a situation with an awareness of their possibilities for doing what would be wrong as well as right. A person's psychic center is the place where they keep their capacities for doing good and evil in equilibrium by bringing them into consciousness. Like the Indian god Vishnu, people are ideally joined with, and balanced by, the opposites of Brahma (the god of creation) and Shiva (the goddess of destruction). Both powers can be used to do both good and evil since people may need to create and destroy in order to do what they believe to be right.

Pretend play makes visible what in everyday life might be considered only appropriate as inner thoughts or narrated events. In conversations children are often shielded from difficult topics like death or oppression. Death tends to be a taboo topic in polite conversation. Death is often referred to in ways that distance people emotionally, using words like 'passing' or, for example, by discussing a funeral as an event rather than talking about the meaning of loss. Oppression tends to be regarded as an adult topic that is inappropriate for young children or to be treated as something that happens to other people.

In pretend play children can say and do what would never happen in everyday life. When children play they can, for example, pretend to kill, oppress others, and die. They can imagine that they are killing dragons or questing knights. They can imagine being a dying Beast and a nurturing Beauty. Or a Wolfman asking for release through death. Or a vampire who will die if he does not drink blood. Or a person facing a zombie who was dead but is about to kill again remorselessly. Pretend play allows children to explore possible selves and over time possible identities as they imagine 'what they might become, would like to become, or are afraid to become' (Marcus and Nurius, 1986, p. 73).

It is much easier to recognize our capacity to create evil as well as good when we read and enter into the worlds of myths. By playing in mythic worlds and identifying with the actions of all characters we can know, not only in the abstract, but also personally, in focused, intense, and powerful ways more about possible good-and-evil selves. We can know how we could use power over others in inhuman ways at the same time as knowing how we could use power with, and for, other people in loving and nurturing ways. When we evaluate our potential use of power as right-and-wrong we are authoring and shaping our ethical understandings and identities.

In arguing for the experiences of good-and-evil deeds via mythic play so that children can continue to author ethical identities, I must emphasize that I am not advocating that young children should be exposed to images and experiences of everyday violence, killing, and hatred. Images of violence of the everyday can not only be extremely disturbing for children but also require complex and often nuanced explanations and analysis about gray ethical areas that young children cannot grasp. Children deserve to live in a joyful, kind, loving environment. As adults, I believe that we should judiciously restrict children's experiences of violence in their everyday world. But that is not to argue that we should protect children from fictional experiences nor that we should ignore or avoid answering their ethical questions about our own and others' everyday deeds.

Unfinalizing

In playing with children, when their possible selves go to the mountaintops, caves, laboratories, or dungeons of mythic worlds we must follow if we want to be able to help them make ethical meaning about facets of life that may seem incomprehensible to them, and sometimes to us. Rather than close down and finalize meaning definitively, playing opens up experiences and prior understandings to new meaning. Playing with children can be a force to unfinalize meaning made by adults and children alike as it creates a sense of completion. When we pretend with children, we do more than explore in imagined spaces because we can assist them to author identities, including ethical identities, that they will carry with them when we shift modes and return to more everyday concerns.

Playing allows people to open up so that they can live and learn from experiences without having to wait for clock time to pass or for crisis situations to arise in daily life. I've spent over twenty years revisiting my upbringing in Northern Ireland in order to author new identities. People like Brian Keenan have done so in hellish experiences that must have seemed more like a never-ending nightmare than real life.

In his book about his four-and-a-half years of captivity and torture as a hostage in Beirut, Keenan tells how 'I was forced to confront the man I thought I was and to discover that I was many people' (1992, p. xv). He forged new understandings about his social, cultural, and ethical selves and identities and how they interwove, often in unexpected ways. In realizing that he was no longer the man who entered captivity, Keenan recognized that people are actually many different self-others. 'We are all made of many parts; no man is singular in the way he lives his life. He only lives it fully in relation to others' (ibid., p. 277).

Keenan was forced to ask, 'Who am I?' while suffering degrading and humiliating torture. He could have finalized his unraveling life by authoring bitterness and hatred toward his captors and his fellow hostages. Instead he chose to speak to their humanity, act with integrity, and answer his situation with his whole life. In contemplating his horrific ordeal he came to realize that 'Humanization is a reciprocal thing. We cannot know ourselves or declare ourselves human unless we share in the humanity of another' (ibid., p. 287).

I was humbled and uplifted by the story of how this man (born Catholic in Northern Ireland two years before I was born Protestant) positioned himself with integrity in relation to evil doers and transformed his rage to create 'a renewed love for the world and its possibilities which, while nascent in us as children, had become buried by the accretions of the conscious worlds we had been brought up in' (ibid., p. xvi).

Brian Keenan's story magnified for me how adults make a difference in the unfolding lives of every child. Rather than ignore or dismiss and thus bury children's desires, when they engage in open-ended play with children they may bring their thoughts, feelings, and questions, no matter how dark, into a shared space of light. If we join children at play we can help them transform their images of good-and-evil into a renewed love for the world.

Chapter 4

Co-authoring ethical selves and identities

> You can be mad but you can't be evil . . . being mad is saying you feel angry but being evil is hurting and you mustn't be evil . . . Sometimes I'm mad but I'm never evil.
>
> 'Would you kill all monsters?'
> 'Oh no, only those that have done many, many, many mean things . . . killing people mostly'
> 'And what would you do before deciding you had to kill it?'
> 'I'd teach it to stop doing those mean things.'

Michael made the above statements when he was about four-and-a-half. They were his articulation of core dispositions in his ethical identity. In previous chapters I examined how particular interactions in and around child–adult play supported ethical action and contemplation. In this chapter I consider the formation of Michael's ethical identity from early childhood into young adulthood. I have shown how Michael authored meaning and authored possible selves and identities. Now I analyze how Michael's ethical identity was co-authored in and around our pretend play as I also discuss the formation of my own ethical identity.

People's ethical identities intersect with their socio-cultural identities to provide them with beliefs about how people ought to act toward one another. My ethical identity provides me with permeable and gradually changing moral lenses. I can use these lenses to look backward to make ethical sense of previous interactions, and to move forward as I act with an ethical self in daily life.

How people identify with others is apparent in their daily practices toward others. Facets of a person's ethical identity are made visible in how they are answerable for their actions, and how they discursively position themselves in their everyday relationships. They will use present deeds as well as narratives of past actions to interpret how they ought to act in relation to others.

In the previous chapter I outlined how socio-cultural and ethical identities are formed and shaped in complementary and simultaneous ways over time. From a cultural point of view people identify with others' actions through shared group practices and narratives. In addition to the family practices of daily living, Michael most often engaged in the practice of pretend play. Through play he projected into and contemplated the actions of possible good-and-evil selves within mythic narratives. From a social constructivist point of view people identify with others because of how they are consistently positioned in relation to them. As well as being positioned as a member of our family and his peer group Michael explored and experienced how people could be socially positioned in heroic and monstrous ways within his mythic worlds.

In the opening quote Michael was ethically evaluating the array of mythic narratives he had explored and improvised upon. When he said that he'd only kill a monster that had done 'many, many, many mean things' and that first he'd try to 'teach it to stop doing those mean things' he meant that killing would only be a last resort if talk and deeds aimed at stopping monstrous action failed. He distinguished between angry feelings and deeds that hurt others when he stated 'you can be mad but you can't be evil'.

Ethical dispositions

In summarizing the academic discipline of ethics (or moral philosophy), Mel Thompson notes that the study of ethics is a rational universalizing activity. 'It studies moral choices, explores their implications and looks at how they may be justified' (1994, pp. 212–213). He then critiques the inherent weakness of the discipline. 'Its ideal is to find a definition of good and bad that will transcend individual preferences, and which therefore will command universal acceptance. This is fine in theory, and yet it does not really do justice to the human complexity of moral choice' (ibid., p. 213).

Thompson argues that, 'The moment of moral choice is . . . informed by the way in which we generally understand and value life' rather than being the product of a person's individualistic objective rational decision (ibid., p. 216). He quotes Iris Murdoch (1970) from *The Sovereignty of the Good* who believes that, 'We act rightly "When the time comes" not out of strength of will but out of a quality of our usual attachments and with the kind of energy and discernment which we have available. And to this the whole activity of consciousness is relevant' (ibid., p. 53). In stressing the uniqueness of every moral decision, Thompson argues that 'the choices we make today define the sort of people we become tomorrow' (ibid., pp. 216–217).

Holland et al. argue that over time a person's everyday choices and their usual attachments form into relatively stable aspects of their identities creating 'sediment from past experiences' (1998, pp. 18, 137). Just as my socio-cultural identities are apparent to others in my dispositions – how I tend to act over time – so is my ethical identity.

Dispositions, including ethical dispositions, develop in the choices and attachments formed when people enter play worlds just as surely as they develop in everyday life. It is almost certain that a disposition to be playful will develop when people play. It was hardly surprising that Michael, who, prior to attending school full-time, spent the vast majority of his waking hours pretending, drawing, reading, or watching movies would become disposed to play with ideas, explore actions in the fictional worlds of literature, video, and gaming, and generally be open to new possibilities. This disposition was encouraged and supported by his parents and by his friends. At the time of writing, Michael is a voracious reader, an accomplished writer, an inveterate debater with a wry sense of humour, and a person committed to serious video gaming.

Projection and being answerable

Over time Michael developed a disposition to project into any person or creature in narratives. When he was six years old he asked me to help him write the names of all the characters he liked. As he laid out over thirty cards on the floor I asked him, 'Which ones are you?' He gestured toward the cards with a sweep of his hand as he said, 'All of them'.

When I played with Michael I followed wherever he went in the mythic worlds that we explored. I didn't censor his desire to imagine. Michael explored many deeds including stopping the attacks of dragons, dealing with the violent anger of Mr Hyde, showing the tenderness of Beauty toward the Beast, and the relentless killing march of zombies.

Aged four, Michael was aware that he could imagine from other positions. I asked him if there was anyone in a story that he could not pretend to be. He thought for a moment and said, 'Only a house because it's not moving.' I reminded Michael of this explanation a decade later and, aged fourteen, he agreed that he could imagine from any point of view. At first he said, 'The only thing I can't get my mind around imagining being is an inanimate object because it wouldn't have senses like us.' But after a moment he added, 'Though I sort of could imagine being the house still and old. It would sense what was going on inside it even though it wouldn't see in the way we know seeing.'

The ethical self arises whenever we are answerable for our own actions and when we address others about the morality of their actions. A person's ethical disposition, following Bakhtin, builds on a disposition to author action by projecting into and evaluating as right-and-wrong the positions of other people and creatures. Michael developed this disposition to be answerable as we played often through improvised dialogue in which each of us was addressed by the other. Within the landscapes and population of the mythic worlds I explored with Michael we did not merely replicate dialogue from the story, we also improvised exchanges from the mythic narratives we read and viewed.

The following example occurred one morning when Michael was four-and-a-half and his sister Zoë was two months old. Michael improvised around encounters from the mythic narratives of *The Hobbit* and *The Ramayana*.

I was lying in bed this morning with Michael and Zoë. Michael was pushing my arm with his foot as I leaned over Zoë.

Michael – I'm Smaug [the dragon from *The Hobbit*] and you are the people on the hill. OK, Daddy? Your hand is the people going down the hill [meaning my arm].
Brian – OK.

[I proceed to walk my hand down my arm. Michael kicks my arm away and giggles. Then he roars and transforms himself into Smaug, snarling and snapping at imaginary people which he devours.]

Michael – Now you're a dwarf and Zoë is a dwarf and I am Bilbo Baggins [all characters from *The Hobbit*]. OK, Daddy?
Brian – OK.
Bilbo/Michael – I have the ring [spoken in a lowered voice].
Dwarf/Brian – What can the ring do?
Bilbo/Michael – It can make us invisible.
Dwarf/Brian – What shall we do about Smaug? He's killed all those people!
Bilbo/Michael – We'll all creep up on him.

[Zoë starts to cry.]

Michael – Smaug put his foot on her that's why she's crying.

[I turn to comfort her. She stops crying and begins to look around.]

Michael – Now Smaug has put his foot on me [lying down as if in agony].
Brian – He's put his foot on me too. Help! Help! What shall we do? [also as if in agony].
Dragon of Goodness/Michael – I am the Dragon of Goodness and I have come to help you.
Dwarf/Brian – Help! We're being crushed by Smaug.
Michael – [as if grabbing and throwing a great weight] I threw Smaug over the mountain.
Dwarf/Brian – He's flying away. Oh, thank you for saving us. How did you know to come?

Dragon of Goodness/Michael – Because your spirit called me.

Dragon of Goodness/Michael – [kneeling down] Climb on my back [flapping his imaginary wings]. We will fly to India. I escaped from the island where all the demons are (i.e. Lanka from *The Ramayana*).

Brian – Thank you Dragon of Goodness for saving us.

[We stop and leave the room for breakfast.]

As he was to do on countless other occasions, Michael authored the deeds of an ethical self in response to an imagined encounter with a monstrous creature. Michael projected into, enacted, and contemplated, the consequences of the actions of a possible good-and-evil self. In this imagined episode Michael invented the Dragon of Goodness in opposition to the evil dragon, Smaug. Michael both projected into the position of the people-devouring Smaug and, when I addressed him in words ('What are we going to do about Smaug?') and deeds ('Help, we're being crushed!'), he was answerable for those actions as the rescuing Dragon of Goodness. By thanking him, and implicitly evaluating his rescuing actions as right, I was affirming his ethical disposition to rescue oppressed people from oppressors.

Inferring intention from appearances

As a very young child, Michael must have believed that by projecting into and contemplating the external features common across characters he could predict intentions. Smiles, frowns, and other non-verbal signals were transformed into the more pronounced demeanor of story characters who were kind and caring or (more often) mean and aggressive. Michael's gaping mouth filled with imagined razor-sharp teeth made T-Rex's violent intentions toward his prey very clear. Similarly, he knew the intentions of the dragons, demons, and creatures like the gorgon Medusa. Michael's unblinking stare and bared teeth as he imagined the power of the hissing Medusa would leave no doubt that Medusa could turn anyone to stone with one glance. Whereas the dragon attacking St George could sometimes be persuaded to use his fire-breath positively, Michael never imagined an alternative life for Medusa.

Michael echoed changes in characters' intentions with changes in their physical appearance. Mr McGregor altered his gruff face to a smile when he was being kind. As the 'mean' giant, Michael would stick out his lower jaw emulating and he made me do the same. When he transformed into a 'nice' giant that would, for example, share with Jack, Michael would completely change his face and posture as he smiled.

Once Michael encountered horror narratives he explored a more complex relationship between physical appearance and an inferred intention.

People, like Dr Jekyll, or creatures, like Dracula, could smile and seem kind yet become oppressive. Jekyll's transformation was more predictable since he turned into a snarling volatile potential killer on taking the potion he created. Dracula was more ominous. Michael loved to dress in a black-and-red cape as he smiled and repeated the words from the movie, 'I am Dracula. I bid you welcome.' He used the same smile when he had me pretend to be asleep so that he could suck my blood and turn me into a vampire. Michael also explored characters like Frankenstein's creature and Quasimodo who could be kind and gentle even though they were hideous to look at and made people fearful. At the same time, Michael felt some sympathy/empathy for many of the monsters he encountered in horror narratives. He was incensed that the respectable Dr Frankenstein abandoned his creation. He recognized that Larry Talbot, the Wolfman, who had killed people, did not want to go on killing. And when he was close to death, he saw that the apparently invulnerable Darth Vader was really a helpless old man.

Aged four-and-a-half Michael knew that appearances could be deceiving. He did not assume that a character that looked monstrous was evil or that one who looked respectable was good. He would engage them in dialogue when I represented them. As Frankenstein's creation he demanded I tell him why I had abandoned him. Once when he was pretending to be Dracula I said I would look into his heart to see if he was evil or not. After that Michael would sometimes enact the metaphor by pretending to look into people's hearts in order to find out their intentions.

Being answerable in daily life

As his parents, we wanted Michael to be answerable for the consequences of his actions in everyday life. When Michael was eighteen months old, as I was holding and talking with him he grabbed my nose. I was in pain and I let out a cry that startled him. A few days later when he grabbed my nose again I gave a cry. This time I held his fingers, placed them round my nose, gave a cry, stopped when I took his hands away, and cried again when I replaced them. Michael found this amusing and over the next few weeks he wanted to play the nose game. Through playing at grabbing my nose with me he was learning to not actually grab my nose.

Michael was a lean and stocky young child and though he could get angry he almost never used his physical strength aggressively. Whenever we noticed that Michael (or another child) had said or done something that we evaluated as hurtful we would immediately stop what we were doing, talk to him calmly, and focus him (or the other child) on what had happened. We would tell and show them why this was wrong and ask if they understood why they shouldn't do that. As a toddler, if it wasn't obvious to

Michael that the other person was upset, I'd re-enact what had happened as I represented the other person's distress. I'd also interact in parallel with him, saying 'I'm so sorry that I hurt you. You say it, Michael.' I'd often do something similar with other children.

As I noted in the previous chapter, from Michael's infancy I was careful to talk about objects being 'ours' and was insistent that he share his toys with other children. When Michael was aged three-and-a-half, a caregiver commented on how he had shared with her children. When I said to Michael, 'Seems you're always thinking about other people', he responded, 'Not always. Most of the time.'

Addressing others

Questioning others' actions by addressing them is the reciprocal disposition to being answerable. Michael knew that he could ask questions and say how he felt. And as we played, Michael could raise high-stakes questions that rarely occurred in everyday life. Michael would take up the viewpoint of those harmed by others' actions and would question oppressive actions even if performed by people in authority. These included: the demon-king, Ravana, in the world of *The Ramayana*, who commanded demons to attack, the jailor of Quasimodo whom Michael told to get another job rather than follow orders to whip the Hunchback of Notre Dame, and the Emperor in the world of *Star Wars* who ordered his battle fleet commanders to destroy entire planets. Acting ethically took precedence over dispositions to behave in a socially appropriate manner or to be culturally compliant.

Why people should develop a disposition to address others, and not accept without question being told what to do by someone in authority, was made very clear by Milgram (1975). His infamous experiments, conducted in the 1950s, showed that humans have a strong tendency to defer to authority. The results of his disturbing study suggest that 65 percent of average Americans would electrocute another human being to death if told to do so by white-coated authority figures. The subjects believed that they were taking part in a scientific experiment. They were told they had been randomly chosen to be a teacher. They were to teach another person (actually an actor) and when the person gave a wrong answer they administered electric shocks.

Michael could be more considerate of others' feelings than I at times and he was prepared to question my use of power and my authority, as the following story illustrates.

Michael could have lost an eye when he was five-and-a-half. I was alone at home with Michael in our living room, writing notes on our play, as he was on all fours pretending. Michael knocked the sofa where Brendan, our cat, had been sleeping and woke him up. The cat mewed and swiped with his front paw. Hearing the noise I looked up to see blood on Michael's eye.

As I bounded to Michael the apparently dire situation combined with several shrill inner voices to feed a rising sense of panic and anger. I had a memory flash of myself at the same age being rushed to the hospital from my great aunts' home where I had been playing largely unsupervised. I almost lost a blood-soaked thumb that had been guillotined in a footstool that I had disturbed. I heard an inner voice chastising me for not watching Michael as he played, instead of writing, and another voice of blame. Though Michael loved to pet the cats, he and I also knew that they could strike out. I had not specifically pointed out the sleeping animal to Michael so that he would be sure to keep away from the sofa.

My anger exploded as I passed the cat. I smacked and kicked him before scooping Michael up and rushing upstairs to examine his eye in the bathroom. There was a cut on the lower eyelid but his eye was intact. As I tended the wound and as Michael sobbed, he asked me, 'Did you smack Brendie?' I said I had and he wanted to know why. I said that I had been angry and scared that he had scratched his eye. Michael got me to clarify that he hadn't. Then he critiqued my action and reminded me of one of our rules, 'You shouldn't smack Brendie. There's no hurting in our home.' I hugged him, felt ashamed and said, 'You're right. I shouldn't have.' Five minutes later the bleeding had stopped and he was sitting on my knee on the sofa. Brendan, who was a little wary of me, had returned to the sofa where he was sitting at the other end from us. We were getting ready to watch a video when Michael reminded me of another one of our rules, 'Daddy, you didn't apologize to Brendie.' 'I will,' I responded. By now my anger had completely subsided and I felt remorse both for hurting the cat and for modeling such a violent outburst. I reached out to stroke the cat and said the 'magic words' that Michael knew were essential for repairing hurt feelings. 'I'm sorry, Brendie', I said, as I scratched him on his ears where he liked me to touch him. Michael formed more meaning about the incident when he explained, 'You were out of control.' He added by way of another question, 'You didn't want to hurt him did you?' I agreed that I didn't intend to hurt the cat. As we cuddled on the sofa I was relieved that Michael's eye was fine. It was only later that I felt grateful to Michael for raising questions.

It was difficult at the time to be told off by my own child. What made it easier was that Michael was not being in the least disrespectful. He talked to me in the way I talked to him about something he had done that I thought was wrong – as one person to another.

Agency

Identities can only be authored and shaped when people have agency. Children, like animals, will respond to situations instinctually and can be conditioned to respond in particular ways. Children additionally can always intend action. Like all humans, children have the capacity for agency.

People have agency when they intend their actions, reflectively make sense of events, and are aware that choices make a difference for themselves and others. Inden describes agency as follows.

> Agency is the power of people to act purposefully and reflectively, in more or less complex interrelationships with one another, to reiterate and remake the world in which they live, in circumstances where they may consider different courses of action possible and desirable, though not necessarily from the same point of view.
>
> (quoted in Holland et al., 1998, p. 42)

When people have little or no agency they passively accept how others want them to behave. Across time this repeated positioning by others forms aspects of their identities without any reflection on their parts. Promoting agency in children is so important because when they have little agency children are, in a sense, being made by other people.

Children have little or no agency if they passively mirror how other people act in accordance with group norms or if they behave by doing what they are told to do. Nor do children have agency if they merely parrot an adult's interpretation of an event rather than engage in dialogue. As Wenger puts it, we have agency 'in the tension between our investment in various forms of belonging and our ability to negotiate meanings that matter in those contexts' (1998, p. 198). But we have no agency if we only act in accordance with predetermined group norms or if we have no opportunity to negotiate as we interact and thereby shape the social context.

The first school I attended was very authoritarian. I had little agency. I remember, aged five, having to sit alone and in silence. The teacher had to give permission for any talking or any movement from our seats. I soon learned to follow routines, and these routines changed only minimally each year. There was little purposeful, reflective action, or negotiation. Following the rules at school became a disposition that I accepted so that I would not be publicly humiliated, or punished and made to stand in the corner, or worse. Though some children chose to use their agency to undermine teachers' authority and were sometimes caned for it, I mostly restricted my agency to volunteering to do things that would allow me to move, like distributing or collecting books or pencils. I often stopped thinking and feeling when I was at school.

I never remember having a genuine conversation with a teacher until I was a teenager. Further, I would characterize most adult actions toward me as amoral. Without discussion or response I was neither addressed nor answered. In contrast, Michael expected to have agency, to be able to ask adults questions as well as answer them. He was used to being addressed and expected to be answerable whether or not we were playing.

Michael's discourse in the bathroom showed both his agency in that moment and his disposition even under stress. He was able to see from another's point of view, to improvise, and to question what he thought was an unfair action. In contrast, my angry outburst when Brendan scratched Michael was an unreflective reactive response in an emotionally charged situation. Michael challenged my behavior as an unacceptable way to position others. I had not positioned Michael as a child who should be 'seen but not heard', he was able to question my anger and address me about actions with which he disagreed. Likewise, if my anger had been commonplace with no one to question me it could have solidified into an angry disposition.

When people improvise they respond in the moment 'using the cultural resources available, in response to the subject positions afforded one in the present' (Holland et al., 1998, p. 18). In doing so, people shape their identities and thus their dispositions. When we played, mythic and other narratives were core cultural resources. In everyday life Michael could draw on cultural resources like our 'family rules' to improvise responses as he did on this occasion. He was not applying rigid decontextualized rules but rather reflectively quoting phrases that referred to living ideas which were part of his, and our family's, history-in-person. For years he had seen them guiding family relationships including those with Brendan, and his sister Ceili, whom we included as members of our family. At preschool he had access to physical and cultural resources that included many book, materials, blocks, and toys as well as indoor and outdoor structures to climb on and move. Likewise, though there were routines to follow at preschool, to a large extent Michael could improvise as he did at home and negotiate with teachers as he did with his parents.

When agency is high, rather than behaving with largely predetermined actions, responses are more contextual and spontaneous. When people exercise little or no agency they rely on other people and social norms to inform them how to behave, or they follow existing dispositions unreflectively. Minimal agency over time creates socio-cultural sediment (and when they are conflated, moral sediment) that will have increasing rigidity and detachment from particular situations.

Agency and the ethical self

When children have agency they exercise choice over their actions and contemplate consequences. Using Bakhtin's metaphor, they are authors of their words and deeds and, over time, of identities that are apparent in their dispositions. When children are answerable, including when they play, ethical selves are evoked. In responding to situations they are guided by their developing ethical identities.

Dispositions of an ethical identity can be regarded as having two reciprocal components that affect how a person is answerable: empathy and sympathy on the one hand and self-management on the other hand. Empathy and sympathy connect me with how other people experience an event and how they will be affected by my own and other people's actions. We act to change how a situation affects others because of how we think and feel with and for other people. Self-management connects me with my self in the moment and with how I will be affected by my own and other people's actions. We act to change how a situation affects us because of how we think and feel about ourselves.

Empathy and sympathy

The philosopher A.C. Grayling in his extended essay on 'the good life' argues for a relational, reflective, and imaginative view of ethical action to counter-balance the prevailing universalizing assumptions about an abstract rational morality. He argues that,

> . . . promoting moral sensibility requires the continued humanisation of ethics – which means rooting it securely in human needs and values. This is a task that requires reflection and continual negotiation; it is always a tentative, exploratory process, aimed at making the best of the sense of moral identity each individual implicitly has and at exploiting properly the human responses, especially sympathy. These responses can fail, not least when insufficient moral imagination is brought into play – which shows how vital is the cultivation of both the social and personal levels of a capacity for moral imagination which works with the grain of human nature.
>
> (2003, p. 187)

As an extreme example of the consequences of the absence of moral imagination Grayling uses Adolf Eichmann, the man responsible for planning and organising transportation to the Nazi death camps. Not only could Eichmann not imagine the fate of the millions who died in the camps, but even after he visited a camp where he was overcome with nausea and had to leave, he still did nothing to question the policies that allowed the Holocaust to continue.

Grayling locates ethics in people's humanity believing that 'morality is natural, a firm property of human social existence'. Rather than regard ethical action as only possible by those who have developed a higher stage of moral reasoning, he argues that morality 'can only be distorted in very extreme circumstances [because] humans can cling to their humanity in the very worst of times, and survive' (ibid., p. 191). Michael's humanity never disappeared when in play he entered into the worst, and best, possible situations that he could imagine.

The social scientists Kristen Monroe and Roy Baumeister, in their extensive analytical and critical academic studies of respectively altruism and evil in both tortuous and commonplace events, show how thoughts and feelings of empathy and sympathy are integral to a morality of compassion. If, on the one hand, we are to be kind or altruistic, and on the other hand we are to avoid hurting another person, we need both to empathise (to think and feel another's pain as if we were the other person) as well as to sympathise (to think and feel badly as ourselves for hurt that we could cause or that we could allow as a bystander). Empathy and sympathy are part of an altruistic ethical framework that 'provides a feeling of being strongly linked to others through a shared humanity and constitutes such a central core to altruists' identity that it leaves them with no [rational] choice in their behavior when others are in great need' (Monroe, 1996, p. 234). Yet, empathy alone is insufficient to avoid doing evil because 'maximum cruelty makes use of empathy without sympathy. To hurt someone, you must know what that person's sensitivities and vulnerabilities are, without having compassion or pity for the person's suffering' (Baumeister, 1997, p. 245).

In her far-reaching cross-disciplinary critique of dominant moral theories in political, economic, evolutionary, social, and educational psychology, Monroe concludes that ethical behavior 'ultimately emanates not from class membership, cost/benefit analysis, utility maximization, or the conscious adoption of an adherence to certain moral values but rather from our fundamental perception of ourselves in relation to others' (ibid., p. 231).

The empirical research both of Oliner and Oliner, and of Glover, who studied those who rescued Jewish people and others in World War II, recognized the significance of family and other long-term caring relationships in developing an identity of empathy and sympathy. Rescuers were ordinary people with 'altruistic personalities' (Oliner and Oliner, 1988, p. 259). They had developed 'connections with others in relationships of commitment and care . . . in which they ordinarily related to other people' (ibid.). It was out of such relationships that 'they became aware of what was occurring around them and mustered their human and material resources' (ibid.,

p. 260) in compassionate acts of rescue that put themselves and their loved ones at risk.

Glover found that rescuers 'tended to be brought up in a non-authoritarian way, brought up to have sympathy with other people and to discuss things rather than just do what they were told' (1999). Similarly, Oliner and Oliner found that in contrast to those who relied on physical punishment to control their children's behavior, the parents of rescuers relied on 'reasoning, explanations, suggestions of ways to remedy harm done, persuasion, and advice' (1988, p. 177).

Oliner and Oliner conclude that 'It is out of the quality of such routine human activities that the human spirit evolves and moral courage is born' (ibid., p. 260). They argue that schools as well as families should be caring places which 'acknowledge diversity on the road to moral concerns. They will invoke emotion and intellect in the service of responsibility and caring' (ibid., p. 259).

Alfie Kohn concurs in developing an educational view of connectedness flowing outward from close relationships. He argues that a social and relational view of morality takes us beyond locating ethics either in an individual who weighs up possible action according to moral principles or in any self-less view of altruism. 'We need a morality of thought and of feeling, of principle and of care' (1990, p. 265). He argues that 'to act compassionately, with sympathy and care, is being moral' (ibid., p. 258). Relying in particular on the ideas of Noddings, he stresses that, 'We are predisposed to help others with whom we feel a personal connection for reasons that are neither egotistic nor altruistic'. He recognizes the need for rules of fairness to guide actions in relation to others with whom we feel no connection. He proposes, as an ethical ideal, 'A model of relatedness that ripples out concentrically from our loved ones to those we know to everyone else' (ibid., p. 266).

Self-management

Monroe's conclusion that 'we do good because that is what makes us fully and richly human' (1996, p. 238) is balanced by Baumeister's argument that our capabilities for doing evil are 'held back by forces inside the person. In a word, self-control prevents a great deal of potential violence' (1997, p. 14).

Self-management controls action by listening to inner voices of restraint which guide the choice of one action over another that is left undone. Once when I would not allow Michael, aged four, to do something, he was so annoyed that he was shaking as he said, 'I feel like hitting you'. When he added, 'Shall I cut your head off?' I responded by saying, 'You could, but you won't, will you?' I extended Michael's awareness of being able to make an alternative choice by acting in a very familiar way. I further diffused his anger by pretending to move an imagined sword saying, 'Quick, if we don't stop the dragon it will attack the people'. Michael soon was also pretending to wield a sword and move as if he was a knight. As he did so his anger quickly subsided.

Michael's ability to manage his self by listening to inner voices of restraint was made very apparent once when he was six-and-a-half. After school he regularly went to the family of his school friend Ben. One day I discovered that Ben had punched Michael in the stomach. Michael explained that they had been arguing over which television program to watch. I asked him if he'd punched him back. He replied in a tone that implied that he would never considering doing that, 'Dad, I know what it feels like.' When I asked if he had wanted to hurt Ben he responded, 'Part of me does but I just say firmly, No, I don't like this.'

An authoring ethical self

Acting ethically, argues Monroe, is a matter of identity and integrity. 'Action is the outcome of identity through the individual's self-defined relation to others' (1996, p. 231). And she concludes her study with these words, 'All we have in the end is the dignity and integrity of the person. But this is enough' (ibid., p. 238). Her understanding parallels Bakhtin's theory (discussed in the previous chapter) of an ideal authoring, relational, dialogic self. A person is most ethical when answerable with his or her whole life for the consequences of his or her actions.

Every time Michael and I played we deepened and extended our parent–child caring relationship while simultaneously acting with compassion to relieve the pain of others. Sometimes Michael chose to return us again and again to desperate situations depicted in particular narratives. At other times we had short-term imaginative rescue missions. For example, one day as I was reading Monroe's *The Heart of Altruism*, Michael, who was almost eight at the time, asked me what I was reading. I started to tell him one of the compelling stories of rescuers that fill the book. As he did countless times, Michael moved into play mode and wanted us to pretend that we were the main characters in the story.

> I had been reading Kristen Monroe's *The Heart of Altruism* and just before dinner I told Michael one of the factual stories which had made such an impression on me – how a sixty-six-year-old grandmother, Lucille, with braces on her leg and back who walked with a stick and had a heart condition had rescued a young woman who was being attacked, robbed, and assaulted by a burly man. As soon as I told him the story he wanted to play it out and started to move like the old woman leaping down stairs four at a time and then brandishing an

imaginary stick at me. Michael shifted position to take on the pose of the young woman victim and asked me to shout the cuss words the man had spoken as he threatened to kill the young woman/Michael. Seconds later, Lucille/Michael swung an imaginary stick at the attacker/me, swore back at the man, and used his Aikido moves to get me off balance. As Lucille had recounted in her story he ran after the attacker/me and pretended to slam his/my leg in the door of the car in which he/I was trying to escape. He yelled at the attacker/me to stop. He pretended to call for the police. Then he imagined he was a police officer and arrested the man/me. As the young woman, I thanked the police officer/him.

After dinner, I asked Michael if he thought that if he had actually been there he would really have gone to help. He said he would. I played devil's advocate and reminded him of comments he had made several weeks previously. As we drove him to school one morning, Michael said that he didn't think about the people he saw on the street any more after we passed them. 'I see them and then they're gone,' he had said. Surely it would make a difference if he did not know the person who was in trouble, I suggested. Wouldn't they be like people on the street? He thought for a moment and then explained that he doesn't think again about people he sees only briefly because 'they don't have a life'. In contrast, he said that the people he knows do 'have a life' and are in his heart. 'You're in my heart. I love you. You'll always be in my heart.' So why would he help someone who is not in his heart, I wanted to know. He paused again and then said, 'I'd have to help them even if I didn't know them.' When I pressed him to explain he said he didn't know why he would but then added, 'I can't bear it when I see someone being hurt.' He drew a connection to a time in the previous summer when he had insisted that the ants which had invaded our bathroom were taken outside. 'That's why I didn't want you to put the ant down the toilet. He'd done nothing. I mean how would you like to be picked up by a giant?'

For his bedtime story, Michael wanted me to read Lucille's story to him, which I did. After describing the events she explains to Monroe why she ran to help: 'Because he was hurting another human being, an innocent human being, I just can't take that. I wasn't trained that way.' Michael stopped me and said 'See. That's what I said.'

Monroe's story, and Michael's response to it in play and in reflection, illustrate how ethical actions are performed with agency in response to the deeds and words of others. The old woman chose to overcome many obstacles on her altruistic path. In play our actions are more intentional than in everyday life because every act is willed. And in reflection on the imagined events, Michael connected his ethical disposition (that was apparent when we played) with his everyday disposition.

In Bakhtin's terms, we are ethical when we are answerable having been addressed by others. If we resonate with the pain that others feel when they are being attacked, we act to rescue them just as we would act to stop ourselves being hurt. We empathetically project into the other person's experience while we remain, or return to being, sympathetically outside. Holding both of those views concurrently puts us in the space of Bakhtin's authoring ethical self.

Michael's ethical identity, and thus his disposition, has been co-authored over years of conversations in and around play and everyday events. When he was fourteen I asked him if he could remember times when he had acted, or thought about acting, to help others. What follows are examples from our conversation.

- I helped a wasp stuck in a swimming pool because I imagine what it would be like to be drowning and I don't want it to die even though you don't technically gain anything by rescuing it.
- When I was in kindergarten I sat next to a kid on the bus that other people thought was weird and I became friends with him.
- I do 'random acts of kindness' helping people with their homework.
- Whenever I see someone obviously struggling with something that I can help them with I always go and try to help them.
- When kids are making fun of another kid, you have to imagine from the point of view of the person who's being horrible and you feel sorry for the person who's being ridiculed. If you intervene and you stick up for them sometimes you don't because you're afraid others will laugh at you.

These examples illustrate a disposition to project into, at the same time as contemplating, the lives of people and creatures. The experiences, whose subjects range from insects to younger children and peers, include those who are being oppressive as well as those who are being victimized. The example of helping the wasp suggests how an ethical disposition is not the product of a rational deliberation. The final example suggests how the possible actions of people in social situations constrained Michael's tendency to reach out to help. Michael didn't engage in reasoned debates to determine how he ought to act. Rather, he was aware of responding to inner voices that might pull him back as well as press him forward to act in response to those in need. Michael articulated how his relationships with others, in Kohn's (1990) words quoted above, were rippling out 'from our loved ones to those we know to everyone else' (p. 266).

Agency in play

Children have high agency when they play. As most theorists have recognized, play is always entered into voluntarily. Play worlds have to be continuously willed into existence and as children play they intend and improvise their actions. If children lose interest then play worlds disappear like a television set going blank in a power cut.

When people act, choosing among different possible ways that they could respond to situations, they will develop a habit or disposition for agency. As Vygotsky puts it, people have 'intellectual responses that fulfill the function of adaptation to new conditions . . . the organizing hierarchy of habits used for solving new problems' (quoted in Wertsch, 1979, p. 154).

In the imagined situations of play, children repeatedly and actively choose their actions to explore whatever interests them by drawing on their cultural resources. Mythic play revolves around improvisation in response to the subject positions available in problematic events where there are life-and-death consequences of acting in particular ways. When children play they do not unreflectively behave in ways expected of them in everyday situations or passively accept how others position them. When they play children can become actively involved in authoring their relationships by exploring how they would be different in imagined encounters.

When Michael first heard a story and began to play, rather than replicate encounters, he explored with me how characters might act differently and adopt different viewpoints. He would both direct me and improvise with me. The giant up the beanstalk sometimes wanted to eat little boys but might also share his food if Jack asked nicely. Jack took gold from the giant but could also return it and help the giant to count his gold. The beast could almost die but he could also fight Gaston (Beauty's suitor in the Disney version) and dance with Beauty. Mr McGregor could catch Peter Rabbit and put him in a pie but he could also share his vegetables. Peter could get caught, but could also escape or talk with Mr McGregor. The following example occurred when Michael was almost three years old.

> Michael stomped down the stairs this morning going 'Fe Fi Fo Fum. I smell the blood of an Englishman.' I started joining in with him but he said 'Only the giant can say that.' He played this on his own as he ran around between the kitchen, the TV room, and the living room. His face grimaced up as the giant and he stomped along with his hands stiff like claws. Then he came to me.
>
> Michael: Daddy, you be Jack. And I'll be the giant.
>
> I pretended to hide from him.

At breakfast he continued to pretend to be the giant as he ate his cereal. He announced that, 'This giant yells.'

After breakfast I played with him. At one point I turned to Michael/ giant and asked:

Brian: Why are you so angry?
Michael/giant: Jack took my gold.
Michael: Daddy you be the giant and I'll be Jack.
Michael/Jack: Why are you so angry?
Brian/giant: Because you took my gold.

Michael produces a bag of gold from behind his back. He beams a big smile as he gives me the gold.

As the giant, I smile, thank him, give him a hug and say in my giant voice, 'If you need something just ask. I'll always share.'

I tell him that I have to go and load up the car. [We were leaving on a trip.] Michael continues to stomp, saying 'Fe Fi Fo Fum.' I tell him that we can play in the car. 'OK' he says and stops pretending to be the giant.

In terms of sex and gender, Michael explored agency from the viewpoints of female as well as male characters. He pretended to be women as well as men, including for example, the giant's wife up the beanstalk, female monsters like Medusa in the world of Greek mythology, female heroes like Princess Leia in the *Star Wars* universe, as well as female victims like Fay Rae in the story of *King Kong* and Esmerelda in the narrative of *The Hunchback of Notre Dame*.

In our home Michael was used to hearing critiques of racial, ethnic, class, gender and other stereotyping. As he grew older he overtly raised questions for himself. For example, when he was six he wanted to know why the Disney studios had dressed Pocahontas in clothes that were so different from ones he'd seen in an informational book on native Americans. We discussed gender portrayals again and how in this movie they overlapped with ethnic stereotyping.

Improvising on characters' actions can undercut the cultural power of narratives to normalize what behaviors and feelings are appropriate for children based on their sex and gender. As Davies has stressed, it is through stories that 'children can learn the patterns of desire appropriate to their gender. They discover what positions are available to members of their sex and how to live the detail of those positionings' (1992, p. 1). Fernie et al. discovered that when young children play they can adopt multiple, changing, and sometimes contradictory gender roles. Yet, it disturbed them to discover that in the preschools where they observed 'children's common humanity, the areas of similarity and overlap between what a male person is and might be and what a female person is and might be, are excluded or even negated' (1993, p. 98).

Through our play, Michael often explored alternatives that cut across the gendered actions depicted in books or movies at the same time as we considered how to act ethically by discovering our common humanity. The giantess up our beanstalk might make Jack breakfast and hide him from the giant but she could also expect him to help with the washing-up. Aged three, Michael loved pretending to be very tiny as he lifted up his bowl and spoon to the sink as I imagined I was the giantess. And when he was five, as he explored the relationship between King Kong and the woman, Fay Rae, Michael transformed her from a passive victim into an active challenger of those who wanted to attack and force Kong to leave the island. As he projected into the position of Fay Rae he would yell at me, as one of the men from the ship, to leave Kong alone.

Michael often pretended that he was very powerful. However, no matter how powerful characters were in one situation, we often explored how they might be powerless to control others or even to avoid death. In other words, he was experiencing how one person's choices could take precedence over another. Jack could be clever but he could also be eaten. The giant could have the strength to pick up children and was so big that he could eat them whole but he could also fall down the beanstalk and die. The giantess could be as powerful as the giant but cleverer by suggesting where Jack could hide. Peter could escape but he might also, like his father, end up in a pie. Mr McGregor could wave his pitchfork at Peter but he couldn't catch a scampering rabbit. The Beast might have learned to be gentle but he would still die if Beauty abandoned him. Kong could grasp airplanes but not stop Fay Rae falling from the Empire State Building. Esmerelda could bring water to Quasimodo in the stocks but she too could be tied up and humiliated.

Michael must have understood when he was quite young that people have choice over their actions and reactions. Once, aged nearly three, after noting that, 'There are two giants, two Jacks, and two Santas,' Michael added that, 'There are two Michaels and two Daddys.' At that age, Michael sometimes pretended to be 'Baby Michael' who wanted a bottle. At other times he said he was 'Daddy Michael' as he articulated command-ing phrases that I had heard myself use, including saying 'No' to the cats when one jumped up on the table.

As we played, Michael explored how all people can have agency. In narrative worlds, as in everyday life, a person has choice over their actions and reactions as well as how they position themselves and others. The giant up the beanstalk could be aggressive, violent, and 'mean' because he would not share his food or his gold. But if you were kind to him he could also be 'nice' and would share. Jack could be called a thief but could also choose to help the giant. Even Santa had agency. Around Christmas time just before his third birthday, Michael said that a 'nice Santa' brought gifts but that the 'mean Santa' broke your toys.

Co-authoring spaces

As I interacted with Michael or Zoë we were often co-authoring meaning in spaces that Vygotsky termed zones of proximal development. A ZPD is the 'distance between independent and collaborative problem-solving' (1978, p. 86). A ZPD is always context specific, expanding and contracting from moment to moment between people as they interact within a particular activity. When people collaborate they make meaning together that they cannot make alone.

Vygotsky theorized that ZPDs always open up when children play together. Piaget regarded play as imitative, with learning limited by whatever stage of development the child had reached. Vygotsky critiqued and inverted Piaget's theory to argue that play is a leading source of development in young children because when they play children can learn in advance of what they can do in everyday life.

Like Emerson I regard the ZPD as a 'practice zone' or a 'test site for moral behavior' (1997, p. 242). Vygotsky recognized the moral significance of play because play is always bound by the implicit social rules of activities creating an internal 'rule of self restraint and self determination'. In a ZPD 'a child's greatest achievements are possible in play, achievements that tomorrow will become her basic level of real action and morality' (1978, p. 100).

Vygotsky's theories are most often used to show how adults and more capable peers can 'scaffold' (Wood et al. 1976) or 'assist' individual children's 'performance' (Rogoff, 1990) in order to support them in learning how to become more expert and independently skillful at socio-cultural activities. Michael learned to tie his shoes with adult assistance. He learned new language use, like how to order at a restaurant, through participating in talking with servers as well as in conversations where adults reflected on appropriate language use. However, rather than focusing on adult scaffolding I want to foreground how adults' authoring of responses to children's actions, especially when they are playing, can support and extend children's authoring including the co-authoring of their ethical identity. And I want to consider how adult understanding is affected by what children do.

Co-authoring with semiotic tools

For Vygotsky, as people interact they use a combination of particular 'tools' or 'signs' in order to mediate the making of meaning. Discourse, as language, is the 'tool of tools' (Coles, 1996) that can be used along with objects, pictures, sounds, gestures, movements, and other non-verbal modes of meaning-making. In stressing the significant difference between technical tools (like a pencil) and psychological or semiotic tools (like language and gesture), Vygotsky noted that psychological tools are used not to affect the actual environment but to affect how we (and other people) think and act.

> The most essential feature distinguishing the psychological tool from the technical tool is that it directs the mind and behavior whereas the technical tool, which is also inserted as an intermediate link between human activity and the external object, is directed toward producing one or another set of changes in the object itself. The psychological tool changes nothing in the object. It is a means of influencing oneself (or another) – of influencing the mind or behavior; it is not a means of influencing an object.
>
> (1978, p. 140)

Signs not only allow us to think and act differently but also change the way we think and how we are able to take action, thereby changing the nature of whatever activities we are engaged in. Signs are transformational in the sense that they alter how we think as well as how we act, because they are continually modified as we use them.

Whereas technical tools are functional objects, psychological (or semiotic) tools are always signs for something else beyond the actual words or images on the page or screen. We can only understand signs within the abstract semiotic systems that organize them and that are used in social interactions. All languages are social sign systems as encountered in formats like the picture book and film as well as in face-to-face interactions.

Michael used technical tools like pencils and scissors to make drawings of characters and weapons: for example, Jedi warriors in the *Star Wars* universe. His drawings became psychological tools when he used them to affect and shape his thoughts and feelings. As he used words, drawings, book illustrations, and movie clips to transform how he enacted what characters from narratives did, he transformed his understanding of their actions.

As children play, Vygotsky characterized them as always 'a head taller'. In imagination they are more competent and capable and can stretch one another's thinking beyond what they can do in everyday life. The tools and signs they use extend in imagination to include anything not actually present but represented by language or the symbolic use of an object or movement etc. As Michael and I imagined, for example, that we were in the *Star Wars* universe, our gestures represented light-sabres in the hands of Jedi warriors Our movements changed when we pretended to fly space ships, and we used language like 'use the force' as we imagined trying to stop Imperial fighters from killing people. As we played and returned to similar encounters again and again we co-authored signs that mediated Michael's (and my) thinking. As Michael and I played, our words and movements in imagined worlds became semiotic tools for making meaning about the discourse we embodied and enacted. Whereas a technical tool, like a pencil, allowed Michael to make meaning by drawing, our bodies and voices, along with any objects we used, became semiotic tools when they represented people and events not actually present. When I pretended to be a person from a narrative for Michael, he made mental images of me as other than myself, and vice versa. And he interacted with me not as myself but as if I were that character. We co-authored meaning, not about the actual space we were in, but about the ideas in the imagined space that we had created together which was populated with people from an imagined world. And as we returned again and again to encounters in particular narratives, as I outlined in the previous chapter, we co-authored possible good-and-evil selves and in doing so we created semiotic tools for thinking about how we ought and ought not to treat other people.

Making discourse one's own

Vygotsky's view of development highlights the relationships between thought, inner, and social speech with an eye toward competency and conceptual development. Vygotsky theorized that people must develop cognitive and affective functions in social spaces for them to be able to use them individually. Social speech, as well as the ideas and emotions that it carries, precedes inner speech and thought.

> Every function in the child's cultural development appears twice: first, on the social level, and later, on the individual level; first between people (interpsychological), and then inside the child (intrapsychological). This applies equally to voluntary attention, to logical memory, and to the formation of concepts. All the higher functions originate as actual relations between human individuals.
>
> (1978, p. 57)

All our discursive interactions within and around our playing, from a Vygotskian point of view, were co-authoring meaning by internalizing understanding that could later be externalized in subsequent interactions.

Michael (and I) were co-authoring signs that shaped ideas as well as ways to think about those aspects of life and shape actions in the future. Thus, Michael and I were both able to think about life-and-death as well as good-and-evil in ways that would not have been possible without our social interactions.

From a Bakhtinian viewpoint, as we played, Michael (and I) used and shaped discourse with an authority that lay along a continuum between the externally authoritative and the internally persuasive. As Bakhtin (1981) stresses, meaning accumulates across time as well as space because language always carries the contextual meaning of previous speakers (or writers). What Bakhtin (1986) characterized as a person's utterance is always in response to previous utterances. Bakhtin uses the word 'utterance' to conceptualize that what a person says and does is always an intentional act in context and in response to the actions of others. If Michael had merely 'ventriloquated' my words, or the language from a text, he would have appropriated and relied on the external authority of that discourse and in effect allowed others to do his thinking for him. That never seemed to happen as we played. Michael continually used words for his own purposes in and around play events so that language became his own, his discourse began to acquire his own 'accent', and it became more internally persuasive for him.

> The word in language is half someone else's. It becomes 'one's own' only when the speaker populates it with his own intention, his own accent, when he appropriates the word, adapting it to his own semantic and expressive intention. Prior to this moment of appropriation the word does not exist in neutral impersonal language, but rather exists in other people's mouths, in other people's concrete contexts, serving other people's intentions,; it is from there that one must take the word, and make it one's own.
>
> (1986, pp. 293–294)

When people have agency, as children have in abundance in the authoring spaces of play, they use language intentionally (as part of their deeds) in order to achieve objectives that they choose to accept or that they set themselves. As we played, and improvised utterances within imagined encounters, discourses became embodied and enacted. And as we interpreted each other's utterances our bodies were perceived as part of the texts of those utterances (Kazan, 2005).

When people play, they author meaning not only because they internalize ideas and transform their way of thinking but also because they make other people's discourse and ideas their own in combining it with prior discourse and previous ideas as they take action in a particular situation.

Over time, discourse becomes more authoritative when a person's utterances in a situation lean supportively on, and are in response to, more and more prior discourses. The more authoritative a discourse becomes for a person as a way of thinking and acting, the more weight it carries for them as a belief or as an assumption about how people ought to act. Discourse that is externally authoritative is resistant to change. More internally persuasive discourse is more open to further transformation in subsequent dialogic interactions. As Bakhtin puts it, 'the semantic structure of an internally persuasive discourse is not finite, it is open; in each of the new contexts that dialogize it, this discourse is able to reveal ever new ways to mean' (1981, pp. 345–346).

The changing context of co-authoring spaces

Co-authoring spaces can be thought of as contexts that change as people interact. The sociolinguist Michael Halliday (1975, 1978) conceptualized that when people use language to get something done, they use particular linguistic registers to create context in relation to other people. Context, for Halliday, is not a fixed environment but is rather an evolving space affected by the changing functions of people's discourse. Playing changes context because people change how they interact.

Halliday theorized that every changing context can be analyzed along three dimensions of register and the three related functions of language. Each affects the meaning being made. 'Field' refers to the nature of the activity as affected by the ideational function of language. Field is an answer to questions like 'What is going on?' or 'What is this encounter about?' 'Tenor' refers to how the social and power relationships among people are affected by the interpersonal function of language. Tenor is an answer to questions like 'How do these people relate to one another?' or 'How are they using power?' 'Modes' are how people try to communicate – the channels and rhetoric of communication used that are affected by the textual function of language. Communication will be multi-modal (Kress and Leeuwen, 2001) when, for example, spoken language is accompanied by movement and sounds, as it inevitably is when young children play.

As I outlined in the previous chapter, play takes place in three spaces simultaneously: the everyday social space, a socially imagined space, and the authoring space formed in the overlap between the other two. Applying Halliday's classification to the context of playful activities, as people play they create three interpenetrating spaces. There they can explore how possible selves might act and how they might identify with others when the field, tenor, and/or mode of the context changes. Playing creates spaces where people may use agency to shift to any topic that interests them. It creates spaces where people can have encounters that captivate them but that they'd never seek out in everyday life and where they can use ways of communication that would rarely be available. Playing with children creates opportunities for co-authoring new depths of their ethical identities.

Refraction among discourses

As we interact with another person, whether or not we are playing, the 'refractive angle' we experience between our discourses (Bakhtin 1981, p. 300) produces thoughts and feelings along a continuum from a sense of being in close agreement to being in intense opposition. Interactions are ideologically unproblematic when there is already much agreement. However, the more divergent people's ideas, the more refraction there is between them and the more discomfort people are likely to feel as they interact.

Adult experience of refraction

Playing with Michael was mostly exuberant and unproblematic. Generally I felt little refraction between Michael's ideas and mine except when I was worried about his safety. Our play became increasingly refractive for me when I found myself improvising words and actions at odds with how I believed I would have behaved in everyday situations. The inner conflict that I experienced at such times made me more aware of the values, assumptions, and beliefs embedded in my language and its related thought. However, when I embraced the dissonance, I was positioned to be more open to changes in my ideas.

One particularly refractive experience for me was the first time Michael wanted me to pretend to be a police officer shooting someone. Fighting as a knight with a sword in an ancient land or as a Jedi warrior with a light-sabre in a far away universe had produced only mild dissonance for me. Holding a gun as a London Victorian policeman was more difficult. As a pacifist and a Quaker I was fundamentally opposed to hurting and killing people. Having grown up in Northern Ireland living in a violently divided society, I believed that I would never use a gun in an aggressive act. I did not anticipate on that day, when I felt such antipathy, that our play and my subsequent inquiry would allow me to examine, clarify, and develop those and other beliefs.

Playing in the world of Jekyll-and-Hyde

From the set of stories of classic movie monsters that a librarian directed him to when he was four-and-a-half years old, Michael discovered Robert Louis Stevenson's story of *Dr Jekyll and Mr Hyde* (1992). He was particularly captivated by the tale of the kind, respectable, and socially responsible physician Dr Henry Jekyll who turned into the monstrously egotistical Mr Edward Hyde when Jekyll drank a potion that he had made in his laboratory. As soon as he realized that we could rent the movies illustrated in the books he begged to borrow them. Within days we had re-read many of the stories several times and watched extracts from the Universal Studios film of *Dr Jekyll and Mr Hyde* as well as *The Wolfman*, *Frankenstein*, and *Frankenstein Meets the Wolfman*. We had also pretended to be characters from the stories.

A central condition and problem of the story of Dr Jekyll and Mr Hyde that appealed to Michael, was how to react to the violent, and eventually deadly, deeds of Hyde. As we began to play I felt little dissonance as we imagined that I was Hyde confronting Michael who pretended in quick succession to be a werewolf, a child, and an adult. I was happy wrestling with Michael. After all, I had enjoyed rough-and-tumble-play with him since he had been a toddler. In initiating our play he improvised from the narrative of *The Wolfman* as he imagined who might encounter Hyde. (He had discovered that story at the same time as the tale of Jekyll-and-Hyde.) By pretending to push the Wolfman/Michael, I confirmed by my actions that I thought no child or adult, and not even a powerful werewolf, could stop Hyde being violent.

> Michael – You're Mr Hyde and I'm Dr Jekyll. We're the same person.
>
> [In quick succession he imagines he is a werewolf who tries to attack Mr Hyde/me, a little boy asking me/Hyde for money, and an adult sitting in front of Hyde/me. Michael tells me/Hyde to push him out of the way. As the werewolf he tries to wrestle me. As the boy and the adult he falls over.]
>
> Brian/Hyde – Get out of my way.
> Michael – Now I'm Mr Hyde and you're a person.
> Michael/Hyde – Get out of my way [pretending to push me and repeating the words I've just said as Hyde].
> Brian/person 1 – Please help me.
> Michael/Hyde – Get out of my way. I'm a monster.
> Michael – You're another person who helps him [i.e. the victim].
> Brian/person 2 – Can you help me?
>
> [He changes to imagine he is my wife and we talk about what to do. He tells me to phone the police. He imagines we are police officers and wants to write in a book what has happened. He wants us to look for Hyde and imagines that we go into a house. He looks up and points.]

Michael/police officer – It's Mr Hyde. Come on. Shoot. Shoot.

Brian – Wait a minute. You have to be very careful it's the right person.

Michael/police officer – Yea. Come on. Shoot.

Brian – Wait a minute. You have to be very careful it's the right person.

Michael/police officer – Oh dear. It's him, his claws (inaudible).

Brian – Shall we have it that he's up on the roof tops and you . . .

Michael – and I (inaudible) yes.

[He changes to pretend to be Dr Jekyll.]

Halliday's sociolinguistic theory illuminates the complexity of the changing context created as we played. In the everyday social space we were playing, sharing power, and using multi-modal discourse as we enacted and embodied encounters between Mr Hyde and people in his way. In the socially imagined spaces within the world of Jekyll-and-Hyde, Hyde was overpowering whoever tried to stop him. He was embodying a monologic discourse of oppression. In authoring spaces I was, as usual, supporting Michael as he made internally persuasive meaning about the actions of the people he imagined. Michael was mostly using his authority to direct me while I also made suggestions and raised questions.

Refraction in inner and social speech

When Michael wanted us to pretend to be police officers I found myself resisting using the imaginary police officer's gun. My words 'Wait a minute. You have to be careful it's the right person' reveal this hesitation that soon became an inner struggle among the voices of inner and social speech. I heard different voices that I felt pulled me between pretending to shoot, and not shoot. In one ear I heard a voice insist that because I was pretending to be the police officer I should pull the trigger. This was a powerful voice that had developed since I had first played with Michael. It now urged me to enact whatever Michael wanted to experience if it was consistent with the fictional world of the narrative; it felt quite appropriate for an armed police officer to shoot Hyde in order to stop him killing. In my other ear I heard the equally powerful Quaker pacifist voice developed over a lifetime that was adamantly opposed to killing people.

My utterance, 'Wait a minute. You have to be very careful it's the right person,' along with my lack of movement was an improvised response or answer to Michael's utterance. It was as if he were a police officer who had addressed me as he pointed and used the commanding words: 'It's Mr Hyde. Come on. Shoot. Shoot.' But my utterance at that moment was also in answer to the other voices by which I felt addressed.

Table 4.1 Field/tenor/mode in the spaces of play

	Field (What is going on)	Tenor (The relationship between the people)	Mode (How language and other signs are being used to communicate)
EVERYDAY SPACE	Michael and Brian are playing	Brian and Michael are sharing power	Dialogic discourse is being enacted using words, sounds, and movements.
SOCIALLY IMAGINED SPACE	Mr Hyde is overcoming anyone in his way	Mr Hyde over-powers others as he egotistically does not listen to anyone else	Monologic embodied discourse: Hyde is pushing or wrestling with anyone in his way.
AUTHORING SPACE	Michael and Brian are co-authoring meaning. Brian raises a question about the use of a gun that Michael explores with him	Brian supports and assists Michael in his meaning-making. Michael does the same	Authoritative discourse as Michael directs Brian. Internally persuasive discourse as Michael and Brian co-author meaning.

As Bakhtin's collaborator Voloshinov notes, 'the immediate social situation and the broader social milieu wholly determine – and determine from within, so to speak – the structure of an utterance' (1986, p. 86). My hesitation was my conflicted answer to, on the one hand, Michael's utterance resonating with an inner voice in the 'immediate social situation' which addressed me with a demand that I shoot; and, on the other hand, an inner voice in my 'broader social milieu' that demanded I not shoot.

At the same time, our interactions were for me both inner speech and social speech. My utterance was 'double-voiced' because in our improvised dialogue I was answering more than one voice. My discourse was directed both toward Michael and toward inner voices that he did not hear. I experienced when the voices 'encounter one another and coexist in [my] consciousness' (Bakhtin, 1981, p. 291). As I struggled to pretend to be the police officer holding a gun that I pointed at an imagined Hyde I felt dissonance. As Bakhtin notes, 'What matters is the dialogic [or refractive] angle at which [voices] are juxtaposed or counterposed' (Voloshinov, 1984, p. 182). At this moment they felt oppositional.

Easing refraction

The refractive angle of our exchange eased significantly as Michael shifted to pretend to be Jekyll. But my utterances were still double-voiced and I was still focused more on my inner speech than on the social speech with Michael. It was only later as I returned to this moment and compared it with other similar moments that I was struck by the meaning that Michael was making.

Having announced that Mr Hyde had changed back into Dr Jekyll, Michael stood still looking puzzled.

> Brian/Utterson – Henry. What are you doing?
> Michael/Jekyll – I can't remember.
>
> [I pretend to read in a newspaper about the people who had been killed.]
>
> Brian/Utterson – Who could have done this, Henry? Do you know?
> Michael/Jekyll – I changed into Mr Hyde.
> Brian/Utterson – Henry, you mean that was you?
> Michael/Jekyll – I don't want to do all this mean stuff.
>
> [I pretend to read in the newspaper that the police say Mr Hyde should be killed.]
>
> Brian/Jekyll – Henry, what do you think should happen? Should Mr Hyde be killed?
> Michael/Jekyll – No, because if Mr Hyde is killed that means me myself is going to be killed.
> Brian/Utterson – But you're not Mr Hyde, Henry.
> Michael/Jekyll – Well I change into him.
> Brian/Utterson – Only when you drank this potion.
> Michael/Jekyll – Yea. I'm going to lock it up. Right now. Here.
>
> [He pretends to lock it in a safe and I help him.] . . .

I was still thinking about the previous episode when the police officer/I was holding the imagined gun. I was answering this voice when I improvised that there was an account in the newspaper that said the police thought that Hyde should be killed and I asked Michael if he agreed. When he said 'No, because if Mr Hyde is killed that means me myself is going to be killed' he was restating the idea that he had articulated as we began to play 'You're Mr Hyde and I'm Dr Jekyll. We're the same person.'

It was only later as I reflected on our play that I realized Michael had captured a central understanding of the story that I did not carry with me as we imagined. I was treating Jekyll and Hyde as separate people whereas he understood that they were two sides of the same person, a concept that he enacted by pretending, with no apparent preference, to be both of them.

Relative power and authority in play

As we played, Michael effortlessly moved among multiple points of view as he took up the perspectives of different people along with their relative power and authority. Michael's utterances from these different positions examined a major theme of the story: How do you interpret and respond to Hyde's actions? In addition to pretending to be altruistic Dr Jekyll and egotistic Mr Hyde, and other characters in the story he also improvised by drawing on other narratives. He imagined that he had great physical strength (a werewolf), someone with expertise and mechanical power (Dr Frankenstein), a person with social authority (a police officer), someone like me (an adult), his mother (a wife), and himself (a little boy).

He explored different ways to use power to deal with Hyde's deeds. Immediately after pretending to be Jekyll locking up the potion and hiding the key in a hole, he pretended to be Dr Frankenstein operating his machine. In response to my question 'Is there anything we could do so that maybe you [Dr Jekyll] won't turn into the beast [the word he had used for Hyde]?' he improvised a response using images from the movie *Frankenstein Meets the Wolfman* (that we had just watched) in which Dr Frankenstein uses his machine both to give and to remove the life force. He wanted Dr Frankenstein/me to connect Jekyll/him to the machine to 'break the power.' I proceeded to do this. After being disconnected Jekyll/he tried taking the potion and it did not turn him into Hyde. When I asked 'What are we going to do about the people who got killed?,' he replied, 'Put them in Dr Frankenstein's machine and I'll bring them back to life.'

Through play, Michael would soon, in effect, address me again with the question that he had raised earlier: Should a police officer shoot Hyde? After pretending to restore Hyde's victims to life I had expected that Michael would likely want to pretend that we were inside a different narrative world as I felt a sense of resolution and order being restored. However, he turned his attention again to the Jekyll-and-Hyde relationship and how to deal with Hyde. Toward the end of the movie that we had watched, Hyde's shadow is shown on a wall. Michael seemed to be thinking about this image when he said 'The Shadow of Mr Hyde remains' and then 'the Shadow gets killed but not Dr Jekyll.' As he began to enact his thoughts he wanted me to pretend to be Jekyll.

> Michael – You're Dr Jekyll finally dead at the end of his life.
> Brian/Jekyll – [I lie down and pretend to die.] Goodbye everybody. I had a good life.

Michael – Now you're all the people that he's destroyed. I'm the Shadow.
Brian/people [pretending to beg] – Please help me.
Michael – But the people aren't beggar men. They're all young men.

[The Shadow/Michael pretends to kill three people/me in quick succession as he shouts 'Get out of my way.' I want to stop playing as I suddenly feel overwhelmed with all the killing.]

Brian – Can we stop for a moment? I don't want to pretend we're killing.

[I hug him and he hugs me back.]

Michael – Knock, knock.
Brian – Who's there?
Michael – Boo.
Brian – Boo who?
Michael – Don't cry, it's only a joke.

[I laugh.]

My conflicted feelings intensified to such an extent that I had to stop pretending. I felt Hyde's evil power viscerally when I looked into Michael's gruesome face, saw his violent movements, and imagined that he was killing me/three men. Having read the story many times I was well aware that Hyde killed people, but seeing Michael for the first time show how Hyde used his physical power to kill, coupled with experiencing killing from the position of the victims was overwhelming.

As soon as I asked to stop playing, Michael transformed into the sweet, concerned little boy who would 'kiss boo-boos' and sing lullabies to his one month-old baby sister. The grimaces disappeared as we hugged. In seconds he had me laughing as he told me a knock-knock joke that he had just learned.

As I chuckled, the understanding that we were just pretending became more prominent. Later, as I analyzed our play, I realized that I had heard his joke as a reminder that no one is ever actually hurt by imagined actions, even if they pretend to kill. Michael's utterance brought other voices and discourses to our exchange. I recalled that though play activities may be deeply meaningful and emotionally intense they are always non-literal. Though we may resist pretending to hurt or kill we are not actually going to be hurt or die if we imagine death by shooting. My laughter and change in mood were part of my answer to Michael's utterance and the voices he had amplified for me.

The past and present voices of inner speech

Michael was eager to continue playing and as I no longer felt a resistance to pretending I was ready to re-enter the world of Jekyll-and-Hyde. He took us almost full circle back to the encounter with which we had begun our play. Again we imagined that I was Hyde with Michael having the authority of the police officer with the power of life-and-death in his gun.

> Michael – Now I'm the little boy. OK, daddy?
> Brian – OK.
> Michael/boy – Police. There's a monster who's killed some people.
> Brian/police officer – Yea we know. Have you seen him? Do you know where he is? We've been looking for him.
> Michael/boy – Yea. He tried to kill me.
> Brian/police officer – Are you all right?
> Michael/boy – Yea.

[He tells the police officer/me that Hyde is on the roof of a building.]

> Michael – Daddy, you be Mr Hyde up on the rooftop.

[I climb half-way up the stairs.]

> Michael/police officer – Get down from that rooftop.
> Brian – No. Who are you?
> Michael/police officer – I'm a police.
> Brian/Hyde – What do you want?
> Michael/police officer – Stop doing all those mean things.
> Brian/Hyde – Why should I?
> Michael/police officer – Because they're all mean.
> Brian/Hyde – Huh. What will you do to me if I do come down?
> Michael/police officer – Well if you don't come down I'll shoot you.
> Brian/Hyde – And if I do? What will you do to me?
> Michael/police officer – I'll send you away to jail.
> Brian/Hyde – Jail? Why should I go to jail?
> Michael/police officer – Because you know. Because you're mean that's why. Huh.

[We talk back-and-forth about rules until Michael refocuses us.]

> Michael/police officer – Just no talk about it. Now get down or I'll shoot you.
> Brian – How do you want it to end? Do you want to shoot him or do you want him to come down?
> Michael – I want to shoot you.

Brian/Hyde – No [laughing]. I can get away, I'm too clever for you.

[Michael shoots and I pretend to die.]

Michael – Now change back into the Shadow.

[I lie down and transform my body into Hyde's. Michael stands over me pretending to hold the gun. Pat enters the room]

Pat – Are you going to use that gun to shoot other people?
Michael/police officer – I only use my gun to shoot monsters [said with a tone of this being obvious].

To understand some of the layers of complexity of our dialogic inter-actions it is important to recognize that my utterances resonated with and answered many past utterances and voices in addition to the voices Michael used in the present moment. As Bakhtin notes, in extending his definition of utterance:

> Each utterance is filled with echoes and reverberations of other [past] utterances to which it is related by the communality of the sphere of speech communication. Every utterance must be primarily regarded as a response to preceding utterances of the given sphere (we understand the word 'response' here is the broadest sense). Each utterance refutes, affirms, supplements, and relies on the others, presupposes them to be known, and somehow takes them into account.
>
> (1986, p. 91)

As I projected again into the encounter between the police officer and Hyde I experienced complex refraction between voices. Unlike when I imag-ined holding the gun I no longer felt an oppositional resistance to killing Hyde. I experienced more complex inner speech. Jekyll/Hyde was a human being but so were his victims. He was a human who was capable of mon-strous actions that I had seen with gruesome intensity in imagination. His violent deeds refracted my view of him as a human being. If he was not stopped I could see him killing again. As I stood on the stairs imagining that Hyde was on the rooftop I heard multiple inner voices that had been uttered as we played. I could hear the cries of the victims of his heartless violence including those that he had killed and those that he would kill if he were not stopped. Jekyll was a kind physician but I also saw Jekyll using the potion to change into Hyde because Jekyll knew where the key to the safe was. Jekyll might be reformed using Dr Frankenstein's machine. But if Jekyll died, and the shadow-of-Hyde remained then it/he would have to be stopped. Killing Hyde was now an option. I knew this because as I climbed the stairs I did not resist forming an image of the police officer shooting Hyde.

Authoring as the police officer, Michael took a different tack than I had expected. He threatened to shoot Hyde but at first wanted him to 'stop doing all those mean things.' He wanted to arrest Hyde and 'send him away for jail.' As in response to other creatures or people who did monstrous deeds, Michael was exploring alternatives to killing. I started to talk about jail and what he meant by the rules of jail. However, as Michael wanted more action and less talk I asked him to choose what he wanted to experience. He enacted shooting Hyde and then wanted me to show the Shadow remaining. Hyde had died but the oppressive power embodied in Hyde had not been killed.

Co-authoring ethical understanding

Our play on this occasion had been more refractive for me than ever before. But because I was able to embrace refractive experiences, after about twenty minutes I had begun to author a more complex understanding of the story of *Dr Jekyll and Mr Hyde* along with a new understanding about my belief in non-violence. My earlier feelings of intense discomfort as I imagined shooting a gun had been the product of extreme refraction between a principle of pacifism and a desire to play. As we played, additional views were given voice in situations that modified the idea of not killing; I recognized that killing someone who kills (in the context of an immediate struggle) had to be an option.

Michael's experience of the same play events would have been quite different. Whereas I had felt refraction as strongly authoritative prior discourses pulling me away from the imagined space, Michael did not. From a Vygotskian point of view he was not engaged in inner speech in the same way as I was. And from a Bakhtinian viewpoint he did not have the sort of historical discursive weight that I had. He only stopped his projection into the world of Jekyll-and-Hyde because I asked him to do so.

Michael did embrace dissonances, both those inherent within the imagined world of Jekyll-and-Hyde as well as any that I introduced. Whereas I authored more internally persuasive discourse in subsequent reflection, Michael did so in-the-moment with me, as he projected into different consciousnesses, embodied action in each case, and then contemplated the consequences of those actions from the consciousness of other people. In doing so we were co-authoring ethical understanding that shaped our ethical identities in two main ways. First, we did this via our ongoing ethical evaluation of each other's utterances. As we interacted I was implicitly (and sometimes explicitly) answering his utterances and thereby evaluating them. Similarly, Michael answered any evaluation I might make as I addressed him about imagined actions. Second, we engaged in what I have called positioning-play.

Ethical evaluation

Discourse always has an ethical evaluative edge in the sense that every utterance is always implicitly affirming (if it is not disputing) the morality of another's actions. But a person's ethical position is only apparent when it becomes 'an object to be perceived, reflected upon, or related to' (Bakhtin 1981, 286). One person's words or deeds are objects for other people to reflect on and evaluate. As happened for me, an ethical positioning of which I was unaware was exposed and tested as Michael and I interacted. Similarly, for Michael, characters' positionings of others in narratives became more apparent as we interacted to make them visible. If one of my utterances refracted significantly for Michael with the discourse he was embodying Michael would answer and dialogue with me. In doing so the meaning he was making was affected.

As we interacted in imagined spaces I provided Michael with new ethical viewpoints on the ideas we were exploring as objects that he could contemplate and respond to. Buzzelli (1993) stressed the ethical significance of an adult's ethical evaluation of events in interactions with a child. As Bakhtin theorized, one person always has a 'surplus of seeing' relative to other people. Since I am in a unique physical space, I can literally see what others can't see. I could see, for example, the look on another's face, like the hatred on Hyde's face. But I also have unique conceptual and ideological points of view. One person always understands and interprets present, past, or future events differently than other people. In dialogue, another person's views will make a difference to the meaning I make, and vice versa. However, this will only happen if we each can hear and respond openly to one another, and not exclude another's consciousness from entering our own.

My discourse always had authority for Michael because he responded to it. When I asked him in our everyday social world to stop playing he did so without any resistance. However, my discourse in imagined worlds never remained externally authoritative for Michael as we played. He did not simply accept a view that I might present but rather set it against other viewpoints as he engaged me in dialogue about a refractive discourse. Michael and I each co-authored innerly persuasive meaning as we explored the import of an authoritative discourse and as Michael shifted field, tenor, and mode to move among multiple intersecting contexts.

When I questioned Michael's insistence that as police officers we should shoot Hyde, Michael shifted his consciousness, and mine, among several positions and relationships. Then about ten minutes later he returned us to a parallel encounter with him as the police officer and me representing Hyde. In succession we moved among the following encounters: Jekyll and his friend Utterson, Jekyll locking up the drug, Jekyll's viewpoint as he dies, and the reactions of a host of victims of Hyde's violent acts including children. I was positioned to evaluate Hyde's deeds from the viewpoint of various people affected by his violence. I was then placed in a position from which I had to answer those evaluations from Hyde's viewpoint as Michael addressed me as a police officer.

Our playful though very serious exploration had dialogized the discourse I had introduced that Hyde should not be shot. The discourse had been placed in a dialogic relationship with other viewpoints. Given the fact that Jekyll would turn into Hyde again, and that he could kill again, and that he refused to surrender, I evaluated it as right that Hyde should be shot. Michael's final comment to his mother was in agreement. Hyde was a monster because he would not, or could not, stop hurting and killing others. He had to be stopped.

Positioning-play

Michael could take up multiple positions within a narrative and move among them because I could always embody and give voice to whatever conscious-nesses Michael wanted to interact with. I made it easy for him to shift field, tenor, and mode.

Michael could also in effect trade places with me as he did when we first projected into the world of Jekyll-and-Hyde. He could thus experience any encounter from both points of view. At first I was Hyde and he represented all those people and creatures that Hyde could defeat as objects in his way. Then he imagined he was Hyde with me as his victims.

Positioning-play made all positionings in a narrative potential subject positions. In the world of Jekyll-and-Hyde Michael was both victim and perpetrator. There were no amoral bystanders in Michael's version of the tale because everyone was a potential victim of Hyde's violence. Positioning-play meant that in Michael's experience and exploration of the narrative, no characters' viewpoints remained outside his consciousness including those positions that adults might avoid projecting into. Through positioning-play Michael could identity, positively and negatively, with all subject positions. As he adopted subject positions he evaluated actions from those viewpoints through his interactions with me.

The complexity of ethical understanding

From a Bakhtinian viewpoint, as we interacted Michael was authoring internally persuasive, or dialogized, discourses on the good-and-evil nature of humanity. He was making his own, those discourses that we had embodied and extended from the narrative of Dr Jekyll and Mr Hyde. Michael followed one idea, enacted it, and then placed it beside another idea allowing them to refract and intermingle with one another.

Applying Halliday's theories, as we played on this occasion and others, Michael shifted the field to explore one of the central ethical ideas in Stevenson's novella. Henry Jekyll, writing a confessional reflective letter before he commits suicide, comments on the impossibility of achieving the desire he had had: he had thought he could separate his evil nature from the good by taking a potion that was to divide himself into separate identities. 'Of the two natures that contended in the field of my consciousness, even if I could rightly be said to be either, it was only because I was radically both' (Stevenson, 2002, p. 56). Unlike Jekyll, who reached this realization on his death-bed, Michael was living it in his sixth year of life.

Rather than enact a single narrative with a tidy moralistic resolution, by repeatedly shifting the tenor and modes of our interactions, Michael embodied, as a possible good-and-evil self, the unraveling contradictory post-structural narrative threads of Stevenson's tale. The same person could help people in one context yet hurt and even kill in another. Some people escaped Hyde's wrath while others were attacked. Jekyll wanted to stop taking the potion yet took the drug to turn him into Hyde. Michael extended Stevenson's idea by embodying the unstoppable nature of evil. Hyde could defeat even the most powerful creatures. And even when Hyde died the Shadow remained to continue its remorseless attacks.

Bakhtin stressed that complex ideas, and the language that shapes our understandings, are never one person's simple decontextualized monologic statements but are rather always experienced as an ongoing dialogic interplay between many consciousnesses.

> The idea . . . is not a subjective individual-psychological formation with 'permanent resident rights' in a person's head; no, the idea is inter-individual and inter-subjective – the realm of its existence is not individual consciousness but dialogic communion between consciousnesses. The idea is a live event, played out at the point of dialogic meeting between two or several consciousnesses. In this sense the idea is similar to the word with which it is dialogically united. Like the word, the idea wants to be heard, understood, and 'answered' by other voices from other positions.
>
> (1984, p. 88)

From a Vygotskian viewpoint, through these interactions, as well as all the others in the world of Jekyll-and-Hyde, we were developing a complex evolving sign. Jekyll-and-Hyde was a possible good-and-evil self. He had many voices as we embodied and enacted deeds across many intersecting and interrelated contexts in the narrative world.

For Michael, as well as for me, social speech became inner speech and thought. These were then externalized as we played. As Michael repeatedly enacted possible selves in play he could objectify and experience different ways of being in the world. The triple context of play combined with positioning-play provided Michael with experiences of watching and evaluating possible selves in action.

Jekyll-and-Hyde was one powerful way of conceptualizing for Michael (and for me) the possible moral-amoral-immoral ways of relating to other people. We can all be kind, nurture, and protect others. But we also all have the capacity to hurt and kill others. And if we cannot or will not stop ourselves oppressing others then we must be stopped. Further, in imagination there are no amoral bystander positions to take up because, in ethical imagination, when we project into others' lives we are always implicated.

Forming ethical identities with heuristic devices

Many of the signs we co-authored as we played, and their related discourses, became both conceptual ethical constructs for making sense of imagined and actual deeds as well as pragmatic tools for guiding future action. They were integral to Michael's ethical identity. Michael was able to understand one dimension of what it meant to do 'good' because of how we had acted, talked, and evaluated deeds as if we were people like St. George or Una (and the dragon) interacting in a world where people were terrorized by a relentless killing monster. Other dimensions of understanding 'good-and-evil' were formed through our deeds and discourse in and about the other imagined worlds we inhabited over the years.

Not all fictional events became significant for Michael. He repeatedly returned to experience again and again only some of the complex signs that were shaped over time in and around our play in every narrative world. These became what Holland has described as 'heuristic devices'. They were heuristics in the sense that they allowed Michael to think about ideas and feelings and to develop understanding that he could not have done merely by talking about books or everyday life. They were devices because he chose to use them by returning to them both in play and by referring to them as he made sense of daily events. As Holland et al. argue, heuristic devices in imagination both 'turn toward self-understanding' of thoughts and emotions in situations, and as facets of identities they 'are social forms of organization, public and intimate, that mediate the development of human agency' and self-management (1998, p. 282). In other words, both in particular interactions and across time, Michael used core play events to access, shape, manage, and understand his thoughts and feelings about how he might relate to others. By revisiting particular play encounters and experiencing how he might act and be affected by those actions Michael was authoring aspects of identities that in turn became new tools for shaping his sense of agency.

Our forming ethical identities mediate the development of our ethical agency. The signs and discourses of the heuristic devices we co-author as we identify with the deeds of others, shift among consciousnesses in positioning-play. What we evaluate in particular contexts as right-and-wrong, all connect us emotionally and intellectually with other people empathetically and sympathetically, and provide us with tools for self-management. As Michael used signs heuristically across social interactions in and around our play he authored facets of his ethical identity that became apparent in his ethical dispositions.

Authoritative ethical heuristic devices

Ethical heuristic devices become more individually authoritative for a person over time when they are authored as dialogized, or internally persuasive, discourses. As I showed above, in our dialogic interactions as we played Michael was able to fill discourse with his own intentions and dialogize ideas across time and space to make them his own.

At the same time, heuristic devices become authoritative for us when they are tied to deeply emotional experiences. The signs that children create as they play are not necessarily going to form very authoritative ethical heuristic devices. However, just as some everyday life past experiences are so emotionally highly charged that we return to them to make meaning about past, present, and future deeds, so are some experiences in imagined worlds. As Vygotsky (1969) argued, thoughts and deeds are always tied to feelings and emotions.

> Thought is not begotten by thought; it is engendered by motivation, i.e. by our desires, and needs, our interests, and emotions. Behind every thought there is an affective-volitional tendency, which holds the answer to the last 'why' in the analysis of thinking. A true and full under-standing of another's thoughts is possible only when we understand its affective-volitional basis.
>
> (1969, p. 252)

From a cognitive psychology viewpoint on the development of ethical concepts, Mark Johnson shows how a person's early intense experiences create what he calls 'base-level experiences' that experientially and emotion-ally ground the idea of heuristic devices. Over time people construct, in what Johnson argues is their moral imagination, 'idealized models and [moral] frameworks that grow out of their experience and that they bring to their understanding of situations' (1993, p. 9). A person's moral concepts, models, and frameworks are unavoidably connected with their experiences of deepest pain and pleasure, harm and well-being etc. They are 'proto-typical' or 'base-level experiences' that become identified as 'good' and 'bad', 'right' and 'wrong' etc. As these basic experiences are metaphorically and heuristically applied to subsequent events they affect the sorts of life narratives that people tell which collectively shape their ethical perspective on life.

Michael's experiences as we played were, more often than not, deeply emotionally charged and gained emotional weight over time. The following cameos give an inkling of how Michael's experience of play was deep, often intense, and repeated across time and imagined spaces to create signs that were used as heuristic devices.

- Physical power. All monstrous creatures and people were noisy and physical. The giant up the beanstalk stomps his feet coming down the stairs crying out 'Fee Fi Fo Fum'; the dragon flies around breathing fire.
- Protective righteous anger. All heroic people demanded that oppressors stop. St. George commands the dragon to stop breathing fire on people; Luke Skywalker points and yells at Darth Vader 'I tell you at the top of my voice to stop killing people'.
- Nurturing attention/visceral pain. For months, most often when we were in the car and he had to lie still, Michael would pretend to be the Beast dying as I/Beauty told him how much I loved him. Esmerelda brought water to Quasimodo, the Hunchback of Notre Dame, when he had been mercilessly whipped.
- Good and evil transformation. Jekyll changed into Hyde when he took one potion and back again when he took another.
- From death to life. Frankenstein's creature comes to life; Dracula wakes up in his coffin; the Mummy wakes up after thousands of years.

Forming ethical heuristic devices from life events

Play, and especially mythic play, provides young children with base-level experiences that are likely to be much more intense and deeply felt (yet more emotionally protected) than their everyday experiences. Some children's lives will have traumatic events that might approach the experiences of one of Hyde's victims. Some children have experienced violence, witnessed brutal murders, or lived through the ravages of war. But for Michael, who has led a relatively sheltered life in a safe middle-class home and in supportive care settings, his most anguished (and unconditionally loving) experiences occurred as we played.

The car accident that I described in chapter two was one emotionally memorable everyday experience that was dialogized as Michael chose to return to it over several months and that developed in and around out play into a heuristic device. Michael used his transformation of that event in play to make sense not only of the danger of cars but also to mediate his exploration of how people ought to be rescued from dangerous accidents via ambulances and helicopters and then cared for if hurt.

Adult-initiated creation of heuristic devices

Occasionally I used play to give Michael an emotional experience that became an authoritative internally persuasive heuristic device for him in terms of his self-management. For example, I wanted him to have a strong sense of self-preservation in relation to cars on the road. Between when Michael was eighteen months and two-and-a-half years old we lived near a street on which speeding cars could suddenly appear. When Michael was about two we were worried that he might run into the road. I talked with Michael about why he should never run into the road. Knowing how important agency is, as well as telling him what might happen I asked him what he thought could happen. He wasn't hearing me. He wanted to pretend that he was a back-hoe.

I was using the semiotic system most often used by adults – talking to children. But two-year-olds can't make a lot of meaning about what cars do just because you tell them. Asking them what they ought to do won't work if they've lost interest. And conceptualizing a future is hard enough work aged two, let alone about events that have never happened and that bear little relation to your safe world. I tried a different tack. I pretended and in doing so shifted communication modes.

> I start to pretend I am driving a car. I hold my body stiff and look forwards. I make car sounds and narrate what I am doing. I say, 'I'm driving down our street. I'm looking ahead. I don't see us here.'
>
> I see a car coming so I point it as it comes round the corner. I mimic its sound and run parallel to it as fast as I can as it zooms on by. Michael is watching me intently. I go over to him.
>
> 'If you ran out in the street and that car was coming and the driver didn't see you, do you know what could happen?'
>
> Michael shakes his head.
>
> 'It could hit you and kill you,' I say seriously.
>
> Michael starts to turn away.
>
> 'You pretend to be the car and I'll pretend to be you. OK?'
>
> He starts to run as I had done.
>
> I narrate as if I'm Michael. 'I'm playing and I don't see you. I run out.'
>
> 'Now, Michael, you run into me. Pretend the car has hit me.'

He runs into me. I fall over screaming. I whimper, close my eyes and go still and quiet. Michael is very still. He comes over to hold me.

'It's OK. I'm just pretending.'

He looks relieved.

'But that's what could happen if you ran into the road'

I hold his face in my hands and look him in the eyes. This signals a serious conversation for him. I've used this before when telling him not to pull the cats' tails or not to go behind the barrier where we have the stereo equipment and CDs.

'Never never run into the road. OK? Because you might get killed and then I'd be so so so sad.' I start to pretend to cry. I feel pretty upset just thinking about the possibility of Michael being killed. I start to parody being upset and weeping and Michael starts to laugh. I do too.

I walk over with him to the edge of the road where there is a sidewalk [pavement] and then a stretch of grass.

'If you stay on the sidewalk you'll be safe. Don't go on this grass. OK?' Another car comes by and Michael flinches.

'It's OK we're safe here.' I get down and hold him as the car speeds on by. 'It was really fast, wasn't it?' He nods. 'But we're safe here,' I repeat. He relaxes.

'I've thought of a good game,' I say standing up. 'I'll walk on the sidewalk and if you see me touch the grass you shout, 'Not safe!' but when I'm on the sidewalk we can say, 'Safe.'

I walk along saying 'Safe, safe, safe . . .' Michael watches me, also saying 'safe' but shouts 'Unsafe' when I touch the grass. He likes playing this for a minute or two. Then we go in.

My authoritative discourse about not running into the road became much more dialogic and internally persuasive for Michael as soon as I shifted into play mode. By pretending with him we were able to contextualize the abstract arguments and references I had tried to make using only words. We were able to enter into an imagined world where the authoritative discourse not only made sense to him but that he could begin to make his own. Michael could project into and embody a car being hit. He could also stand outside the event and author meaning with me that connected my ethical evaluation with his experience. The words 'safe' and 'not safe' now had personal authoritative meaning for Michael that connected with his imagined experience of why he shouldn't run into the road.

After the time we played Michael never ran into the road. That play event became a heuristic device that Michael used in self-management. Michael sometimes wanted to play the 'safe/unsafe' word game when we walked along the road. He also used his experience of my hands on his face, his words, and the safe/unsafe game all as pivots to remind his self of the abstracted but emotionally charged meaning that we made that day. Without interacting with me he would make the sound of cars, and hold his own head with his hands as he said, 'No run in the road'. Michael was illustrating Vygotsky's idea that, 'What a child can do with assistance today she will be able to do by herself tomorrow' (1978, p. 87).

Use of heuristic devices for everyday self-management

Michael's use of a heuristic device for self-management was most obvious in his social behavior. Dracula was one of the possible good-and-evil selves that we, and then Michael, used as a heuristic device to mediate the development of his social identity.

Getting Michael to sit down to eat was often a challenge when he was young. Playing with him was paradoxically more effective than discussion or directives for mediating his shift from intense movement and noise to more stillness and quiet. When words alone were not working I pretended that we were gentlemen. Michael would often play along imagining that he was the gentlemanly Count Dracula. I would often talk as if I was the character Renfield asking if he had something to eat. We would then sit down and behave very politely at the table.

Before he was five, on his own Michael initiated the use of a violent encounter from Dracula as a heuristic device. He had not wanted to stop walking around in his Dracula cape and sit down for breakfast. When we asked him for the third time to sit down at the table Michael said very melodramatically, 'Whichever one of you has a wooden stake pound it into my heart. I hate what I do.' When I posed my often-asked question, 'Isn't there any other way?' He replied, 'No. I am evil.' I suppressed a giggle as I pretended to tap in a stake and he came smiling to the table.

After that day Michael increasingly initiated pretending, or shifted with minimal suggestion, to imagine that he was transforming from one of the evil-doers he knew and/or that he was one of the people he knew from narratives who sat at tables politely. The following examples were most common: Count Dracula; Mr Hyde turning into Dr Jekyll, or as the characters Poole or Utterson from the tale; pretending to be Dr Livesey or Long John Silver eating with the captain from *Treasure Island*. Michael gradually remained as a gentleman for longer periods of time and by the time he was seven he only sporadically imagined that he was someone else as we ate.

Child-initiated creation, exploration, and use of heuristic devices

The creation, exploration, and use of heuristic devices in the vast majority of cases was initiated by Michael through play. He sought out the stories, focused on those particular encounters that captivated him, and then pursued explorations with me often across weeks or months. Pretending and discussing about play events intermingled as Michael returned to particular encounters and then used them heuristically to co-author understanding as we explored ethical dimensions of particular social relationships in imagined worlds.

One narrative world that engrossed Michael between the ages of about four and four-and-a-half, was formed from his projection into encounters in the original *Star Wars* trilogy of movies. Michael discovered Jedi knights on the heels of a fascination with other knights and warriors including : St George, Beowulf, Perseus, Theseus, Rama, and Bilbo Baggins.

Michael most often pretended to be Luke Skywalker but he also imagined that he was the Emperor, Darth Vader, Obi-Wan Kenobi, and others. He relished making the noises of imaginary light-sabres as we pretended to do battle. He liked to pretend to be Luke Skywalker learning to use his light-sabre with the former Jedi warrior, Obi-wan Kenobi, as well as Luke fighting Darth Vader, and both of them fighting the Emperor. As Obi-Wan he would quote from the movie and tell me to 'feel the force, Luke.' As Darth Vader Michael would often wear his cape and cover his mouth to make the machine-like sound of breathing as he used words from the movie like, 'Turn to the dark side, Luke'. As the Emperor he would make crackling electrical sounds as he imagined using power flowing through his fingers to try to force me, squirming on the floor as Luke, to 'turn to the dark side.'

We projected into and contemplated only a few core encounters from the vast array available in the *Star Wars* universe: dueling with light-sabres between a Jedi warrior (usually Luke or Obi-Wan) and an Imperial leader (usually Darth Vader or the Emperor); rescuing people threatened with destruction on Princess Leia's planet; and the Emperor's torturing of Luke and his rescue by Darth Vader.

Through these explorations Michael chose to project into and contemplate with me over and over facets of the following embodied, enacted, contextualized, ethical ideas:

- When killing someone is (or is not) necessary
- The authority of family ties in relation to other power relationships
- The meaning of words like 'hate', 'cruelty', 'destiny', 'good', 'evil' and 'wisdom'
- Using the force as a 'Jedi' warrior

Michael asked me one day when I was driving him in the car to pre-school, if Jedi were real. I told him that they were in the world of *Star Wars*. He said, 'I wish I was a Jedi. Do you think I'm a Jedi?' I gave Michael a psychological interpretation that I don't think made much sense to him. 'You're getting there because you stand up to the powers of the dark side and face your fears'. He didn't understand what face meant in the context so I added that 'you face your fears when you don't pretend that they don't exist'.

As I pulled into the parking lot [car park], Michael switched tactics, and as he often did, he asked me to apply my thinking to myself. He asked me, 'Are you a Jedi, Daddy?' As I turned off the ignition I paused for a few seconds thinking about what I had said about the need to face our fears. I didn't take the position that I couldn't be a Jedi because I didn't actually live in the world of *Star Wars*. As I would say to Michael when he was older about anything that we could interpret in a non-literal way, I recognized that metaphorically I could be a Jedi. As he was doing, I used the idea of being a Jedi heuristically. I was honest with him when I said that I thought I was sometimes a Jedi because I usually didn't run away from my fears.

I got out of the car and went round to open the door for him. Michael's response, as was often the case when I started to get too abstract for him, was to contextualize our conversation in a play event. He seamlessly pro-jected into an event in the *Star Wars* universe in parallel with lifting up his arms in the everyday world to let me unbuckle the belts in his car seat. 'We're being shot at. I'm not running away'. As I helped him out of the straps Michael said, 'I'm Luke and you're Han Solo, OK? You've been shot.' He perceived Luke and Han Solo as friends. Michael wanted me to squat down beside the car. I checked to see that there were no other cars coming into or moving in the lot and said, 'OK. No cars coming'. I crouched down making a groaning noise as if I had been shot. Michael made shooting noises as he jumped down, put his arms out and then around me pulling me up. 'We've got to rescue Princess Leia. Use the force. Get into my space ship.' And off we went toward the preschool building. As we arrived at the outdoor play area where children were swinging, sliding, and running, Michael wanted to continue to pretend with me. However, I initiated my leave-taking by saying, 'I need to talk to Michael now'. I got down on my knees, held him, and repeated words I used every day as a ritual goodbye, 'I love you. You're always in my heart and I'll see you this afternoon'. He scampered off to the swing set.

Later that day at home I had been angry with Michael about something insignificant. I think he had left caps off the markers. I felt bad about raising my voice in annoyance and I apologized to him and gave him a hug. I had been thinking again about the metaphors of being a Jedi and using the force against the dark side. I said, 'Everyone gets angry at times. That's the dark side. When you get wiser you use your anger less to hurt other people. Wisdom is on the light side.'

Though he didn't say anything at that time, to my surprise later that evening, Michael asked me 'Daddy, what is wisdom?' as we were watching *Return of the Jedi*, the third *Star Wars* movie. In reply I said, 'Well, I suppose, being wise is knowing how to make good decisions'. Michael said no more. As we were watching a scene in the movie when the aged Jedi knight, Obi-wan Kenobi, is training Luke how to use a light-sabre, I asked Michael whom he thought was wise in the movie. Without hesitation he said Obi-wan Kenobi. I agreed. Michael asked me why and I said, 'Well, he went to confront Darth Vader even when people said it was useless'. Michael responded and I nodded in agreement that, 'He was wise because he confronted the dark side. Right?'

The next evening I noticed a scratch on Michael's cheek and I asked him what had happened to his face. Michael told me that Colin, one of the other boys at the preschool, had told him to move, had hit him, and scratched him. Michael became upset as he remembered the incident. 'He told me to move off the spot.' I said I didn't understand. He added, 'He said I was in his way, but I didn't know I was.' I asked Michael if he had 'used the force' and he replied as he began to cry, 'I didn't hit him back'. Following that incident Pat and I talked with his teachers telling them the story and asking that they mediate negotiations between Michael and Colin. They must have helped the boys because Michael did not report another painful event.

In the *Star Wars* universe, using the force for good deeds is an oppositional position to turning to the dark side. Though Michael used those core phrases as we played, understanding their meaning required a great deal of inference even by myself as an adult viewer. As we played we created contexts in which the meaning of key phrases became situated and where Michael could connect with them across imagined and other experiences.

Michael knew that saying 'stop' or 'no' meant a person had to stop without negotiation whether or not they thought they were playing. In our *Star Wars* play he contextualized this imperative in a mythic life-and-death situation to experience the horrific or deadly consequences of not stopping. In this socially imagined space the power of the Emperor could not be overcome by words. The Emperor illustrates Baumeister's example of extreme cruelty (a word we talked about at another time in reference to this encounter) where a person empathizes, knowing what pain he is causing, yet does not sympathize with his victim. Michael chose to author this experience and did not want me to stop pretending that the Emperor was intentionally inflicting pain.

We're in the living room.
Michael: Daddy, I'm Luke and you're the Emperor. We're fighting.

[We pretend to use our light-sabres for a minute.]

Brian/Emperor: Turn to the dark side, Luke.

Michael/Luke: No, I'll never turn to the dark side.

Michael: Say 'Feel the hate'.

Brian/Emperor: Feel the hate flowing through you boy. Turn to the dark side.

Michael/Luke: I'll never turn to the dark side.

Brian/Emperor: Feel the hate.

Michael: Daddy you can't say anything good about the Emperor, can you?

Brian: Not in this version of the story no but in another version maybe he'd not want to kill, kill, kill.

Michael: Daddy, now you make the cracking sound, like this (making the sound and hand movement of the Emperor and then lying down on the floor).

Brian: (making the sounds and hand movements).

Michael: Daddy say, 'Feel the hate' and laugh.

Brian/Emperor: (laughing) Feel the hate flowing through you boy. Fulfill your destiny. Turn to the dark side.

Michael: What does destiny mean?

Brian: He means that because his father turned to the dark side he ought to as well.

Michael: But he doesn't, does he?

Brian: No. He's a Jedi.

Michael/Luke: (contorting himself, pretending to be shocked) I'll never turn to the dark side.

We continue for two or three minutes until Michael wants to go outside.

On this occasion, Michael chose to focus on interpretation of two words used in context in the original scene from the movie: destiny and hate. I interpreted the word destiny with the meaning I thought the Emperor inferred. I also connected Luke's resistance with a steadfast view of what it meant to be a Jedi warrior.

To interpret the phrase 'Feel the hate', Michael referenced what I had stated on several previous occasions about usage of the word 'hate'. I had made comments like the following: 'Hate is a very strong word. You should only use it when you can't say anything good about the person'. Michael was personifying the meaning of the word hate in the actions and discourse of the Emperor and I concurred with Michael's ethical evaluation. Additionally, to stress that the meanings of words are always contextualized I made an authoring reference to the notion I had introduced months previously that as we played we were making up our own versions of the narratives we read or viewed.

On other occasions Michael enacted versions of the following encounter from the movie when Darth Vader enters. The Emperor assumes that Vader will assist him in forcing Luke to join them or in killing Luke. But this moment is a crisis point for Vader. He refuses to follow orders. He then stops the torture by attacking the Emperor, lifting him up, and casting him to his death in the vortex of the spaceship. In doing so Vader's life force dissipates. He collapses. Luke removes his mask and he dies in Luke's arms.

> Michael: Daddy, you be the Emperor making the crackling sounds. Say 'Feel the hate'.
> Brian/Emperor: Feel the hate.
> Michael/Vader: Stop hurting and killing.
> Michael: You laugh and say 'No'.
> Brian/Emperor: No!
>
> Michael walks over and pretends to lift me up.
>
> Brian/Emperor: Vader. Stop. I command you.
>
> Michael pretends to throw me down and I yell with the sound as if I am falling down a bottomless hole.
>
> Michael: Now you're Luke. You take off my mask.
>
> He lies down, I enact taking off his mask, and he lies still with his head in my lap.
>
> Michael/Vader: I had to kill the Emperor. He wouldn't turn to the good side.
> Brian/Luke: I know.
> Michael/Vader: I'm glad I killed the Emperor. I couldn't let him kill you.
> Brian/Luke: Thank you, father.
>
> [I am thinking that if necessary I too would have done this to save my son.]
>
> Michael/Vader: Be a good emperor.
> Brian/Luke: How will I do that?
> Michael/Vader: Be trustworthy and good and tell the people what to do only when you need to.
> Brian/Luke: How can I be good?
> Michael/Vader: I was evil very much. Don't be like me.
>
> Michael closes his eyes.

Brian/Luke: Goodbye, father. Thank you for saving my life. I wish you
   didn't have to die.
Michael: Let's watch the movie.

I look for the scene in *Return of the Jedi* to view.

When Michael evaluated why Vader believed he had to kill the Emperor
he was recontextualizing the ethical position that the Emperor had to be
stopped from killing others. Michael/Vader was answerable not only to the
Emperor but to Luke. In a tug between following orders and saving his
son's life Michael/Vader chose the later even when it meant the loss of
his own life. Michael/Vader's choice was also in answer to all the times
when Michael/Luke had been answerable to the people he had rescued so
many times from planets the Emperor had destroyed.

Michael's response to the Emperor's deeds paralleled and extended the
many other monstrous actions he had stopped and which as heuristic
devices he had embodied and enacted and referenced in his synthesizing
words that I quoted at the beginning of this chapter:

'Would you kill all monsters?'
'Oh no, only those that have done many, many, many mean things . . .
killing people mostly.'

Ethical imagination

When Michael was thirteen we discussed a conscience struggle he had
experienced. One Saturday, the day after a Friday evening school skiing
trip, Michael showed me a $20 bill that he had found on the ground near his
bus. He said he didn't know whether to keep it or not. He told me the story
of where he had found it. I didn't tell Michael what to do but rather I raised
some questions for him and talked as if I was the person who had lost
the money. Michael took the money to school the next Monday and gave
it to the teacher who had been in charge of the trip. As no one had told her
that they had lost money she returned it to Michael at the end of the day.

In a subsequent conversation a week later Michael told me about his
experience of what had been for him an ethical dilemma.

I thought maybe I shouldn't have told you because at first I was
thinking I could have kept it without my conscience being tested. But I
was glad because if I hadn't told you I would probably have had an
inner battle with my conscience over the weekend. Over the weekend
I'd have been thinking should I turn it in or keep it. Personally I think I
would have decided to turn it in.

I asked Michael if what I had said had made him turn in the money. He responded, 'No. But it sort of speeded up the process and made me realize I should turn it in sooner.' Michael had experienced an inner struggle between competing inner and outer voices. He told me that when I had initially asked him what he thought he should do, and why, he was pulled in different directions.

• Other students had found money and kept it without turning it in.
• Someone had lost the money.
• It was impossible to know for certain who had dropped it.
• He had money in his hand.

As I had talked with him he said it was as if I had amplified these voices. In particular I had created a personal voice for the person who had lost the money. This voice had become more demanding than the decontextualized voice of 'finders keepers' and the dominant peer culture voices of others who had previously kept money for themselves. Finally, I had focused him on the golden rule question of what he would want someone else to do if he had lost the money.

Morson and Emerson's description of an evolving, relational, intersecting view of consciousness illuminates how Michael's ethical dilemma and our conversations about it were part of a life-long evolution of competing voices of conscience that we both experience and that in our interactions we have assisted in co-authoring.

> Consciousness takes shape, and never stops taking shape, as a process of interaction among authoritative and innerly persuasive discourses.
>
> (1990, p. 221)

All inner voices are not equally insistent as they pull on our desires to act, or not act, in the encounters we experience in particular situations. The more authoritative one voice is, the more pressing it will be in attempting to guide our actions. At the same time, the more innerly persuasive (as opposed to externally authoritative or authoritarian) a discourse is, the more it is our own but also the more open it is (as opposed to being resistant) to other's ideas and to development in new interactions. Play creates spaces where we can co-author innerly persuasive discourses that form into personal authoritative guides for ethical action.

The Chinese ideogram for listening consists of the symbols for two eyes, one ear, undivided attention, the heart, and you. When we really listen we have our full attention on the other person whom we hold in our heart. However, only one ear is on the other person because the other ear is turned inward.

Listening with compassion requires us to project into the lives of other people and to contemplate actions from their viewpoint. Listening with the heart is the beginning of ethical action because we can't treat people or other creatures as objects when we view the world as if we were them. Listening to people who aren't actually there requires an act of the ethical imagination, a human faculty that develops in play, and especially child-adult play

The co-authoring of play creates opportunities for children and adults to encounter and dialogue with viewpoints that would never be faced in everyday life. Over time and across imagined and everyday social spaces we co-author ethical identities that ground our conceptual ethical under-standing and guide moral interpretations of present dilemmas, past events, and possible futures.

I asked Michael, aged sixteen, what he thought makes a deed right or wrong, good or evil. He made clear a core aspect of his ethical disposition.

> You have to take it on a case by case basis. I agree with Baumeister in *Evil* [that he had just been reading] that's something's wrong if it's intentionally causing harm to someone else. I'd like to say that evil is just serving yourself and good is serving other people but that doesn't make sense because you do have to pay attention to yourself as well.

Being ethical is being answerable which means struggling to hear and see the world from the position of the perpetrators of deeds that cause pain or suffering as well as those who are the victims of oppressive actions. But in addition, we pay attention in ethical imagination to those inner voices of conscience that connect us with the deeds of people across time and space and which have developed heuristically to form more complex ideas about right-and-wrong. Collectively they are our evolving ethical identity.

My conversation with Michael turned to the question of when it might be right to kill someone.

> I don't think anyone really deserves to die, I don't think it's right, but I think it's sometimes necessary. I think it can be justified if you have no other option or if you've already tried all the other options and they haven't worked. You can kill someone in self-defense, if the person is directly threatening to kill you or somebody else particularly if that person isn't capable of defending themselves. It's always more complicated than that but that's the basic principle.

Michael's discourse had clear threads of connection to positions he had enacted in our mythic play and articulated aged four-and-a-half.

You can be mad but you can't be evil . . . being mad is saying you feel angry but being evil is hurting and you mustn't be evil . . . Sometimes I'm mad but I'm never evil.

'Would you kill all monsters?'
'Oh no, only those that have done many, many, many mean things . . . killing people mostly'
'And what would you do before deciding you had to kill it?'
'I'd teach it to stop doing those mean things.'

Michael's ethical identity connected him with people beyond those he might encounter face-to-face. I asked him about war and how some people argue that it's right to kill people in war because it's unavoidable.

War and individual conflict are completely different. War is institutionalized for one thing and it involves people who are not directly involved in the fighting, doing the shooting. The people who make the decisions are the ones with conflicts but the people who actually do the fighting are not. War also has the doctrine of collateral damage that it's justifiable to sacrifice a person's life without their consent 'for the greater good'. I don't think that's right. I think if someone's going to sacrifice their life they should at least have a say in whether they're going to die or not.

As I looked for a quotation to end this chapter that would illustrate the heart of co-authoring ethical identities through play, I shared several possibilities with Michael. He had recently been reading about Buddhism and chose this quote from the Dalai Lama.

The key to genuine world peace . . . is inner peace, and the foundation of that is a sense of understanding and respect for each other as human beings based on compassion and love. Some may dismiss love and compassion as impractical and unrealistic, but I believe their practice is the true source of success. Compassion is by nature, peaceful and gentle, but it is also very powerful. It is a sign of true inner strength. To achieve it we do not need to become religious, nor do we need any ideology. All that is necessary is for us to construct our fundamental human qualities such as caring for others, respecting them, and being just and honest.

(1999, p. xi)

Chapter 5

Play as ethical pedagogy

Ethical pedagogy

Play as an ethical pedagogy creates spaces in early childcare settings for child–adult co-authoring of ethical selves and identities. The practice of an ethical pedagogy requires a 'pedagogy of listening and radical dialogue' (Dahlberg and Moss, 2005, p. 98) that is fundamental to the approaches in the preprimary schools and infant-toddler centres within the Italian city of Reggio Emilia (Edwards et al., 1994; Rinaldi, 2005). The Reggio philosophy is discussed in detail by Dahlberg and Moss (2005) in a companion volume in this series.

Pedagogy that develops from such philosophical assumptions 'encompasses learning and caring within a broad concern with all aspects of life' (ibid., p. 91). In using the term pedagogy I reject false dichotomous beliefs that would attempt to separate the social constructivist processes of learning from teaching, conceptualize them as divided between adult and child, or view caring relationships as optional in classrooms. In doing so, early childhood care can be conceptualized as creating 'spaces in civil society where children and adults can engage together in a potentially wide range of possibilities' around 'the locus of the ethics of an encounter' where children and adults might collaboratively examine 'the question of being together' (ibid., pp. 91, 95).

Reggio Emilia classrooms are physically, emotionally, socially, culturally, and intellectually like extended families and communities where children mostly learn alongside adults about matters of mutual interest (Katz, 1994, p. 31). Learning in Reggio classrooms revolves around collaborative long-term inquiry projects, as well as short-term activities, all of which involve 'joint exploration among children and adults who together open topics to speculation and discussion' (Edwards, Gandini, and Forman, 1994, p. 5). Long-term projects are 'open-ended spirals' that revolve around the core socio-cultural and ethical question of what it means to be together in the changing physical and social environment of the preschool (ibid., p. 7). Access to a wide range of materials and supportive relationships with adults promotes use of 'the hundred languages of children' as children explore ideas and express themselves, often working in small groups, using words, movement, drawing, painting, building sculptures, collage, music etc. (ibid., p. 3). In one project the children's study of dinosaurs led to a desire to represent what they had discovered through models. When a group of children wanted to build a life-size dinosaur they engaged in an extensive inquiry not only into how to build their model to accurately represent the dinosaur but also into where they should house it (Rankin, 1994).

Children in Reggio classrooms are viewed as 'powerful, active, competent protagonists of their own growth' (Edwards et al., 1994, p. 180) while adults are 'fully attentive to the children, and at the same time, taking responsibility for recording and documenting what is observed and then using it as a basis for decision-making shared with children and parents' (ibid., p. 181). Adults view themselves as 'partners, nurturers, and guides in children's learning' (Fu et al., 2002, p. 6). Through close observation of children, representations of the children's work, extensive documentation, and repeated revisitation of children's understanding, teachers co-create knowledge with children. Adults in Reggio classrooms view those in their care as young people with unique needs and desires, not as children whose classroom activities are likely to be judged according to predetermined standards of what is 'developmentally appropriate' for them.

The pedagogy of listening and radical dialogue, practiced by adults in Reggio classrooms, resonates with Bakhtin's theories of ethics and the self. To be addressed by a child means that we must be listening. To be able to answer, and to create spaces for children to address one another, we must be in radical dialogue with children.

> In radical dialogue, based on listening, as a teacher you have to participate together with the child, entering a space together where both teacher and child are actively listening and trying to construct meaning out of the situation.
>
> (Dahlberg and Moss, 2005, p. 101)

Listening in Reggio, as the premise for any learning relationship, is active, respectful, open, sensitive, question-forming, tied to close watching, and always contextualized. Listening is not easy because it 'can make us both surprised and shocked as we find out how rich and intelligent children's thoughts are' (ibid., p. 101).

Vivian Gussin Paley also placed listening and adult curiosity at the core of her pedagogy. She puts it like this:

> The key is curiosity, and it is curiosity, not answers, that we model. As we seek to learn more about a child, we demonstrate the acts of

observing, listening, questioning, and wondering. When we are curious about a child's words and our response to those words, the child feels respected. The child is respected.

(1986, p. 127)

Readings (1996) argues that we should 'listen to thought' and we can only do so by listening to the voice of an Other. He turns to Levinas to develop the idea of ethical responsibility toward a person as an Other. This theory parallels Bakhtin's theory of answerability. Dahlberg and Moss note the apparent paradox between a pedagogy that positions an adult as both open and welcoming of children while creating a sense of difference so that children's actual ideas can be heard and responded to as Other than theirs.

> To leave room for radical difference and the singularity of the Other, the pedagogical relationship must also leave space between, it must be a dissociating relationship. . . . The child becomes a complete stranger, not a known quantity through classificatory systems and normative practices whose progress and familiar development must be steered to familiar and known ends.
>
> (p. 93)

Playing with children creates spaces for listening and radical dialogue in the ethics of encounters with Others that children imagine. In the projective space of an imagined world, as well as in the contemplative co-authoring space formed in the overlap with the social spaces of everyday life, children can appear very strange as they project into the possible selves of play to move and talk in ways that are quite Other than the selves developing for participation in everyday life. Listening to children who are imagining monstrous actions or exuberant heroic deeds can be difficult. It's understandable why adults would not only wish that children would conform to the norms of sameness and predictability that a Reggio philosophy resists but even chastise children who are being boisterous or loud.

Ethical identities can be co-authored in classroom play, but only if supported by the sort of radical dialogue envisioned for Reggio classrooms. As adults, we must be ready to answer children who address us and in turn address them with the expectation of an authentic exchange within the narrative worlds that captivate their imagination.

To really listen to children and be curious we must be able to project into how they view the world. All young children play not only to understand the world they observe, but also to think about how their experience of the world might be different. When Michael was about two he pushed a plastic truck along the carpet making a truck sound and asked, 'When is a truck?' Only by joining in as if I too were driving a truck and talking with him did I discover that he wanted to know what makes a truck a 'truck' rather than a car or a bus. Weeks later Michael was using blocks and his toy truck to wonder about the power of a machine that he had seen knock down a wall. As I talked with him, enacted imagined events, and pretended to be knocked down, we imagined what it might take to demolish a house, a road, or a city. A few months later when we read an illustrated flap-book, *Piggy at the Wheel*, Michael focused on a picture where Piggy had inadvertently covered someone up when dumping a load of sand. As we played inside, and then outside in a sandpit, he loved to pretend to cover me up, sometimes say 'Sorry', and check to see that I was not hurt. When we switched positions to dump sand on him, he giggled when we pretended that I didn't see him, that he had been hurt, and as I made extravagant apologies.

In one classroom in Reggio Emilia, a child-created poster hangs on a wall. It lists the rights of children that include the following:

> Children have the right to have friends, otherwise they do not grow up too well.
>
> Children have the right to live in peace.
>
> To live in peace means to be well, to live together, to live with things that interest us, to have friends, to think about flying, to dream.
>
> (Gandini, 1994, p. 135)

Everyone has the right to live in peace with friends in the everyday social world of the classroom. It is adults' responsibility to nurture, maintain, and negotiate a peaceful community. At the same time, in the imagined spaces that open up in parallel with everyday classroom spaces, I believe that children have the right to explore what might happen to them or their friends if they met a careless truck driver, a giant, or a vampire. And children who want to pretend to fly as a dragon, make friends with a wolfman, or be chased by a dinosaur surely have that right as much as a child who wants to pretend to be a princess, have a tea party with friends, or be safe-and-sound at home. Paley's contrasting analysis of imagined and everyday worlds illuminates how play creates possibilities not present in adult everyday life. 'A different reality coexisted beside my own, containing more vitality, originality, and wide-open potential' (1986, p. 124).

Play is an attitude to communication and community in which hundreds of additional languages can become accessible, appealing, and productively used to explore how the world might be, as well as how it is. Michael could talk dinosaur when he was three as he discovered the destructive power of Cretaceous predators and their relationship with their prey. At the same age, Zoë talked on the phone before she ever actually made a call. At four, she dressed up to speak and move as a woman going to Australia, and

Michael at that age conversed as a Jedi while he explored how he might stop Imperial forces from destroying planets.

Playing with children allows adults to co-author meaning, including ethical understanding, but only if they can use the languages of imagination. Play as ethical pedagogy requires adults to do more than observe children and facilitate in the creation and documentation of their work. Adults who listen have to do more than talk about ideas from the outside. Adults may have to be able to talk dinosaur or Jedi, imagine being a different gender, or talk as if they are driving a truck or using a pretend phone.

Ethical pedagogy means that as adults we have to be prepared to act on what we hear and follow children into whatever imagined worlds they choose to enter and explore. We have to allow our selves to be positioned by children and then talk and move as if we were any of the imaginary people or creatures that populate those other worlds. We must also be ready to be addressed, expect to be answerable, and provide children with ethical evaluations of events that can then be explored and dialogized in authentic conversations.

Co-authoring ethical identities

A Bakhtinian approach to the co-authoring of ethical identities embraces whatever ethical questions arise for people in the particulars of a situation. Such a poststructural view recognizes that ethical dilemmas can be explored in fractured intersecting dialogized narratives told from multiple viewpoints in discourses that do not resolve into neat moralistic conclusions.

I have argued that the core long-term ethical pedagogical goal is to promote children's agency along with relational dispositions of answerability and addressivity. We want children, as ethical beings, both to take responsibility for their actions, and to be ready to question other people's actions, in particular events and specific relationships. Play extends contexts beyond the everyday to the often more problematic events in narrative worlds.

A dialogic approach places one discourse in relation to another as people are addressed with how to act in particular contexts. When children embrace refractive experiences, as past and present discourses collide, they author ethical understanding.

Over time, some discourses become more authoritative. Beliefs about how to be 'good' or how to do the 'right' thing are never static if they are internally persuasive because they are open to being affected by another situation, another viewpoint, or another person's interpretation both in imagined worlds and in everyday life.

Discourses of moral development

Early childhood educators who rely on the dominant modernist theory of moral development, as I argued in chapter one, have a very different goal for children. Their view of agency is limited to autonomous, rational, self-regulation. Without a Vygotskian perspective on learning, children are viewed as locked into their interrelated stages of cognitive, affective, and moral development. Without a Bakhtinian view on ethics, the self, and discourse, young children are regarded as not-adult individuals at the start of a long march toward a mature application of universal ethical principles.

The discourse of developmental theories assumes that because children construct understandings, moral and otherwise, it takes individual children time to learn how to be 'good' and that what is considered 'appropriate' behavior varies by stage of development. Play, as I noted in chapter two, is largely regarded in opposition to or as an escape from reality, and though valued as a useful activity for generic development, the imagined spaces of play are not embraced as sites for the exploration of ethical issues or for moral development via child–adult play.

Moral development, it is assumed, will be promoted by children's involvement with adults in abstract rational activities like the agreement of rules, decision-making processes, and the acceptance of consequences for unacceptable behavior (DeVries and Zan 1994, pp. 126–144). However, moral perspective-taking (the ability to decenter and see from another person's viewpoint; the ability to think abstractly about the morality of a deed) is judged as an individual ability rather than anticipated as the product of child–adult interactions. The moral ability to take another's point of view is not expected until the preschool years are long passed. As Edwards and Ramsey put it, 'Before the age of about seven, children cannot simultaneously coordinate the perspectives of different people. Instead they focus on the perspective of one person at a time'. Young children are to a large extent regarded as amoral because it is assumed that they are unable to engage in moral perspective taking and thus cannot 'resolve moral conflicts by balancing competing claims' (1986, p. 152).

An implicit acceptance of these assumptions will affect how adults approach and interpret their interactions with children. Adults are likely to assume that children are largely unable to see from another person's point of view. When combined with a rational choice approach to morality, adults may conclude after talking rationally to a child that he or she just cannot shift their perspective. This may explain the approach by the preschool teachers I observed once when Michael was about five.

I was present during preparations for a class photograph. There was a disruption when a boy, Jeremy, appeared to deliberately hit a girl,

Sophie, in the face with a ball. The young teachers remained calm but seemed very emotionally detached. Jeremy was told 'use your words' to explain why he had hit the now sobbing girl and he was asked how he thought Sophie felt. He did not visibly respond. Sophie was in floods of tears. She was removed from the room while Jeremy sat alone at a table for a few minutes until the photograph was taken when Jeremy was brought into the group. Sophie was still too upset to join in.

All adults want children to be responsible for their everyday actions. Moral developmentalists view interpersonal conflict as inevitable and productive since its resolution may lead to moral growth through attempting to take another person's perspective. Where there is conflict between children, teachers are advised to mediate the conflict. Typically teachers ask individual children to calmly explain why they did something. They help them to try to see cognitively from another's perspective by asking how the person directly affected feels about what happened, by attempting restitution, and by having the children accept consequences (DeVries and Zan 1994, pp. 79–103).

Perspective-taking is typically promoted with questions like 'How do you think she feels?' Ideally, the classroom is an example of Kohlberg's 'just community' (Power et al., 1989) where the principle of justice is used to guide the resolution of conflicts, with such questions as 'What would happen if everyone did that?' However, rational talk may not be successful in promoting perspective-taking even when it focuses on feelings, moral principles, and future behavior.

In an example given by DeVries and Zan, a teacher (T) mediates a conflict between two boys who minutes previously have been playing together (ibid., pp. 94 – 95). Both had used tape to cover their mouths and had been happily playing together until M had pulled the tape off D's mouth. D had pinched M in retaliation. After the teacher had established the facts, and M had accepted that he had indeed pulled the tape off 'hard', negotiations continued until the children were no longer visibly angry with one another.

M: I pulled it off hard.
T: How did you feel?
M: I didn't feel anything.
T: You didn't feel anything. Well, D did, and it really made him angry, and that's why he chose to pinch you. It's not really okay. What should you do instead of pinching?
D: I don't like (inaudible).
T: You don't like what? What did he do that you didn't like?
D: I didn't like when he took that tape off hard.
M: I don't like it when you pinched me.

T: Can you understand why he did that? I know he probably should have used his words, but do you understand why he did it?

M: (nods)

T: You didn't use your words. So what should you do, M, the next time if you see that D has tape on his mouth again? What should you say to D?

M: Take the tape off?

T: And what do you think D would probably do? Is it okay now? You guys are not angry any more? Is it okay?

(The boys assent, and return to their play.)

In contrast with the incident I had observed, in this example the teacher worked hard to get the children to feel responsible for their actions. She managed to get each child to say what each did not like about the other's actions. She interpreted M's nodding to mean that he understood D's position. She evaluated D's pinching reaction as 'not really okay', got M to accept that he should 'use his words' rather than use physical violence, and presumably would have got D to similarly agree. Finally, she approved of M's suggestion that the next time he would say 'Take the tape off' rather than pull at it.

The children probably felt somewhat responsible for what had happened, but applying Bakhtin's theory, were they answerable for their actions? The teacher was very skilfully using rational talk but how much did the children shift their positions? They stated their prior views but did they change those views by seeing and feeling from the perspective of the other? They knew that the teacher evaluated the tape pulling and pinching as wrong but did they each evaluate their own behavior as wrong? Did they shift from monologic positions to more dialogic ones? They accepted the plan that the teacher suggested for the future but did they author it too?

Child–adult positioning-play could have been used at the time, or more likely at a later time, in order to promote perspective-taking and co-authoring understanding. In chapter four I gave several examples of how I was able to use play in everyday situations to assist Michael to see the consequences of his everyday actions. Our nose-play when he was eighteen months old showed him the pain he had not intended but that I had felt when he grabbed my nose. A similar approach could have been used with Jeremy. The positioning-play that I used with our running-into-the-road play when Michael was about two could have been used with M and D to re-enact their exchange and allow both boys to project into the other's experience.

In play, a discourse about a past event can be made visible and present. Talking about a past (or future) event can be very difficult for young children especially when their attention becomes more focused on present discourse because it is more immediate (as it is likely to be when a crying child leaves the room as a photograph is being taken) or more intense (as it may be when a teacher is talking to you). In any event, play can make discourse about a past event more present.

Child–adult play can promote co-authoring identities. Play can create the productive experiences of refraction between children's interpretations of a prior event and present adult (or child) discourse about its physical or emotional consequences. Over time, pretending to be other people can assist children to take up other perspectives that refract with previous discourses, not to advance them through a particular moral stage of development, but rather to become answerable for their actions as part of developing a disposition to answer people who address them.

Discourses of character education

In their historical overview, and accompanying discourse analysis of character education proposals for funding, Smagorinsky and Taxel (2005) analyze two pervasive contrasting views of character that inform approaches to moral education. They characterize these approaches using Lakoff's (2002) political metaphors of the nurturing parent and the strict father.

The nurturing parent approach encompasses Noddings' ethic of care, Dewey's theories of democracy and progressivism, as well as Kohlberg's idea of the school as a just community. A nurturing parent discourse is founded on assumptions that 'the focus of character education needs to be on the way the school environment works and feels . . . emphasis ought to be on transforming the educational structures rather than on forming individual characters' (Smagorinsky and Taxel, 2005, p. 45).

An approach to moral education for older children using classroom drama, outlined by Joe Winston (1998), is in alignment with a nurturing parent discourse. Winston grounds his pedagogy for school-aged children in neo-Aristotelian theory of virtue ethics with its view of a rational, atomistic self and the creation of a classroom that is a 'community of virtue' via evolving conversations about the complexity of moral life (p. 174). It was Aristotle who, in Western philosophy, first argued that people become ethical by becoming virtuous. In other words, we become kind or brave by repeatedly being kind or brave. Aristotle argued that virtues develop through nurturing the habits of being virtuous rather than by moral reasoning. Using this theory (as developed by e.g. MacIntyre, 1981), Winston gives useful extensive examples of how teachers can project into narratives alongside children through dramatization. However, his view of action in drama (or play) is only as a rehearsal of virtuous behavior. He does not value imagining and enacting immoral action. For Winston, contemplation for moral meaning is in relation to predetermined virtues that are more concerned with moral judgment on others' actions than with evaluation of one's own action through positioning-play. Rather than dialogizing ethical discourse to promote a disposition of answerability, Winston's approach could tend to allow children to dichotomize actions as moral or immoral and thus distance their selves from exploring the morality of their possible actions.

In contrast with nurturing parent approaches to character education, Smagorinsky and Taxel argue that the dominant 'traditional values' approach of the strict father arose out of a desire 'to restore the more authoritarian approach to character' by critics of the values clarification project and what they perceived as a pervasive liberal view of moral freedom of choice. They reject what they regard as 'moral relativism and feelings and endorse a more didactic role for adults in teaching values to their society's young' (ibid., p. 31).

Like the theory of moral development, this dominant character education approach to moral teaching assumes that children become ethical through rational discussion and individual responsibility. Unlike developmentalism, this approach to character education advocates consequences that are largely externally dictated and imposed.

The character education movement (Lickona, 1991) combines a theory of virtue ethics with the modernist and Enlightenment assumption (outlined in chapter one) that to know how to behave people should rationally identify and follow universal moral rules. Teachers using character education methods adopt a behaviorist didactic approach (rather than a cultural or social constructionist one). Character educators argue that children develop good character when teachers and schools instill good habits in children that they practice over time.

In describing character education as 'the new moral education', Ryan (1989) argues that 'The role of the school is not simply to make children smart, but to make them smart *and* good. We must help children acquire the skills, the attitudes, and the dispositions that will help them live well and that will enable the common good to flourish'.

The aims of the character education movement are laudable and are ones that I support. Character educators argue from the reasonable premise that people can agree on which values children should learn. For example, the American Institute of Character Education identified these virtues to be taught K-6 [Years 1–7]: being honest, generous, just, kind, and helpful; having courage and convictions along with tolerance of the views of others; making good use of time and talents; providing security for self and dependents; understanding and fulfilling the obligations of citizenship; standing for truth; and defending basic human rights under a government of law (McClellan 1999, p. 90).

Law, a philosopher who values rational discussions of morality, notes inherent dangers in character education. 'Many people believe that simply getting kids to do what they're told is character education. This idea often leads to an imposed set of rules and a system of rewards and punishments that produce temporary and limited behavioral changes, but they do little or nothing to affect the underlying character of the children'. As Law notes, some adults, 'want the opportunity to drill children mindlessly accepting their own religious and moral beliefs . . . while their intellects are firmly switched off' (2006, p. 129).

Few character educators believe that a child has any more responsibility than to learn to name values and then to apply them in virtuous behavior. 'Like arithmetic, the teaching of character values such as "responsibility" and "respect" must be purposeful and direct. Students should hear and see the words, learn their meanings, identify appropriate behaviors, and practice and apply the values' (Brooks and Kann, 1993, p. 20). Though Lickona advocates cooperative learning, teaching conflict resolution, the need for cognitive perspective-taking, and democratic classrooms, he operates on the premise that teaching should be a 'recovery of shared, objectively important [universal] ethical values' to 'define our responsibilities in a democracy' (1991, p. 9).

William Bennett, former US Education Secretary in the Reagan Administration, has been highly influential in promoting the character education movement that has received federal funding since the 1990s. Bennett (1993; 1995) synthesizes core assumptions about the character education approach that I find highly problematic.

- children will become virtuous if they are rationally instructed in morality by being told what is right and wrong;
- instruction comes through exposure to the modeling of virtuous behavior in classrooms and the moral content of carefully selected stories which are read and discussed to identity moral rules;
- obedient behavior equals moral action.

Bennett believes that 'Moral education must involve following rules of good behavior. It must involve developing good habits, which come only through repeated practice.' He argues that children will achieve 'moral literacy' if they rationally 'identify the forms and content of the traits of character we most admire'. They can do so through reading virtuous stories that 'can be important moral influences' (1993, pp. 12–13). Horror literature did not make it into his collections of stories (ibid., 1993; 1995).

Character educators view adults as moral 'trainers' and children as the recipients of adults' superior moral understanding. Bennett argues that 'character training must provide examples by placing children in the company of responsible adults who show an allegiance to good character, who demonstrate the clear difference between right and wrong in their own everyday habits' (1995, p. 12). Bennett has been highly criticized for his moralizing tone and paternalistic attitude. Ayers (1994), for example, asks who is to decide whether or not an adult is adequately 'responsible' or of sufficient 'good character'? Further, because adults are assumed to be moral but children are not, there is no recognition that children might already have developed ethical understanding or that adults might have anything to learn about their own ethical identity as they interact with children.

Though this approach to character education adopts a culturalist view of learning, assuming that virtue is acquired across time through participation in practice, character educators' behaviorist approach to teaching is inconsistent both with a social constructivist theory of learning and with ethical pedagogy. Ayers captures the ethical vacuum in character education. As he notes, 'youngsters remain in effect passive recipients rather than active constructors of values' (1994, p. 10).

The caring relationships of ethical pedagogy

Play as an ethical pedagogy must be grounded in active caring relationships among adults and children. In proposing the need for developing caring relationships in school, as well as at home, Noddings begins with the recognition that 'all people everywhere want to be cared for' and be in a positive relation with other beings (2002, p. 21). Over two decades, Noddings (1984; 1992; 2002) has extended Gilligan's (1982) work, to lay out a manifesto that all child–adult relationships should be guided by an ethic of care. Noddings stresses that caring relationships benefit adults as well as children, because 'Caregiver and cared-for enter a mutually satisfying relation' in which a young child learns to be cared for and later how to care for others while a caregiver learns how to respond and then receive care (2002, p. 15).

When caring adults project into imagined worlds with children they collaboratively create whatever landscape they explore with imagined people and creatures. Play is ideally a workshop for life constructed in parallel with, and supported by, the emotional, social, and physical safety of daily living. Play won't be regarded by children as an escape from everyday life if they know that they are cared for by the adults in their lives who are supportive of, and participate in, their explorations of how the world might be.

As Diana Kelly-Byrne (1989) and Maureen Kendrick (2003) both discovered in playing with young girls they had not previously known (aged respectively eight and six), authentic, caring, trusting, intimate relationships can develop quickly when adults play with children. Over periods of only a few months they were each able to communicate with a child to co-author understanding about life in ways that did not happen in everyday exchanges even with loving parents and caring teachers.

I too have found that deep relationships can begin to be forged with previously unknown children when I have played with them even for short periods. In one school where I have been a regular visiting teacher for over a decade, children are invariably eager to see me on return visits when we play together. Some children continue to engage with me in imagined worlds as we pick up and carry forward previous brief conversations that began in a play world. I had played with one six-year-old girl and her friends for about an hour one day. They had helped me/Baby Bear look for possible foster parents. Baby Bear never found any suitable parents that day. Over the next five years each time I met her in half-a-dozen situations the same girl continued the search. Our play became more jocular as the years passed.

Child–adult power relationships

Child–adult relationships are unavoidably power relationships. As Foucault (1977, 1978, 1980) has shown, power circulates in the discourses of everyday routines, rituals, and interactions like those of classrooms. Power shifts among children as well as adults across time and space. Power ebbs and flows, to accumulate and stabilize with those who are given and/or assume that they have the knowledge, the responsibility, the authority, the right, or the privilege to use discourse to frame and interpret the 'truth' of situations and make decisions to act in ways that affect others' lives. An ethical pedagogy based on Reggio principles undermines normalizing institutional practices, educational discourses, and adult assumptions, all of which can legitimate adult domination of preschool classroom activities.

Adults tend to use power to impose predetermined controls over what activities are 'appropriate' especially how adults and children can use space and move. Controls are particularly apparent in relation to pretend play. Brian Sutton-Smith notes the adult assumption that 'generally we take for granted that in this power relationship we adults will remain in control'. In championing the rights of children to play on their own terms, he notes that 'the central issue for children may be how they can gain sufficient power in the relationship to allow their own deep need for fantasy empowerment to take its course' (1994, p. 33). Mythic play, in particular, is likely to be banned. Rules and prohibitions may be justified in terms of socialization, but Grace and Tobin argue that 'something about children's delight in mock violence threatens adult authority and disrupts socially constructed notions about childhood innocence' (1997, p. 173).

Anne Phelan laments the fact that many teachers turn their experiences of institutional pressures to control into self-discipline that erases their own pleasure in being with children. In advocating playing with children I agree that 'we must no longer allow our worries about order to over-ride our desire to teach and to have pleasure in the doing' (1997, p. 97). Phelan, along with Grace and Tobin, advocates a Bakhtinian (1984b) carnivalesque approach in early childhood classrooms. She would replace the often sterile, closed, and orderly system of controlling adults with 'a complex ambivalent admixture of order/disorder, pleasure/pain, fear/hope, laughter/misery, and freedom/oppression' (ibid., p. 93). Encouraging child–child play, as well as child–adult pretend play that follows children's agendas, will open up such a vibrant, exploratory, pedagogical space.

Power and positioning

Power is exercised in relation to others rather than being an individual possession. One person's power is always relative to the power that other people assume, accept, relinquish, resist, contest, or negotiate. As people use power to position one another they shape each other's identities.

There are inevitably shifts in power when children and/or adults interact. There may be a jostling for power that can escalate into a power struggle. Adults tend to assume that children should be compliant and that adults have the right to impose their prior understandings on situations and decisions. Adults can also easily assume that they possess superior knowledge and interpretive power to understand what children say, do, think, and feel without really listening and talking with children. Adults can interpret children's movements, desires, or verbal responses as 'out-of-control', 'inappropriate', or 'not normal' and then attempt to negate such action. Such adults can easily take resistance to be a challenge to the power they believe they ought to have. Conversely, adults can miss power struggles among children that should be mediated because children are being quiet and still (Paley, 1986).

Child–adult play can feel disempowering for adults because in play landscapes children are more likely to position themselves as much more powerful than adults. Because imagined power relationships are foregrounded over existing ones, adults cannot rely on their pre-existing authority as teacher or parent but must enter an encounter with whatever power and authority flows to them in the discourses of imaginary worlds.

To be able to explore with adults how possible selves could position others, children must feel emotionally as well as physically safe. They must feel free to express themselves with adults who can project emotionally and physically, as well as intellectually, into imagined spaces. As Boler shows so compellingly, because emotion and power are intertwined, adults can easily undermine building the sort of close community that needs to form as people play together. Adult predetermined 'appropriate' physical and emotional responses can create distance from children and a fear of allowing expression of 'inappropriate' emotions like extreme hatred or love (1999, pp. 139–140).

Power gets stabilized in the predictability of relationships, expectations, contexts, and the layout of physical space. From when he first began to bring narratives to life in play Michael consistently had more power in play contexts. Only if I was worried about our physical safely or other people's reactions did I try to control Michael's actions when we played. Invariably I reacted to Michael's imagined use of power within whatever power relationship we were enacting.

How a person uses power to position others makes a difference in terms of how power flows and accumulates among people. Children will experience this social reality as they play. When children and adults project into imagined worlds they can play with and explore how apparently stable power relationships and people's related authority can shift and be challenged or renegotiated. Children can explore what they might do if ethical evaluations led them to want to resist or renegotiate relationships.

Adult power relationship stances

In chapter one I outlined how power relationships can be conceptualized as shifting among three intersecting stances: using power over others, for others, and with others. Adults use power over children, for example, when they control their bodies. They use power for children when they protect them from physical or emotional harm. And when adults negotiate they use power with children. The relative dominance of each relational power stance makes a difference to the quality of the adult–child relationship created over time and thus to the ethical identities co-authored in everyday spaces. Ethical pedagogy requires adults in preschool classrooms to share power with children as much as possible in order to create trusting collaborative relationships and spaces that will support children's ethical explorations with each other and with adults in everyday and playful interactions.

Using power *with* others in dialogic discourse is ideally the dominant relational power stance, within which others are nested. I believe that adults should use power over children most sparingly. I conceptualize an authoritative stance that attempts to control or limit children's actions through largely monologic discourse as ideally dialogically in relationship with, or nested within, a nurturing use of power for others. Authoritarian stances are ethically untenable; they are not dialogic, they impose ideas, can dismiss feelings, and will close down relationships.

Children play with power relationships when they project into imagined worlds shifting among possible uses of power over, for, and with others. Michael used power over me when he attacked as Mr Hyde. He used power

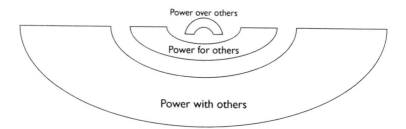

Figure 5.1 Power over/for/with others

for me when as Dr Jekyll he gave me medicine. He used power with me when we negotiated as police-officers what to do about Hyde.

When adults play with children their power relationships are made more complex and fluid as they interact in the imagined and authoring spaces that come to the fore in addition to everyday social spaces. For example, a collaborative dialogic sharing of power with one another in the everyday can be supplemented with power relationships that can range from the oppressive to the altruistic in imagined worlds in addition to an adult supportive position in an authoring space.

Playing with power in caring relationships

When adults establish caring relationships with children, as individuals and as a group, everyone is protected into an exploration of how people could use power and might respond to others' use of power. Adults and children can play with power. Only when children play, and especially when they play with adults, will they be able to experiment with the myriad ways in which they might use power, from the most oppressive uses of power over others to the most supportive and nurturing use of power for other people. And as Michael did, children can then explore how they might answer those users of power and dialogically author facets of their ethical identities.

When I played with Michael we created landscapes for expeditions into worlds where Michael could experience how power circulates, stabilizes, and is contested. Michael experienced how power is never an individual matter, is always contextualized, and shifts among humans (and non-humans) in different situations. Mr McGregor may call Peter a thief but when he cannot catch him because Peter runs faster or hides in a watering can he loses power. Peter gains power if Mr McGregor listens to him when he says that he's taken carrots because he is hungry.

From when Michael first projected into narrative worlds in play he could imagine that he had the power to move, interpret, and evaluate actions just as characters in those stories did in relation to other characters. All possible selves could be addressed and be answerable for the consequences of their actions. Imagining he was Mr McGregor, he could run after me as Peter Rabbit shouting, 'Stop thief!' as he threatened to put me in a pie. As Peter he could improvise and plead with me, as Mr McGregor, to give him food for his family.

Using power over others

Using power over others is the most common way that we conceptualize power relationships – the power to get what you want despite the objections or views of others (Weber, 1962). The histories of oppression, colonization, and environmental degradation as well as the everyday realities of domination, aggression, racism, and sexism are examples of people using power over others in asymmetric power relationships.

Foucault has analyzed how people oppress others through a consistent use of power to discipline and control. Authoritarian adults use power over children, not only to contain their bodies but also to ignore, dismiss, or attempt to restrict their ideas and emotions (Boler, 1999). Leavitt describes a particularly distressing example as she shows how adult rigidity in the management of routines actually creates or exacerbates most problematic situations.

> The caregivers arranged twelve infants between twelve and twenty-four months, on the floor for 'story time'. One caregiver sat before the children and flipped through the pages of the book, pointing to the pictures while repeatedly asking the toddlers, 'What is it? What is it?' A few children in the back of the group stood up in order to better see the pictures. They were pushed down by the second caregiver who had been standing behind them. 'Sit down, Tyler!' she commanded, as she took her hand and firmly pressed it into his shoulder, pushing him to the floor. A few other children attempted to stand up. The caregiver then grabbed each of their arms and pulled them back down to a sitting position. Meanwhile, the first caregiver continued to question the children about the pictures in the book.
>
> (2001, p. 153)

Believing that children need to be told what is right and wrong, moralizing adults can use the power that their authority gives them to tell children what to believe and how they ought to behave. When adults confuse pretend fighting with violent behavior, stop children from playing, and lecture them about not pretending to be bad, they can actually become oppressive while believing that they are being virtuous.

People are not monsters or heroes but their actions can be monstrous or heroic. When we try to force others to do what we want and don't listen but ignore others' views, then we are trying to take power from others and we are beginning to act like a monster. Like all children, Michael and Zoë could stamp their feet, wail, and shout to demand what they wanted. It's no wonder that adults often jokingly refer to children as 'little monsters'. In contrast, when adults think of children as 'little angels' they are likely to remember moments like their spontaneous smiles, loving hugs, or generosity.

Like all parents, at times I forced our children to do something. I could act monstrously at times as I became more authoritarian. I started to become monstrous if I stopped listening and became angry when they didn't comply with demands. One cold winter day Michael, aged four, was in tears when I tried to force him to put on his coat and get into the car because we were late. I hadn't listened to why he wanted to put on his gloves before his coat. Once I stopped pressing him, took deep breaths, and actually talked with him I discovered that he wanted to keep out the cold from the gap between his coat and gloves. He agreed that I'd dash him into the already warm car and that we'd put on his gloves and coat when we arrived at preschool. We had negotiated what I began to refer to as 'win–win' solutions as opposed to the inevitable 'win–lose' outcomes of an oppressive use of power over another.

When necessary I am authoritative so that children will pay attention to other points of view. I do my best to make authoritative moves as dialogic as possible in order to promote children's agency. I would give Michael or Zoë the sort of explanations they needed that ranged from where we were going to why we wouldn't rent a particular movie. I would get their input as much as possible ('You choose the four books we'll take with us to the restaurant'), tell them in advance about necessary changes in activity ('When I've gone up and down stairs it'll be time to go'), give them choices ('Do you want to read a story before you go to bed or when you're in bed?'), and give them another viewpoint on something we had done that had upset them ('I know you wanted to go to Chicago with mom, but you would have had to have been in meetings with her. Do you remember how much you wanted to leave the last time you came to that meeting with us?').

An ethical pedagogy embraces children projecting into imagined worlds so that they can explore how people engage in, encounter, and resist oppression. All the monsters that Michael embodied as we pretended to be in oppressive encounters used power over others. Monsters who only think about themselves force others to comply. They may hurt or kill those who do not. For example, as the dragon, he loved to pretend to fly and swoop down breathing fire on me as St George. I would run terrified and narrate how houses and crops would burst into flames. If I told him to stop and he attacked again he was using the power of an oppressor.

Using power over others is also part of the history of defenders and protectors fighting to stop aggression. However, this authoritative use of power is nested dialogically within using power for others. In other words, defenders use power as allies of the oppressed who are unable to resist as effectively as they are. Michael imagined this altruistic use of power when he embodied all the heroes who, in the stories we read, only think about others. Michael's violence was most often the righteous violence of a heroic champion. When we switched our positions and he pretended to brandish his sword as George he yelled at the dragon to stop hurting people. If I didn't cease he attacked to make me stop. As we played, if I was the dragon and I did stop attacking then he would cease fighting.

Using power for others

Noddings and Gilligan implicitly place using power for others at the centre of their view of school and family relationships and the ethic of care that they propose. Like Levinas (1989) who argued that caring arises out of the need of the other, they stress that it is adults' responsibility to care for children based on their needs. As Noddings puts it, 'We are called upon to listen, to respond to others according to their needs, not according to their membership in a symbolic community or according to "universal" rules that they them-selves may reject' (2002, p. 67). In challenging a masculinist discourse that discounts 'feminine' virtues as soft or weak, they want parents and teachers to balance acquiring individual virtues such as courage and honesty with relational virtues such as kindness, compassion, responsiveness, tenderness, equality, trust, and peace. At the heart of such virtues is the power of love.

The history of love is the history of power used for others. Protectors and nurturers use their power, not for themselves, but to benefit others. Caring defenders are likely to be active and noisy whereas nurturers are most often quiet calm heroes. Parents know how to use power for children in acts of love and protection that are given without an expectation of rewards. From singing him to sleep in the middle of the night to warming his ice-cold hands in the winter, I used my powers for Michael. Fortunately, it was only when we played that I had to experience using my power for him in active confrontational ways as I challenged the monstrous deeds of giants, dragons, vampires, or humans

In mythic worlds the stakes are raised and the consequences more stark for those who care for others in need as there is often a risk to their safety. For example, Una's life was in danger as well as St George's, but if she had not nurtured the knight he would not have been able to fight the dragon for three days. Likewise, Esmerelda brings water to Quasimodo (known as the Hunchback of Notre Dame) and helps him to escape from the stocks, but she also risks being captured and humiliated like him.

Monsters are monstrous because they want all power for themselves. They take what they want and often use violence. They ignore the effects of their actions on their victims. Heroes are heroic because they want to redirect power to the powerless. Heroes act on behalf of victims to stop monsters, to speak the unheard protests of oppressed people, and to mitigate victims' pain. People's deeds lie between the extremities of monsters and heroes. People can become monstrous or heroic at times but are rarely in situations where they are faced with moral choices that have momentous consequences for others.

In mythic play as well as in some significant everyday interactions with Michael as a young child, I would argue that we were often in what Bauman (1993; 1995) has described as a primal state of morality. Bauman argues that from very early childhood every human is in relationship with others. He believes that 'the human condition is moral' because 'well before we are told authoritatively what is "good" and what "evil" (and sometimes, what is neither) we face the choice between good and evil; we face it already at the very first, inescapable moment of encounter with the Other' (1995, p. 2).

How Michael related to me as an infant when he grabbed my nose and how I responded was an ethical encounter. At that moment I was the Other for him and he was the Other for me. If I had intentionally slapped him to 'teach him a lesson' or if he had gone on holding when he knew I was in pain, we would each have been choosing to do an evil deed. For Bakhtin, each of us would have been unethical if we had been unresponsive to the cry of the other. Instead, as I chose to make my pain clear and he chose not to inflict pain, we were each being answerable to one another. Using Bauman's phrase, we were being moral because we were each 'being-for the Other'. Every time Michael (or Zoë) acted in a way that caused pain or discomfort for me, or others, I would evaluate those deeds as wrong. The response was inevitably to cease or modify actions accordingly. 'Being-for me' and for the other people in their lives became a commonplace stance in our children's everyday lives. As they became older it was really only tested when either of us acted in unexpected ways.

Bauman stresses that people author ethical acts as they choose between good and evil (ibid., p. 1). However, as people grow older they tend to explore such choices less often, settling into patterns of interaction. Yet authoring ethical choices forms the backbone for mythic play where the stark choices and the consequences of actions in unpredictable landscapes cannot be overlooked. So every new mythic narrative that Michael discovered provided us with opportunities to imagine, enact, and react to, the heroic and monstrous deeds of new Others who extended the boundaries of comfortable predictability. And I was repeatedly faced with ethically evaluating those deeds.

Using power with others

Bakhtin's overarching theory of dialogism (Holquist, 1996) conceptualizes how all those people who have cooperated, collaborated, compromised, dialogued to reach agreement, and grappled to reach shared understanding have struggled in sharing power with others. These are the largely untold social stories of the ebb and flow of power in people's interactions behind the scenes of historical events. Tales of the tug between pleas to share power and resistance to those desires are the life-blood of fiction, with mythic narratives exploring the extreme consequences of oppressive uses of power and the human cost of struggles to share more power.

When people negotiate with one another they use power collaboratively to create new interpretations of situations as they explore possible actions. Sharing power in this way is ethical from moment to moment if people address and are answerable to one another and to those whose views are made visible and are heard.

All two-parent families have lived the value of using power with one another and with a child. Pragmatically, caring for a child is easier when parents cooperate, collaborate, compromise, and pool their abilities and resources. When parents share power with children there is less of a struggle over potential flashpoints like sitting at the table, bedtime, and changes in activities. But further, using power with children means sharing ideas and creating new understandings for everyone.

When people share power they create spaces where ideas can be co-authored. If adults and children play together then co-authoring spaces become available as collaborative everyday spaces intersect with play spaces. In doing so the potential for creating ethical and other new under-standing is expanded through social imagination to incorporate the views of people and creatures in other worlds with which they can dialogue.

I try to make my discourse with children as dialogic as possible. I want to co-author with them. My intention is to dialogue and explore ideas together, whether or not these come from narrative worlds or the physical and social worlds around us.

In our mythic play as we explored in imagination characters' struggles over sharing power, those encounters tested the limits of relationships. When Michael was nearly six I noted some of the moral philosophical ideas that arose for me because of our play:

- Was the dragon evil if it was hungry?
- Would St George be right to kill the dragon if it said it was sorry?
- Was Medusa only defending herself?
- If King Kong has feelings for a human should he be treated differently than any other gorilla?

- What about a human who becomes a werewolf and thus half wolf?
- Should the Wolfman be able to choose to end his own life?
- How do you react to a vampire like Dracula who needs to drink blood to remain undead?
- Is there a monster in the story of Frankenstein? Is it Frankenstein's creature when he wants revenge or Dr Frankenstein when he wants to kill his creation?
- Is a Mummy still a person after 3000 years? If you'd been a slave in an Egyptian tomb where they were about to sacrifice a human child what would you do?
- A living dead zombie has been human but is it still human as it reaches out to strangle you? Is it OK to use a machine gun to stop it?
- Darth Vader had been monstrous in killing thousands of people. But he'd killed the Emperor and rescued his son, Luke. So how should he be remembered after he dies in Luke's arms?
- As a father, would I shoot my son to stop him blowing up a building? What about if he was Freddy Kruger and he would not stop coming into people's dreams?
- Is Mr Hyde a man or the monstrous nature that we all have as humans? Is it right to kill him?

These were not questions that Michael was interested in discussing. He did not appreciate abstract conversations as an alternative to enacting the encounters in which these questions were contextualized. Yet, as we projected into mythic encounters my changing ideas affected what I said and did and thus the meaning we made together. Michael was open to dialogically exploring ideas like these through play interactions. He was always ready to dialogue from the point of view of any of the creatures or people in the mythic worlds in response to whatever statements or questions I raised. At the same time he positioned me to do the same. As we played we were co-authoring our ethical identities.

Beginnings

I am standing alongside a bronze statue of two figures, titled 'Hands across the divide'. The decade-old sculpture stands in the vibrant and peaceful town of my birth that has been revitalized and transformed since the days of protests, bombings, and shootings that I remember all too clearly from the Northern Ireland 'Troubles'. Both figures stand overlooking the River Foyle that some see as dividing, others see as uniting, Catholic Derry and Protestant Londonderry. Each faces the other as an equal across a wide schism in the plinth of the statue. Their outstretched hands are close to touching.

In imagination I stand with both of the figures. Nothing about the statue locates it specifically in Northern Ireland. People could identify with this statue if it were standing in Johannesburg, Sarajevo, Berlin, or Charleston, South Carolina. One day a copy of the statue might be welcomed in Jerusalem or Baghdad.

Nine years on, at the time of writing, from the 1998 Good Friday Agreement that began a political sea change for everyone on the island of Ireland, politicians from across the religious, ethnic, cultural, and political divide now form a devolved power-sharing government in Belfast. There are people living in the city and country of my birth who are still hurting emotionally and physically from the effects of past actions by discriminating institutions and people, as well as by the twenty-five plus years of violence and killing inflicted by paramilitary groups and the state security forces. Yet people have reached out to one another.

I imagine words, written by the poet Seamus Heaney, engraved on the base of the statue: 'We are the hunters and gatherers of values.' Heaney was born in the same county as I was and these words come from his acceptance speech for the Nobel Prize for Literature.

In Heaney's (1995) speech he tells a story that illustrates the chasms that can open up between people to test their ethical desires for mutual compassion and respect. He recounts a dark hour in the history of sectarian violence when, in 1976, a minibus full of workers was stopped by a gang of men with guns in their hands and hatred in their hearts. The workers were made to line up beside the minibus. A gun was waved in front of them as a man snarled, 'Any Catholics among you step out here.' The lone Catholic man in the group did not move when his hand was gripped by his fellow Protestant worker in a signal that said 'we are in hell, but we are here together'. The story does not have a just ending. After hesitating, he stepped forward, only to see all his friends butchered by the masked executioners.

Yet Heaney finds hope in his belief that 'the birth of the future we desire is surely in the contraction which that terrified Catholic felt on the roadside when another hand gripped his hand'. In reaching out, the hand illustrated 'the power to persuade that vulnerable part of our consciousness of its rightness, in spite of the wrongness all around it, the power to remind us that we are hunters and gatherers of values, that our very solitudes and distresses are creditable, in so far as they too are an earnest of our veritable human being'.

Playing is a human ability that opens us up to worlds of possibilities. When we play with children we can harness, for ethical ends, young people's enthusiastic projection into other people's consciousnesses in imagined worlds. If we meet children in the distressing, or exhilarating, encounters they have chosen to enact, we may begin to co-author with them and strengthen what may be tentative voices of compassion. Children may embrace feeling they are in hell, or heaven, and if they do we should be ready to be there with them. Over time if we explore how possible selves could act and evaluate their imagined deeds, as well as our everyday actions, together we can hunt for, and gather, values including a disposition to be answerable to others.

Along with the Quaker mystic, Rufus Jones (1937), 'I pin my hopes on the quiet processes and small circles in which vital and transforming events take place.' This quote reminds me that though play can seem noisy and exaggerated it often circles around small emotional moments of quiet that in ethical imagination can become highly significant. I pin my hopes on play because all children, and all adults, regardless of their socio-economic background and cultural resources, can play with one another. Play is literally vital in the sense that we are more fully alive, and more fully human, when we play than we often are in everyday life.

In closing, I look forward to a new beginning for the status of play in early childhood. Many children want to explore with parents or teachers in mythic, as well as everyday, play worlds. Many children need adults to play with them and we could answer children with an outstretched hand. In joining with children we could embrace opportunities to play at life and begin to co-author ethical identities with the young people in our care.

Bibliography

Ayers, W. (2004) *Teaching the personal and the political: Essays on hope and justice*. New York and London: Teachers College Press.

—— (1994) I'm talkin' about ethics. *Rethinking Schools* (4)8: 1–10.

Bakhtin, M. M. (1993) *Toward a philosophy of the act*. Holquist, M. and Liapunov, V. (Eds), Liapunov, V. (Trans.). Austin, TX: Texas University Press.

—— (1990) *Art and answerability: Early philosophical essays*. Holquist, M. and Liapunov, V. (Eds), Liapunov, V. (Trans.). Austin, TX: Texas University Press.

—— (1986) *Speech genres and other late essays*. McGee, V.W. (Trans.). Austin, TX: Texas University Press.

—— (1984a) *Problems of Dostoevsky's poetics*. Emerson, C. (Ed. and Trans.) Minneapolis, MN: University of Minnesota Press.

—— (1984b) *Rabelais and his world*. Iswolsky, H. (Trans.). Bloomington, IN: Indiana University Press.

—— (1981) *The dialogic imagination*. Holquist, M. (Ed.), Emerson, C. and Holquist, M. (Trans.). Austin, TX: Texas University Press.

Bateson, G. (1972) *Steps to an ecology of mind*. London: Ballantine Books.

Bauman, Z. (1995) *Life in fragments*. Oxford: Blackwell.

—— (1993) *Postmodern ethics*. Oxford: Blackwell.

Baumeister, R. (1997) *Evil: Inside human violence and cruelty*. New York: W. H. Freeman.

Bennett, W. (1995) *The moral compass: Stories for a life's journey*. New York: Simon and Schuster.

—— (1993) *The book of virtues: A treasury of great moral stories*. New York: Simon and Schuster.

Bennett, N., Wood, L., and Rogers, S. (1997) *Teaching through play: Teachers' thinking and classroom practice*. Buckingham: Open University Press.

Best, S. and Kellner, D. (1991) *Postmodern theory: Critical interrogations*. New York: Guilford Press.

Bettelheim, B. (1976) *The uses of enchantment*. New York: Knopf.

Bredekamp, S. (1987) *Developmentally appropriate practice in early childhood programs serving children from birth through age eight*. Washington, DC: National Association for the Education of Young Children.

Brooks, D. and Kann, M.E. (1993) What makes character education programs work? *Educational Leadership* 51(3): 19–21.

Brown, F. (2003) *Playwork: Theory and practice*. Buckingham: Open University Press.

Bruner, J. (1996) *The culture of education*. Cambridge, MA: Harvard University Press.

—— (1986) *Actual minds, possible worlds*. Cambridge, MA: Harvard University Press.

Bruner, J.S., Jolly, A., and Sylva, K. (1976) *Play: Its role in development and evolution*. London: Penguin.

Bocharov, S. (1999) The event of being: On Mikhail Mikhailovich Bakhtin. In C. Emerson (Ed.) *Critical essays on Mikhail Bakhtin*. New York: C.K. Hall

Boler, M. (1999) *Feeling power: Emotions and education*. New York and London: Routledge.

Bourdieu, P. (1977) *Outline of a theory of practice*. Richard Nice (Trans.). Cambridge: Cambridge University Press.

Butler, J. (2005) *Giving an account of oneself*. New York: Fordham University Press.

—— (1990) *Gender trouble: Feminism and the subversion of identity*. New York: Routledge.

Buzzelli, C. (1997) Origins, differences, and the origins of differences in moral development. *Developmental Review* 17: 101–109.

—— (1993) Morality in context: A socio-cultural approach to enhancing young children's moral development. *Child and Youth Care Forum* 22: 375–386.

Buzzelli, C. and Johnston, B. (2002) *The moral dimensions of teaching: Language, power, culture in classroom interaction*. New York: RoutledgeFalmer.

Campbell, J. (1972) *The hero with a thousand faces*. Princeton, NJ: New Jersey Press.

Cannella, G.S. (1997) *Deconstructing early childhood education: Social justice and revolution*. New York: Peter Lang.

Cannella, G.S. and Bailey, C.D. (1999) Postmodern research in early childhood education. In S. Reifel (Ed.), *Advances in early education and day care* 10: 3–39. Greenwich, CT: Jai Press.

Carlsson-Paige, N. and Levin, D. (1990) *Who's calling the shots? How to respond effectively to children's fascination with war play and war toys*. Philadelphia, PA: New Society Publishers.

Carlsson-Paige, N. and Levin, D. (1987) *The war play dilemma: Children's needs and society's future*. New York: Teachers College Press.

Christian Peacemakers Team (2006) Press release 'We mourn the loss of Tom Fox'. Retrieved October 17 http://www.cpt.org/iraq/response/06-10-03statement.htm.

Cole, M. (1996) *Cultural psychology: A once and future discipline*. Cambridge, MA: Harvard University Press.

Coles, R. (1986) *The moral life of children*. Boston: Atlantic Monthly Press,

—— (1997) *The moral intelligence of children*. New York: Random House.

Cooper, S. (1996) *Dreams and wishes: Essays on writing for children*. New York: Margaret K. McElderry Books.

Corrigan Maguire, M. (1999) *The vision of peace: Faith and hope in Northern Ireland*. Maryknoll, NY: Orbis.

Corsaro, W. (1985) *Friendship and peer culture in the early years*. Norwood, NJ: Ablex.

Coustineau, P. (2001) *Once and future myths: The power of ancient stories in modern times*. Berkeley, CA: Canari Press.

Cupit, G. C. (1996) Superhero play and very human children, *Early Years* 16(2): 22–25.

Dahlberg, G. and Moss, P. (2005) *Ethics and politics in early childhood education*. New York and London: RoutledgeFalmer.

Dahlberg, G., Moss, P., and Pence, A. (1999) *Beyond quality in early childhood education and care: Postmodern perspectives*. London: Falmer Press.

Dalai Lama (1999) Preface. In M. Corrigan Maguire, *The vision of peace: Faith and hope in Northern Ireland*. New York: Orbis Books.

Davies, B. (1993) *Shards of glass: Children reading and writing beyond gendered identities*. St Leonards: Allen and Unwin.

—— (1992) Beyond dualism and toward multiple subjectivities. In L. Christian-Smith (Ed.). *Texts of desire*. London: Falmer Press.

—— (1989) *Frogs and snails and feminist tales: Preschool children and gender*. Sydney: Allen and Unwin.

Davies, B. and Harré, R. (1990) Positioning: The discursive production of selves. *Journal for the Theory of Social Behavior* 20(1): 43–63.

Day, J. and Tappen, M.R. (1996) The narrative approach to moral development: From the epistemic subject to dialogic selves. *Human Development* 39: 67–82.

Delbanco, A. (1995) *The death of Satan: How Americans have lost the sense of evil*. New York: Farrar, Straus and Giroux.

Derrida, J. (1978) The retrait of metaphor, *Enclitic* 5.

—— *Of grammatology*. Gayatri Chakravorty Spivak (Trans.). Baltimore, MD: Johns Hopkins University Press.

DeVries, R. and Zan, B. (1994) *Moral classrooms, moral children: Creating a constructivist atmosphere in early education*. New York: Teachers College Press.

Dewey, J. (1909/1975) *Moral principles in education*. Carbondale, IL: Southern Illinois University Press.

Donald, M. (1991) *Origins of the modern mind*. Cambridge, MA: Harvard University Press.

Donaldson, M. (1978) *Children's minds*. New York: Norton.

Doniger O'Flaherty, W. (1995) *Other people's myths: The cave of echoes*. Chicago, IL: University of Chicago Press.

Dyson, A. Haas (1997) *Writing superheroes: Contemporary childhood, popular culture, and classroom literacy*. New York: Teachers College Press.

Edmiston, B. (2005) Coming home to research. In L. D. Soto and B. Blue, *Power and voice in research with children*. New York: Peter Lang.

—— (2000) Drama as ethical education. *Research in drama education* 5(1): 63–84.

—— (1998a) Ethical imagination: Choosing an ethical self in drama. In J. Wilhelm and B. Edmiston, *Imagining to learn: Inquiry, ethics, and integration though drama*. Portsmouth, NH: Heinemann.

—— (1998b) Reaching out: Ethical spaces and drama. In T. Grady, and C. O'Sullivan (Eds.) *A head taller: Developing a humanizing curriculum through drama*. Birmingham: National Association for the Teaching of Drama (UK), pp. 58–69.

—— (1993) Structuring drama for reflection and learning: A teacher–researcher study. *Youth Theatre Journal* 7(3): 3–11.

Edmiston, B. and Enciso, P. (2002) Reflections and refractions of meaning: Dialogic approaches to classroom drama and reading. In J. Flood, D. Lapp, J. Squire, and J. Jensen (Eds) *The handbook of research on teaching and the English language arts*. New York: Simon and Schuster Macmillan, pp. 868–880.

Edmiston, B. and Wilhelm, J. (1998) Repositioning views/reviewing positions: Forming complex understandings in drama. In B.J. Wagner (Ed.) *Educational drama and the language arts: What research shows.* Portsmouth, NH: Heinemann, pp. 90–117.

—— (1996) Playing in different keys: Research notes for action researchers and reflective drama practitioners. In P. Taylor (Ed.) *Researching drama and arts education: Paradigms and possibilities.* London: Falmer Press, pp. 85–96.

Edwards, C., Gandini, L., and Forman, G. (1994) *The hundred languages of children.* New York: New Jersey.

Edwards, C. P. and Ramsey, P. G. (1986) *Promoting social and moral development in young children: Creative approaches for the classroom.* New York: Teachers College Press.

Egan, K. (1997) *The educated mind: How cognitive tools shape our understanding.* Chicago, IL: University of Chicago Press.

Emerson, (1997) *The first hundred years of Mikhal Bakhtin.* Princeton, NJ: Princeton University Press.

Erickson, F. (1986) Qualitative methods in research on teaching. In M.C. Wittrock, (Ed.) *Handbook of research on teaching* (3rd edn). New York: Macmillan, pp. 119–161.

Erikson, E. (1963) *Childhood and society.* London: Routledge & Kegan Paul.

Evans, K. (2002) *Negotiating the self: Identity, sexuality, and emotion in learning to teach.* New York: Routledge Falmer.

Favat, F. Andre (1977) *Child and tale: The origins of interest.* Research Report No. 19. Urbana, IL: National Council of Teachers of English.

Fernie, D.E., Davies, B., Kantor, R., and McMurray, P. (1993) Becoming a person in the preschool: creating integrated gender, school culture, and peer culture positionings. *Qualitative Studies in Education* 6(2): 95–110.

Flavell, J.H., Botkin, P.T., Fry, C.L., Wright, J.W., and Jarvis, P.E. (1968) *The development of role-taking and communication skills in children.* New York: John Wiley.

Flavell, J., Miller, P.H., and Miller, S.A. (2002) *Cognitive development* (4th edn). Upper Saddle River, NJ: Prentice Hall.

Foucault, M. (1985) *The history of sexuality, Volume 2: The use of pleasure.* New York: Pantheon.

—— (1984) On the genealogy of ethics: An overview of work in progress. In P. Rabinov (Ed.) *The Foucault Reader.* New York: Pantheon.

—— (1980) *Power/knowledge: Selected interviews and other writings, 1972–1977,* New York: Pantheon.

—— (1978) *The history of sexuality, Volume 1.* New York: Vintage.

—— (1977) *Discipline and punish: The birth of the prison.* New York: Vintage.

Freud, S. (1933) *New introductory lectures on psychoanalysis.* Sprott, W. J. H. (Trans.). New York: Norton and Company.

Fromberg, D. (1992) A review of research on play. In C. Seefeldt, *The early childhood curriculum: A view of current research.* New York: Teachers College Press.

—— (1987) Play. In P. Monighan-Nourot, B. Scales, J. VanHoorn, and M. Almy *Looking at children's play.* New York: Teachers College Press.

Fu, V., Stremmel, L., and Hill, J. (2002) *Teaching and learning: Collaborative exploration in the Reggio Emilia approach.* Upper Saddle River, NJ: Merrill.

Gallas, K. (2003) *Imagination and literacy: A teacher's search for the heart of learning.* New York: Teachers College Press.

Gandini, L. (1994) Educational and caring spaces. In C. Edwards, L. Gandini, and G. Forman (Eds) *The hundred languages of children: The Reggio Emilia approach to early childhood education*. Norwood, NJ: Ablex Publishing, pp. 135–149.

Garvey, C. (1977) *Play*. Cambridge, MA: Harvard University Press.

Gee, J. P. (2003) *What video games have to teach us about learning and literacy*. New York: Palgrave Macmillian.

Geertz, C. (1973) *The interpretation of cultures: Selected essays*. New York: Basic Books.

Gibbs, J. (2003) *Moral development of reality: Beyond the theories of Kohlberg and Hoffman*. Thousand Oaks, CA: Sage Publications.

Gilligan, C. (1982) *In a different voice: Psychological theory and women's development*. Cambridge, MA: Harvard University Press.

Glasgow Koste, V. (1995) *Dramatic play in childhood: Rehearsal for life*. Portsmouth, NH: Heinemann.

Glover, J. (1999) Into the garden of good and evil. *The Guardian*, 13 October.

Goldenberg, S. (2004) The stand. *The Guardian G2 magazine*. May, 5. London.

Goldhagen, D. (1996) *Hitler's willing executioners: Ordinary Germans and the Holocaust*. Cambridge, MA: Harvard University Press.

Grace, D. J. and Tobin, J. (1997) Carnival in the classroom. In J. Tobin (Ed.) *Making a case for pleasure in the classroom*. New Haven and London: Yale University Press, pp. 159–187.

Grayling, A.C. (2003) *What is good? The search for the best way to live*. London: Phoenix.

Grieshaber, S. and Cannella, G. (2001) *Embracing identities in early childhood education: Diversity and possibilities*. New York: Teachers College Press

Hall, S. (1996) Introduction: Who needs identity? In S. Hall and P. du Gay (Eds) *Questions of cultural identity* London: Sage Publications, pp. 1–17.

Halliday, M.A.K, (1978) *Language as social semiotic. The social interpretation of language and meaning*. London: Arnold.

—— (1975) *Learning how to mean*. London: Arnold.

Harré, R. (1993) *Social being*. Cambridge, MA: Blackwell.

Harré, R. and Langenhove, L. (Eds) (1999) *Positioning theory: Moral contexts of intentional action*. Malden, MA: Blackwell Publishers.

Hauser, M. and Jipson, J. (1998) *Intersections: Feminisms/early childhoods*. New York: Peter Lang.

Heaney, S. (1995) *Crediting poetry*. New York: Farrar Strauss Giroux.

Heathcote, D. (1984) *Collected writings on education and drama*. L. Johnson and C. O'Neill (Eds.). Melbourne: Hutchinson.

Hodges, M. (1984) *Saint George and the Dragon*. Schart Hyman, T. (Illus.). New York: Little, Brown.

Hoffman, M.L. (2000) *Empathy and moral development: Implications for caring and justice*. Cambridge: Cambridge University Press.

Holland, D., Lachicotte, W., Skinner, D., and Cain, C. (1998) *Identity and agency in cultural worlds*. Cambridge, MA: Harvard University Press.

Holland, D. and Lave, J. (2001) *History in person*. Santa Fe, NM: School of American Research Press.

Holland, P. (2003) *We don't play with guns here: War, weapon, and superhero play in the early years*. Maidenhead, England, and Philadelphia, PA: Open University Press.

—— (2000) Take the toys from the boys? An examination of the genesis of policy and the appropriateness of adult perspectives in the area of war, weapon, and superhero play, *Children's Social and Economic Education* 4(2): 92–108.

—— (1999) Is zero tolerance intolerance? *Early Childhood Practice* 1(1): 65–72.

Holquist, M. (1990). *Dialogism: Bakhtin and his world*. New York and London: Routledge.

hooks, b. (2003) *Teaching community: A pedagogy of hope*. New York: Routledge.

Hughes, P. and Mac Naughton, G. (2001) Fracture or manufactured: Gender identities and culture in the early years. In S. Grieshaber and G.S. Cannelle (Eds) *Embracing identities in early childhood education: Diversity and possibilities*. New York: Teachers College Press, pp. 114–130.

Huizinga, J. (1955) *Homo ludens: A study of the play-element in culture*. Boston, MA: Beacon Press.

Ingebretsen, E.J. (1996) *Maps of heaven and hell: Religious terror as memory from the Puritans to Stephen King*. Armonk, NY: M.E. Sharpe.

Jackson, P.W., Boonstrom, R.E, and Hansen, D.T. (1993) *The moral life of schools*. San Francisco: Jossey Bass.

James, A., Jenks, C., and Prout, A. (1998) *Theorizing childhood*. New York: Teachers College Press.

Johnson, M. (1993) *Moral imagination: Implications of cognitive science for ethics*. Chicago, IL: University of Chicago Press.

Johnson, R.A. (1991) *Owning your own shadow: Understanding the dark side of the psyche*. New York: Harper Collins.

Jones, E. and Reynolds, G. (1992) *The play's the thing: Teachers' roles in children's play*. New York: Teachers College Press.

Jones, G. (2002) *Killing monsters: Why children need fantasy, superheroes, and make-believe violence*. New York: Basic Books.

Jones, R. (1937) Quoted in Britain Yearly Meeting (1995) *Quaker Faith and Practice*. London: Religious Society of Friends, 24.56.

Katch, J. (2001) *Under deadman's skin: Discovering the meaning of children's violent play*. Boston, MA: Beacon Press.

Katz, L. (1994) What can we learn from Reggio Emilia? In C. Edwards, L. Gandini, and G. Forman (Eds) *The hundred languages of children: The Reggio Emilia approach to early childhood education*. Norwood, NJ: Ablex Publishing, pp. 19–37.

Kazan, T.S. (2005) Dancing bodies in the classroom: Moving toward an embodied pedagogy. *Pedagogy: Critical Approaches to Teaching Literature, Language, Composition, and Culture* 5(3): 379–408.

Keenan, B. (1992) *An evil cradling*. London: Vintage.

Kelly-Byrne, D. (1989) *A child's play life: An ethnographic study*. New York: Teachers College Press.

Kendrick, M. (2003) *Converging worlds: Play, literacy and culture in early childhood*. Bern: Peter Lang.

Kessler, S. and Swadener, B.B. (1992) *Reconceptualizing the early childhood curriculum: Beginning the dialogue*. New York: Teachers College Press.

Kilpatrick, W. (1992) *Why Johnny can't tell right from wrong: Moral illiteracy and the case for character education*. New York: Simon and Schuster

King, R. (1978) *All things bright and beautiful*. Chichester: Wiley.

Kitson, N. (1994) Please Miss Alexander: will you be the robber? Fantasy play: a case for adult intervention. In J. Moyles (Ed.) *The excellence of play.* Buckingham: Open University Press, pp. 88–98.

Kohlberg, L. (1984) *The psychology of moral development: The nature and validity of moral stages.* San Francisco, CA: Harper and Row.

Kohn, A. (1990) *The brighter side of human nature: Altruism and empathy in everyday life.* New York: Basic Books

Kress, G. and Leeuwen, T.V. (2001) *Multimodal discourse: The modes and media of contemporary communication.* London: Arnold.

Lakoff, G. (2002) *Moral politics: How liberals and conservatives think.* Chicago: University of Chicago Press.

Lather, P. (1991) *Getting smart: Feminist research and pedagogy within/in the postmodern.* London: Routledge.

Lave, J. and Wenger, E. (1991) *Situated learning: Legitimate peripheral participation.* New York: Cambridge University Press.

Law, S. (2006) *The war for children's minds.* London and New York: Routledge.

Leavitt, R. (2001) Critical inquiry and children in day care. In M. Pacjer and Mark Tappan (Eds) *Cultural and critical perspectives on human development.* New York: State University of New York Press.

—— (1994) *Power and emotion in infant toddler day care.* Albany, NY: State University of New York Press.

Le Guin, U, (1979) *The language of the night: Essays on fantasy and science fiction.* New York: Putnam.

Lehr, S. (1995) *Battling dragons: Issues and controversy in children's literature.* Portsmouth, NH: Heinemann.

Lévi-Strauss, C. (1996) *The structural study of myth.* New York: Garland Publishers.

—— (1978) *Myth and meaning.* Toronto: University of Toronto Press.

Levinas, E. (1989) Ethics as first philosophy. In S. Hand (Ed.) *The Levinas reader.* Oxford: Blackwell.

Lickona, T. (1991) *Educating for character: How our schools can teach respect and responsibility.* New York: Bantam Books.

Lloyd, B. and Duveen, G. (1993) *Gender identities and education: The impact of starting school.* Hertfordshire: Harvester Wheatsheaf.

Lurker, E. (1991) Zen and the art of playing. *Play and Culture* 4: 75–79.

McAdams, D. P. (1993) *Stories we live by: Personal myths and the making of the self.* New York: William Morrow.

McCadden, B.M. (1998) *It's hard to be good: Moral complexity, construction, and connection in a kindergarten classroom.* New York: Peter Lang.

McClellan, B.E. (1999) *Moral education in America: Schools and the shaping of character from colonial times to the present.* New York: Teachers College Press.

McElroy-Johnson, B. (1993) Giving voice to the voiceless. *Harvard Educational Review* 63: 85–104.

MacIntyre, A. (1981) *After virtue: A study in moral theory.* London: Duckworth.

Mac Naughton, G. (2005) *Doing Foucault in early childhood studies.* London and New York: Routledge.

—— (2000) *Rethinking gender in early childhood.* Sydney: Allen and Unwin.

Maguire, M. C. (1999) *The vision of peace: Faith and hope in Northern Ireland.* Maryknoll, NY: Orbis Books.

Marcus, H. and Nurius, P. (1986) Possible selves: The interface between motivation and the self-concept. In K. Yardley and T. Holness (Eds.) *Self and identity: Psychosocial perspectives*. Chichester: Wiley, pp. 157–172.

Maxwell, M. (1991) *Moral inertia: Ideas for social action*. Niwot, CO: University Press of Colorado.

Meadows, S. and Cashdan, A. (1988) *Helping children learn: Contributions to a cognitive curriculum*. London: David Fullton.

Midgley, M. (1981/2003) *Heart and mind*. London and New York: Routledge.

Milgram, S. (1975) *Obedience to authority*. New York: Harper-Colophon.

Milton, J. (1644 [1968]) Areopagatica. In J. Max Patrick (Ed.). *The prose of John Milton*. New York: New York University Press.

Monroe, K. R. (1996) *The heart of altruism: Perceptions of a common humanity*. Princeton, NJ: Princeton University Press.

Morris, P. (1994) *The Bakhtin reader: Selected writings of Bakhtin, Medvedev, Voloshinov*. London: Arnold.

Moyles, J. R. (1989) *Just playing? The role and structure of play in early childhood development*. Milton Keynes and Philadelphia, PA: Open University Press.

Morson, G.S. and Emerson, C. (1990) *Mikhail Bakhtin: Creation of a prosaics*. Stanford, CA: Stanford University Press.

Nash, R. J. (1997) *Answering the 'virtuecrats': a moral conversation on character education*. New York: Teachers College Press.

Noddings, N. (2002) *Educating moral people: A caring alternative to character education*. London: Teachers College Press.

—— (1992) *The challenge to care in schools: An alternate approach to education*. New York: Teachers College Press.

—— (1984) *Caring: A feminine approach to ethics and moral education*. Berkeley, CA: University of California Press.

Norton, B. (1997) Language, identity, and the ownership of English. *TESOL Quarterly* 31: 409–429.

Oliner, S.P. and Oliner, P.M. (1988) *The altruistic personality: Rescuers of Jews in Nazi Europe*. New York: Free Press.

Packer, M.J. and Tappen, M.B. (Eds) (2001) *Cultural and critical perspectives on human development*. Albany, NY: SUNY Press.

Pagels, E. (1995) *The origin of Satan*. New York: Random House.

Paley, V. (2004) *A child's work*. Chicago, IL: The University of Chicago Press.

Paley, V.G. (2001) Introduction. In J. Katch *Under deadman's skin: Discovering the meaning of children's violent play*. Boston, MA: Beacon Press.

—— (1988) *Bad guys don't have birthdays*. Chicago, IL: University of Chicago Press.

—— (1986) On listening to what children say. *Harvard Educational Review* 56(2): 122–131.

—— (1984) *Boys and girls: Superheroes in the doll corner*. Chicago, IL: University of Chicago Press.

Palmer, P. (2004) *A hidden wholeness: The journey toward an undivided life*. San Francisco, CA: Jossey-Bass.

Pateman, T. (1991) *Key concepts: A guide to aesthetics, criticism, and the arts in education*. London: Falmer Press.

Pelligrini, A.D. (1991) *Applied child study: A developmental approach.* Mahwah, NJ: Lawrence Erlbaum.

Phelan, A.M. (1997) Classroom management and the erasure of teacher desire. In J. Tobin (Ed.) *Making a case for pleasure in the classroom.* New Haven, CT, and London: Yale University Press, pp. 76–100.

Piaget, J. (1975) *The equilibration of cognitive structures: The central problem of intellectual development.* Chicago, IL: Chicago University Press.

—— (1962) *Play, dreams, and imitation.* New York: Norton.

Power, C., Higgins, A., and Kohlberg, L. (1989) *Lawrence Kohlber's approach to moral education.* New York: Columbia University Press.

Pullman, P. (2002) Interview. *To the best of our knowledge.* Wisconsin Public Radio, December 29.

Rankin, B. (1994) Curriculum development in Reggio Amelia: A long-term curriculum project about dinosaurs. In C. Edwards, L. Gandini, and G. Forman (1994) *The hundred languages of children.* Norwood, NJ: Ablex, pp. 189–211.

Rawls, J. (1971) *Theory of justice.* Cambridge, MA: Harvard University Press.

Readings, B. (1996) *The university in ruins,* Cambridge, MA: Harvard University Press.

Rest, J., Narvaez, D., Bebeau, M., and Thoma, S. (1999) *Postconventional moral thinking: A neo-Kohlbergian approach.* Mahwah, NJ: Lawrence Erlbaum.

Reynolds, G. and Jones, E. (1997) *Master players: Learning from children at play.* New York: Teachers College Press.

Rinaldi, C. (2005) *In dialogue with Reggio Emilia.* London and New York: Routledge.

Rogoff, B, (1990) *Apprenticeship in thinking: Cognitive development in social context.* New York: Oxford University Press.

Rosen, H. (1985) *Stories and meaning.* Sheffield: National Association for the Teaching of English.

Ryan, (1989) The new moral education. Available on line at http://www.hi-ho.ne.jp/taku77/refer/ryan.htm

Scarlet, W.G., Naudeau, S., Salonius-Pasternak, D., and Ponte, I. (2005) *Children's play.* Thousand Oaks, CA: Sage Publications.

Schechner, R. (1988) Playing. *Play and Culture* 1: 3–10.

Schwartzman, H.D. (1991) Imagining play. *Play and Culture* 4: 214–222.

—— (1978) *Transformations: The anthropology of children's play.* New York: Plenum Press.

Selman, R. L. (1980) *The growth of interpersonal understanding.* New York: Academic.

Selman, R.L. and Shultz, L.H. (1990). *Making a friend in youth: Developmental theory and pair theory.* Chicago, IL: University of Chicago Press.

Sevenhuijsen, S. (1998) *Citizenship and ethics of care: Feminist considerations on justice, morality, and politics.* London: Routledge.

Shefatya, L. (1990) Socioecomoic status and ethnic differences in sociodramatic play: Theoretical and practical implications. In E. Klugman and S. Smilansky (Eds) *Children's play and learning perspectives and policy implications.* New York: Teachers College Press.

Smagorinsky, P. and Taxel, J. (2005) *The discourse of moral education: Cultural wars in the classroom.* Mahwah, NJ: Lawrence Erlbaum Publishers.

Smilansky, S. (1990) Sociodramatic play: Its relevance to behavior and achievement in school. In E. Klugman and S. Smilansky (Eds) *Children's play and learning perspectives and policy implications.* New York: Teachers College Press.

Sockett, H. (1993) *The moral base of teacher professionalism*. New York: Teachers College Press.

Soto, L. D. and Swadener, B.B. (2002) Toward liberty in early childhood theory, research, and praxis: Decolonizing a field. *Contemporary Issues in Early Childhood Education* 3(1): 38–66.

Spencer, H. (1873) *The principles of psychology*. New York: D. Appleton.

Stevenson, R.L. (1992/1886) *Dr Jekyll and Mr Hyde and other stories*. New York: Knopf.

Sutton-Smith, B. (1994) Does play prepare the future? In J. Goldstien (Ed.) *Toys play and child development*, pp. 130–146.

—— (1988) War toys and childhood aggression. *Play and Culture* 1: 57–69.

—— (1993) Dilemmas in adult play with children. In K. MacDonald (Ed.) *Parent–child play: Descriptions and Implications*. New York: SUNY Press, pp. 15–40.

Tappen, M.B. (1997) Language, culture, and moral development: a Vygotskian perspective. *Developmental Review* 17: 78–100.

Tappen, M.B. and Packer, M.J. (Eds) (1991) *Narrative and storytelling: Implications for understanding moral development*. San Francisco, CA: Jossey-Bass.

Thompson, M. (1994) *Ethics*. London: Hodder and Stoughton.

Thorne, B. (1993) *Gender play: Girls and boys in school*. New Brunswick, NJ: Rutgers University Press.

Tizard, B. and Hughes, M. (1984) *Young children learning: Talking and thinking at home and in school*. London: Fontana.

Tobin, J. (2000) *Good guys don't wear hats*. New York: Teachers College Press.

—— (1997) Playing doctor in two cultures: The United States and Ireland. In J. Tobin (Ed.), *Making a place for pleasure in early childhood education*. New Haven, CT: Yale University Press, pp. 119–158.

Todorov, T. (1996) *Facing the extreme: Moral life in the concentration camps*. New York: Metropolitan Books.

Tronto, J. (1993) *Moral boundaries: A political argument for the ethics of care*. London: Routledge.

Turner, V, (1992) Morality and liminality. *Blazing the trail: Way marks in the exploration of symbols*. Tucson, AZ, and London: University of Arizona Press.

Voloshinov, V.N. (1986) *Marxism and the philosophy of language*. Matejka, L. and Titunik, I.R. (Trans.). Cambridge, MA: Harvard University Press.

Vygotsky, L. (1986) *Thought and Language*. Kozulin, A. (Ed.) (revised edition). Cambridge, MA and London: MIT Press.

—— (1978) *Mind in society*. Cole, M., John-Steiner, V., Scribner, S. and Souberman, E. (Eds and Trans.). Cambridge, MA: Harvard University Press.

—— (1969) *Thought and language*. 2nd edition.

—— (1967) Play and its role in the mental development of the child. *Soviet Psychology* 5: 6–18.

Walkerdine, V. (1988) *The mastery of reason*. New York: Routledge.

Warner, M. (2003) Introduction. *World of myths*. Austin, TX: University of Texas Press.

—— (1994) *Managing monsters: Six myths of our time*. London: Vintage.

Weber, M. (1962) Secher, H.P. (Trans.). *Basic concepts in sociology*. Secaucus, NJ: Citadel.

Wedden, C. (1997) *Feminist practice and poststructural theory*. Oxford: Basil Blackwell.

Wegner-Spöhring, G. (1994) War toys and aggressive play scenes. In J.H. Goldstein, (Ed.). *Toys, play, and child development.* Cambridge and New York: Cambridge University Press.

Wenger, E. (1998) *Communities of practice: Learning, meaning, and identity.* New York: Cambridge University Press.

Wertsch, J. (1979) The concept of activity in Soviet psychology: An introduction. In James V. Wertsch (Ed.) *The concept of activity in Soviet psychology.* Armonk, NY: M.E Sharpe.

Winnicott, D. W. (1971) *Playing and reality.* Harmondsworth, Middlesex: Penguin Books.

Winston, J. (1998) *Drama, narrative, and moral education.* London: Falmer.

Wolf, J.M. and Walsh, D.J. (1998) 'If you haven't been there, you don't know what it's like: Doing day care'. *Early Education and Development* 9(1): 29–47.

Wolf, S. and Heath, S.B. (1995) *The braid of literature: Children's worlds of reading.* Cambridge, MA: Harvard University Press.

Wood, D., Bruner, J., and Ross, G. (1976) The role of tutoring in problem solving. *Journal of Child Psychology and Psychiatry* 17: 89–100.

Wood, E. and Attfield, J. (2005) *Play, learning, and the early childhood curriculum.* London: Paul Chapman Publishing.

Wortham, S. (2006) *Learning identity: The joint emergence of social identification and academic learning.* New York: Cambridge University Press.

Index

addressing others 127–9, 174, 177
aesthetic activities 69–74; aesthetic
    potential of play 72–4; authors
    69–70; and ethical actions 70–2;
    self and other 69
agency 21, 129–40; definition 129; and
    the ethical self 131–6; and identity
    81, 82; moral agency 16; in play
    137–40
American Institute of Character
    Education 182
answerability 24, 92, 177; and
    compassion 85, 111; in daily life
    126–7, 192; definition 17; and
    ethical identity 22; and integrity
    82–4; and projection 123–5
Aristotle 181
authoring ethical identities 21–2, 23,
    134–6
authoring selves and identities 23,
    81–96; agency 81, 82; answerability
    and integrity 82–4; authoritative
    and internally persuasive discourses
    85–7; children's selves and identities
    87–96; self as self-others 84–5, 120
authoring selves and identities in play
    23, 96–107; exploring possible
    identities 102–5; playing as
    projection into interrelated
    viewpoints 106; playing with
    possible selves 97–102; positioning
    in everyday and play worlds 105–6;
    shifting embodied discourses 106–7
Ayers, W. 184

Baba Yaga 43, 48*t*
Bakhtin, M.M. 16–18, 19, 21, 30, 62,
    66, 69, 70, 72–3, 77, 83, 84, 85, 87,
    92, 98, 143–4, 145, 148, 153, 157,
    186, 193
balance 118
Bateson, G. 6, 99
Bauman, Z. 14, 16, 192
Baumeister, R. 109, 114, 132, 133,
    166, 171
Beauty and the Beast 38, 39, 43, 48*t*, 52,
    137, 139
Bennett, N. et al. 6
Bennett, W. 183–4
Beowulf 25, 31, 48*t*, 53, 56
Bettelheim, B. 29, 63, 66
Bocharov, S. 84
Boler, M. 186–7, 189
Bredekamp, S. 8
Brooks, D. and Kann, M.E. 183
Bruner, J. 5, 11
Bruner, J.S. et al. 8, 9
Bush, George W. 110

Calvin & Hobbes 25, 25*f*, 26
caring relationships 184–5; playing
    with power 188–94
Carlsson-Paige, N. 59, 61
Cashdan, A. 4
character education 181–4
Chesterton, G.K. 67
child–adult play: as aesthetic
    experience 69, 70, 72–3; concerns
    about 5; ethical meaning-making
    19, 97, 119; interactivity 18, 23, 71;
    positioning and protection 105–6,
    112; and power 186–7
child–adult power relationships 17,
    185–8; adult power relationship